Five
in a Row

Volume Eight
Inspired learning through great books.

Ages 12+

By Becky Jane Lambert

Introduction by Jane Claire Lambert

Five in a Row Volume Eight

ISBN 978-1-888659-30-6

Published by:
Five in a Row Publishing
312 SW Greenwich Dr.
Suite 220
Lee's Summit, MO 64082
816-866-8500

Thank you to Carrie W. for her contributions to volumes 5-8.

Send all requests for information to the above address.

The units for *Neil Armstrong: Young Flyer, Marie Curie and the Discovery of Radium,* and *Hitty: Her First Hundred Years* were originally published in *Beyond Five in a Row, Volume 3,* and *Above and Beyond Five in a Row.* All of these units have been revised for inclusion in Volume 8.

Many Five in a Row units contain go-along titles that complement the FIAR book selection. Since every family and every child is different, it's important to preview these additional titles before reading aloud or giving to your child to read.

To Mary M.
For your great help and encouragement on this project

Contents

Introduction

Good books have always been the doorway to learning. That doorway leads to growth and an appreciation for the wonders around us. The *Five in a Row* curriculum was created to bring excitement and fun to learning and to enrich children's lives through wonderful children's literature. This foundation is evident in every volume, beginning with *Before Five in a Row*.

Continuing this unique and effective way of learning, **Five in a Row Volume 8** contains **complete units for three chapter books and accompanying lessons** (selections that were formerly published in *Beyond Five in a Row Volume 3* and *Above and Beyond Five in a Row*). These units are designed for students aged 12 and above; many of these students will have used earlier *Five in a Row* volumes and both teacher and student will be familiar with the very similar approach to learning in Volume 8.

Just as in previous FIAR volumes, the chapter book units in Volume 8 are intended to be extremely flexible, allowing you the option to do any combination of the lessons for each chapter. You may elect to skip over certain lessons which do not fit the needs of your student and you may place additional emphasis on certain ones which seem appropriate. You will find more exercises than you can use, so enjoy choosing just the right lesson elements for your students.

You can adjust school time to fit your needs as well. By using only one lesson element each day, you can work through *Five in a Row* in as little as 30-60 minutes daily, including the time to read the chapter. If you choose to use all or most of the lesson elements, field trips and follow-up exercises, you could easily spend several hours daily. Use *Five in a Row* however it best suits your needs and the needs of your students. The more lessons you do together, or that your student does independently, the more skills that will be acquired—skills which will benefit them through high school, college and throughout life!

Five in a Row chapter book units are complete studies that cover Social Studies (including History, Geography, and Career Paths), Science, Language Arts (including Writing and Discussion Questions and Vocabulary), Fine Arts, and Life Skills. You'll also find Teacher's Notes pages for every title, providing a place to record lessons, go-along resources, favorite memories, and more; and Activity Sheets for every chapter that support and add to the lessons.

As with all volumes of *Five in a Row*, the purpose and mission remain the same: to provide students with "inspired learning through great books." You are the leader for this adventure, so gather the children around you and have a great time!

Jane Claire Lambert, author and creator of *Five in a Row*
October 2022

Tips and Advice for Five in a Row Chapter Book Studies

• There is **no right or wrong order** for covering the material or ordering the books. You will find that throughout the Five in a Row curriculum, some subjects are revisited once, and some several times! This repetition is intentional to remind your student of other books' lessons that have a similar theme or lesson topic. Covering the same topic in new ways or in greater depth at an older age is of great benefit to students.

• Following the individual units in this manual, you'll find **Sample Lesson Planning Sheets** (and a blank sheet for your use). These sample sheets demonstrate how you might organize your studies for two weeks of a sample unit. You can also make your own planning sheets or simply work directly from the manual.

• Keep in mind that there are **more lessons in the manual than you can use**. For each chapter, you'll be choosing the lessons that are especially suited to your student. You might choose topics you've never covered, topics you want to cover again, topics of particular interest to your student, etc.

• You'll occasionally be using **other resources such as your library or the internet** for further information or research. You may want "go-along" titles that match up with a particular lesson, a video that explains or illustrates a certain principle, or a website or book where your student can research additional information. Many times you'll find suggestions for other resources right in the lessons, but you may also desire additional resources depending on the needs of your particular student.

• These chapter book units do not include math; therefore, **you'll need to provide a separate math curriculum** for your child (this is true of all levels of Five in a Row). You'll also want to **add in the narrower language arts subjects** of grammar, spelling, and possibly continue with handwriting (printing and/or cursive) at some point (the timing on language arts may be different for different students). These subjects don't lend themselves to a unit study approach and you'll want to be sure to include them each week.

• Five in a Row was created to be gender-neutral and you'll find a wide variety of **fascinating lessons that appeal to both boys and girls**. Don't assume that a boy may not enjoy a book that has a girl as the main character, or vice versa! And, please note that we've referred to "teacher and student" in the singular. Many of you will have more than one student.

In Five in a Row chapter book units, you'll no longer be studying certain **academic subjects** on particular days of the week, as you did in early volumes of the FIAR curriculum. Instead, you'll be guiding your student into **a variety of areas each week**; some weeks will have a heavier emphasis on science while others may have a greater emphasis on fine arts, for example. What you study each week derives directly from what chapter you have just read at the time. Overall, your student will receive a comprehensive education in five principal areas:

- **Social Studies** (includes history, geography, and career paths)
- **Science**
- **Language Arts** (includes writing and discussion questions and vocabulary, among other topics)
- **Fine Arts**
- **Life Skills** (includes human relationships, problem solving, and personal development, among other topics)

If you have previously studied picture books in Five in a Row, you're already familiar with many of these subject areas. The following are areas that are new or unique to the chapter book units:

Career Paths are lessons that allow your student to explore and learn about various professions that tie in to the chapter. Use these in a way that fits the needs of your student. You may choose to skip some career paths, while others you may choose to investigate in depth, including a field trip to meet and interview someone in the profession.

Writing and Discussion Questions are found in every chapter, and can be used in different ways. You may choose to simply discuss the question together, or you may assign it as a writing topic. The length is dependent upon your student's age and ability; it may range from a few sentences to several paragraphs or a couple of pages. You can adjust the assignment length depending on your academic goals and what works best for your student.

Fine Arts lessons include such diverse topics as cooking, visual and performing arts, fabric arts and needlework, design and architecture, drama, and other creative arts.

Life Skills lessons cover a wide variety of topics and can be used as springboards for discussion or as writing assignments. The topics are especially appropriate for students ages 10 and up who are growing in maturity and learning to navigate human relationships, develop critical thinking skills, and practice problem solving for upcoming teen and adult years.

With chapter book units, you'll likely vary in the **number of chapters you read each week and the amount of time you spend each day**. Some chapters are brief and you might finish the chapter and activities in one day, but some are longer or more complex and could take up to a week to explore thoroughly. Many families find that they average about two chapters per week, but again, this is a generalization and some weeks may not follow this pattern. In addition, you'll find that amount of time varies per day with your chapter book activities. Some lessons may take only 30 minutes to complete, while some could take an hour or two, or extend to a long-term study or project.

Because chapter books vary in length and number of lessons, the **amount of time it will take you to complete a chapter book study will vary**, as well (two families could easily spend different amounts of time on the same book, even!). Each Five in a Row chapter book could take you as little as 4 to 5 weeks to finish, or as many as 8 to 9 weeks—it's up to your daily and weekly lesson plans, your student's needs, and your academic calendar. The flexibility of Five in a Row is great in all areas, including length of time spent on each unit!

Should you be reading the chapters to your student or should the student read silently? Either way works! Your student may want to read alone, or may want you to read aloud, and that's a decision you can work out together, depending on your child's reading ability and personal preference. Many children who are perfectly capable of reading to themselves still wish to be *read to*, and this could be a perfect opportunity for you to share that time together. Or, you may have a student who is more than willing to read alone—this is also just fine. A **Teacher Summary** has been provided at the beginning of every chapter for your convenience. You can take turns reading, listen while your student reads, read it aloud, let your student read alone … there's no right or wrong way to do it. You might employ a combination of all these approaches.

Whatever method of reading you choose, you and/or your student will **read each chapter only once**. Unlike the Five in a Row picture book units, no repetitive reading is necessary with the chapter books unless you are simply rereading a small section for a particular lesson, etc. This means that on some days, you'll read a chapter and also do a lesson; on other days, you will only do a lesson (from the same chapter) and not start a new chapter. Be sure to see the **Sample Lesson Planning Sheets** following the unit studies in this manual for a clear picture of how this works.

In each chapter's list of "What we will cover in this chapter," you'll see that one lesson is marked with an **asterisk** (there is an asterisk on the actual lesson, as well). This indicates that there is an **activity sheet** for this lesson at the end of the chapter book unit.

Please note: Five in a Row Volume 8 contains a longer chapter book unit that you may choose to row in a different manner than the previous FIAR chapter books. Please see the separate introduction to *Hitty: Her First Hundred Years* on page 169, as well as a note to your student about this special unit.

12

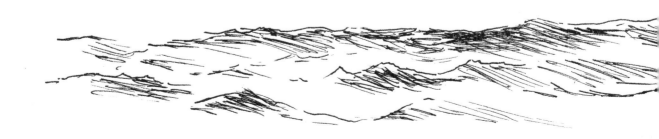

Neil Armstrong:
Young Flyer

Title: *Neil Armstrong: Young Flyer*
Author: Montrew Dunham
Copyright: 1996

14

Chapter 1—The Tin Goose

Teacher Summary

Our first chapter begins with an introduction to Neil Armstrong at age six. His father, Stephen Armstrong, works as a city accountant. Neil's mother, Viola, cares for the family, which also includes a three-year-old sister, June, and a baby brother, Dean.

One day, Neil's father tells the family an interesting plane has come into their town—the Ford Tri-Motor. Neil is thrilled and asks his father if they can go to see the plane. Although hesitant because it is Sunday, his parents grant permission and father and son soon head off to view the Ford Tri-Motor, also called "The Tin Goose."

Neil and his father not only get to see the magnificent plane, but the pilot offers to take them for a ride! Neil couldn't be more excited, and is soon taking his first plane ride.

What we will cover in this chapter:

Social Studies: History - Tri-Motor Airplanes
Social Studies: History - Our Story's
Time Frame: 1936*
Science: Aluminum and Alloys
Science: The Eardrum
Language Arts: Dialogue - Correct Punctuation
Language Arts: Vocabulary Enrichment -
Numerical Prefixes
Language Arts: Writing and Discussion Question

Social Studies: History - Tri-Motor Airplanes

Neil and his father were fortunate enough to ride as passengers on a Ford Tri-Motor airplane. Share with your student more information about this plane.

The term 'tri-motor' simply refers to the number of engines used in this style of airplane. First developed by German engineers, these three-engine planes began their flights in 1924. They were more powerful than previous aircraft and quickly gained popularity. American designers began working on their own models. Henry Ford, eager to expand his holdings from automobiles to airplanes, began production on a Tri-Motor of his own in 1926.

The original Ford Tri-Motor airplanes were able to carry ten passengers and travel at 100 miles per hour. They were more efficient than their predecessors and were more comfortable for passengers. As an interesting side note, the first flight over the South Pole was made in a Ford Tri-Motor in 1929.

Social Studies: History - Our Story's Time Frame: 1936*

In all levels of Five in a Row, we always try to determine our story's time frame. Understanding when a story takes place can give us clues about the characters and the situations they encounter. Knowing who was president, what the fashions were and even what books and songs were popular can enrich our comprehension of the story. Even if the author of our story doesn't write a direct description ("Our story takes place in 1908," for example), we may still deduce the story's time frame from other clues. For instance, in our story about Neil Armstrong, the opening line tells us that Neil is six years old. A few paragraphs later, we learn that the year is 1936. Now we know what year it is and that Neil was born in 1930.

With this information, take some time to discuss with your student what was happening in America in 1936. Perhaps your student can research on his own which president was in office, the main national and international political issues being discussed, a popular entertainer and so on. With some creativity and work, your student could put together a collage or presentation discussing the year 1936, or do a retrospective on the 1930s as a decade. Encourage him to find a song from the 1930s, or a video from the time period.

A few background facts your student might uncover in his study of the 1930s:

• Social and Political Issues—The Great Depression, the New Deal, and the Social Security Act in the U.S.; global events leading up to WWII

• President—Franklin Delano Roosevelt

• Entertainment—Two new genres of motion picture (musicals and slapstick comedy)

• Actors who rose to fame—Cary Grant, Katharine Hepburn, Gene Kelly, Fred Astaire and others

• 1936 Nobel Prizes—The Nobel Prize in Literature was given to Eugene O'Neill (United States) for his plays. The Nobel Peace Prize went to Carlos Lama (Argentina) for negotiating a peace settlement between Paraguay and Bolivia during the Chaco War.

• Popular Music—A new style of music was born: swing. Benny Goodman and Glen Miller were both popular artists using this style of music.

• Fashion—The 1930s was the first decade in which women began to wear pants (slacks) on a regular basis.

Encourage your student to explore the decade in which Neil Armstrong was raised. It will give him a greater understanding of this unit. He will learn many fascinating details about his country and the world in general. He could compile this information on a poster, write a paper, prepare a slide show or presentation, or think of another way to show what he has learned.

Science: Aluminum and Alloys

Neil's father tells him the Ford Tri-Motor is made from aluminum. Take advantage of this opportunity to delve into a bit of science with your student. To begin your discussion, draw your student's attention to the passage on where Neil's father describes the Tin Goose.

Stephen Armstrong says, "Aluminum is a rigid metal, and makes the plane very strong." Aluminum in its pure form is, in fact, not very rigid. It is quite soft and

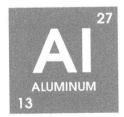

16

would not make a very good body for an airplane. But pure aluminum does have some good properties. It is easily molded to any shape. It can be as thick as a big dictionary or as thin as a narrow wire. It is also lightweight and won't rust.

With all of these excellent properties, engineers were quick to think that aluminum would work well for planes. But what about the softness of the metal? When scientists and engineers combine one or more metals together, it is called an "**alloy**." And that is precisely what engineers do with aluminum. The Ford Tri-Motor was not fashioned from pure aluminum, but instead from an aluminum alloy comprised of small amounts of zinc, copper, magnesium and other elements. These elements help the aluminum stay strong and more rigid, but still maintain flexibility and light weight. In an aluminum alloy, the aluminum is referred to as the base metal. The other elements are called components.

If you are able, locate an aluminum sheet or wire and let your student bend and shape it. Try crushing a soda can to demonstrate this principle. Ingenuity and creativity help inventors to create better and more efficient materials for us to use every day. Alloys are an example of this kind of creativity.

Science: The Eardrum

As Neil and his father are beginning their flight on the Ford Tri-Motor, the pilot hands each of them a piece of gum. He tells them it will help to ease the pressure on their eardrums as they take off and land. Does your student have any idea why this works? Has he ever flown on an airplane? Did he experience that popping feeling in his ears? Did he chew a piece of gum?

How does a piece of chewing gum affect the pressure in our ears? It has to do more with a tube in the body than with the eardrum. A narrow tube, called the Eustachian [yoo STAY shion] tube, connects the middle ear (behind the eardrum) to the back of the throat. It works in a very simple way. Most of the time it is relaxed and closed. Whenever the mouth is opened (to yawn, swallow or blow one's nose), it opens as well. When it opens, it makes the air pressure behind the eardrum equal the air pressure outside the body. When you experience a popping sensation, it is caused by air escaping or filling the space behind the eardrum. That air is allowed in or out by the Eustachian tube. The Eustachian tube is important to keep your eardrum from rupturing if the air pressure changes.

So why chew gum? Why does your student think it helps? When gum is chewed, saliva accumulates in the mouth repeatedly and swallowing must occur on a regular basis. When swallowing, the Eustachian tube is opened and the air pressure is equalized around the eardrum.

Even if your student has never experienced this ear-popping phenomenon on an airplane, he may have had a similar experience in a long elevator ride up or down, or even while riding in a car up mountains. The next time he feels that funny sensation, your student can pop a piece of chewing gum into his mouth and think about the Eustachian tube, the eardrum and Neil's first plane ride.

Language Arts: Dialogue - Correct Punctuation

Communicating effectively through creative writing takes two important skills: imagination and technical expertise. Thinking up delightful, original stories is vital. But authors must also understand how to correctly use the English language and grammar. One area is learning to correctly write dialogue. Spend some time with your student to learn (or review) dialogue punctuation.

Draw your student's attention to the page where the pilot begins speaking to Neil and his father. Have him look over the page and ask him what he notices about the dialogue (the portion where characters are speaking). What happens each time someone speaks? What begins and ends each sentence?

When we write dialogue, there are two main things about punctuation to remember. The first is the quotation mark.

Quotation marks ("_____") are used in several ways. They may begin and end a direct quotation. For example, in this conversation, we see the following:

"No, not up close like this," Neil's father answered. Quotation marks are placed at the beginning of Stephen Armstrong's statement and at the end. The quotation marks do not include the phrase: Neil's father answered. Why not? Because this is not spoken by Neil's father. Only what is directly said is included. Note also that a comma is used after "like this" even though it's the end of the sentence spoken by Neil's father. This is because the entire sentence includes the ending phrase "Neil's father answered." However, if Neil's father was asking a question or speaking very excitedly, a question mark or exclamation point would be used here.

The second important punctuation rule to remember when writing dialogue is that if more than one paragraph is spoken, quotation marks are placed *before each* paragraph and *at the end of the last* paragraph quoted. The following is an example of this from E.B. White's book, *Stuart Little*.

"My dear Miss Ames, I am a young person of modest proportions. By birth I am a New Yorker, but at the moment I am traveling on business of a confidential nature. My travels have brought me to your village.

"Yesterday, the keeper of your local store, who has an honest face and an open manner, gave me a most favorable report of your character and appearance.

"Pray, forgive me, Miss Ames, "continued Stuart, "for presuming to strike up an acquaintance on so slender an excuse as our physical similarity; but of course the fact is, as you yourself must know, there are very few people who are only two inches in height.

"Being an outdoors person, I am camped by the river in an attractive spot at the foot of Tracy's Lane. Would you care to go for a paddle with me in my canoe?

"If you wish to accept my invitation, be at the river tomorrow about five o'clock. I shall await your arrival with all the eagerness I can muster."

As your student can see, at the beginning of each new paragraph the section is indented and a new set of quotation marks is used to open the paragraph. There are not, however, quotation marks placed at the end of the paragraphs, which indicates that the same person (Stuart) is still speaking. When your student sees quotation marks end a section of dialogue, he can assume that a new speaker will begin the next section of dialogue.

After teaching or reviewing these two rules, encourage your student to write a short story or simply a page of dialogue and implement both rules. Learning and practicing proper punctuation allows writers to clearly communicate their thoughts, which helps the reader easily follow what is happening in the story.

Language Arts: Vocabulary Enrichment - Numerical Prefixes

The plane in which Neil and his father fly is called a Ford Tri-Motor. Does your student know what the prefix "tri" means? It means three. In other words, the plane has three motors. What are other words that tell us about the number of things? Can your student think of more?

Take this opportunity to enrich your student's vocabulary by sharing with him several of the basic numerical prefixes.

mono or **uni**—one
bi—two
tri—three
quad—four
quint, pent—five
sex, hex—six
sept—seven
octa—eight
deca—ten
cent—one hundred

What are some examples your student can think of which use these prefixes? Here are two to get you started: triplets—three siblings; octagon—eight-sided shape. Encourage your student to try to think of an example for each of the numerical prefixes above.

Language Arts: Writing and Discussion Question

Neil's father, Stephen Armstrong, helps cities straighten, organize and correct their financial situations. He deals with numbers and money, and his job requires his family to move every few years. Do you think that would be an interesting and fulfilling job? Why or why not? Explain.

Chapter 2—The First Plane

Teacher Summary

Neil continues to think about the glorious flight in the Ford Tri-Motor. His mother even buys him a model plane kit and he eagerly builds the tiny aircraft. As time passes, Neil learns about King Edward VIII and his abdication of the throne of England. He thinks it's interesting that Kind Edward VIII was the first king to ride in an airplane. Neil begins to do his own research on planes and finds a book on the Wright brothers. Neil learns all about the first airplane and the brothers' hard work.

What we will cover in this chapter:

Social Studies: History and Geography - Kitty Hawk and the Wright Brothers
Social Studies: History - King Edward VIII
Social Studies: History and Geography - England: An Introduction
Science: How Airplanes Fly*
Language Arts: Writing and Discussion Question
Language Arts: Vocabulary*
Fine Arts: Your Own Model Airplane
Fine Arts: Designing a Book Cover
Fine Arts: Cooking - Yorkshire Pudding
Life Skills: A Sense of Duty
Life Skills: What Makes Some Decisions Difficult

Social Studies: History and Geography - Kitty Hawk and the Wright Brothers

Neil is eager to learn all that he can about airplanes and their history. He finds a book about the first successful airplane. The book is about Wilbur and Orville Wright. This chapter offers a perfect opportunity to explore some new information with your student about the Wright brothers, Kitty Hawk and the first successful flight.

Teacher's Note: As with so many lessons in Five in a Row, there are many excellent videos and go-along books on the Wright Brothers available to complement this topic. If you wish to enrich this lesson or extend it into a long-term project, locate one or more of these resources.

To get your student started, you may wish to briefly introduce the Wright brothers and their lives. A fabulous book on the subject is entitled *The Wright Brothers: How They Invented the Airplane* by Russell Freedman. This resource includes dozens of original photographs taken by Orville and Wilbur Wright of each other and their various aircraft.

Wilbur and Orville Wright were not twins, although many people assumed that they were. They were brothers, but they did so many things alike and spent so

much time together that they often acted alike. Neither of the brothers ever married, and both loved to spend every spare minute in their workshop working on various scientific projects.

Wilbur was born in Millville, Indiana in 1867. His brother, Orville, was born in 1871 in Dayton, Ohio. They had three siblings—two older brothers and a younger sister. Their father was a minister in the United Brethren Church and their mother was a homemaker. Susan Wright, their mother, was the handy person in the family. When the boys had a question about building something, they went to their mother. She enjoyed working with her sons on a variety of projects.

The Wright brothers became interested in flight and airplanes in 1899, after reading about others' attempts at flight. Orville and Wilbur worked diligently on various gliders. In just one year they had built a glider that could carry one person. But where could they test it? It would need to be a long piece of land, fairly flat and preferably have a soft terrain (like sand). They contacted the Weather Bureau and found a sandy strip of land called Kill Devil Hills (near Kitty Hawk, North Carolina). It was perfect.

Unfortunately, neither their first glider nor the second, larger, glider was successful. The gliders just didn't have the power to lift themselves and a pilot. The brothers continued to work on their design and finally designed an entirely new wing shape. These wings could withstand air pressure and deflect it properly, ensuring a lift-off.

In the following year, 1902, their first glider covered nearly 600 feet in the air. It was better balanced, but it was just a glider. It did not have any power source to provide thrust. Wilbur and Orville continued to work on a powered plane. In just under one year, by

1903, they were ready for what they hoped would be a successful flight. The plane cost less than $1,000. The wings were 40 1/2 feet across. With the pilot, the entire aircraft weighed around 750 pounds. On December 17, 1903, the two persistent brothers made the world's first flight in a power-driven plane. The aircraft covered 120 feet and was in the air for 12 seconds. It was a major accomplishment! Suddenly, the names Wilbur and Orville Wright, Kitty Hawk and Kill Devil Hills became famous. However, the two brothers were not distracted. They continued to work on their airplanes, increasing flight times and flight altitudes.

Wilbur Wright died in 1912 of typhoid fever, but Orville continued the work of the brothers alone until he died in 1948. Both brothers are now in the Hall of Fame for Great Americans.

If you live nearby, your student might be fascinated by a visit to Kill Devil Hills, North Carolina. Your student can stand on the lonely, windswept strip of land where Orville and Wilbur tested their experiments. In Washington, D.C., the original 1903 Wright Flyer hangs in the Smithsonian Institution. Your student can gaze on the actual plane that Orville and Wilbur built. The plane is really an impressive sight!

Social Studies: History - King Edward VIII

Neil hears the live radio address of King Edward VIII on December 11, 1936, with his mother and father. What is the background of this famous Duke and his beloved wife?

Take some time to share with your student some interesting and important facts about this King of England and his life.

King Edward VIII was born in 1894 in London. He was the son of King George V and Queen Mary. He was, by birth, a part of the House of Windsor and an heir to the throne. For nearly forty years he was groomed for the position—and he fully intended to become king upon the death of his father. On January 20, 1936, the day finally arrived. But it was to be a short reign.

Edward had fallen in love with a woman named Wallis Warfield Simpson—an American. The fact that his girlfriend was not English was not as much of a problem as the fact that she was divorced.

England is a country where the separation of church and state has not historically been as clearly defined as in America. Many of the future King's subjects and advisors did not believe it was morally or spiritually right for the King of England to be married to a divorced woman. They would not accept Mrs. Simpson as their queen. King Edward VIII thought about his dilemma for just short of one year. On December 11 of the same year he was crowned (1936), he delivered a speech which stated that he was giving up (**abdicating**) his throne and handing it over to his brother, George VI (you and your student can listen to this radio speech online). He would no longer be King of England, but instead would be the Duke of Windsor. The following June, he married his love, Mrs. Simpson.

What does your student think? Should the Duke of Windsor have been allowed to marry the woman of his choice? Does he think the Duke made the right decision? What would he have chosen?

Social Studies: History and Geography - England: An Introduction

In this chapter, we are introduced to the topic of England and King Edward VIII. An entire unit study could be built around the massive subject of England, but take some time to give your student a brief, but interesting, introduction to this country.

Begin by locating England on a world map. (If your student has rowed *How to Make an Apple Pie and See the World*, *Mr. Gumpy's Motor Car*, or *The Hatmaker's Sign* in previous volumes of Five in a Row, he may be able to find this country easily and be able to tell you what he remembers about it.) Point out to your student the odd shape of England and the fact that it is indeed part of an island, completely surrounded by the Atlantic Ocean. Your student may have heard different names for this section of land: the British Isles, Great Britain, Britain or the United Kingdom. Is he clear on the definition of each name?

The term "British Isles" refers to England, Scotland, Wales and the entire island of Ireland. When people talk about "Great Britain," "Britain," or the "United Kingdom" (U.K.), they are talking about England, Scotland, Wales and Northern Ireland. The southern region of Ireland is the independent Republic of Ireland.

England is the largest of the four political divisions in Great Britain. England is a diverse country. Much of the land is countryside, with small villages and gardens nestled every few miles. Most of the people in England, however, live in larger cities. London, the country's capital, is the largest city in England.

England boasts many famous historic people, including William Shakespeare (the playwright and poet) and Sir Isaac Newton (one of the greatest scientists of all time).

England is ruled by a constitutional monarchy. This form of government is different from the United States (which includes a President, Senate, House of Representatives, governors, etc.). In a constitutional monarchy such as in England, the king or queen is the head of state. However, he or she does not govern the country. Instead, a group of politicians, called ministers, govern the country and their group is called the cabinet. The head of the cabinet is referred to as the Prime Minister. With your student, look up the current king or queen of England, and also the name of the current Prime Minister.

The official language in England is English. Although the accent differs, most Americans have no trouble understanding someone from England. Sometimes, however, you will hear words that differ. The following is a list of English terms and their American equivalents. Has your student heard any of them?

English	American
jumper	sweater
lift	elevator
biscuit	cookie
loo	restroom
petrol	gasoline
post	mailbox
queue	to wait in line, or the line itself
tube	subway
cheerio	goodbye
to ring	to call someone on the phone
car park	parking lot
flat	apartment

For fun, try to include a few of these words in your conversation with your student.

The food in England is fairly simple. Not many hot spices are used, and sauces tend to be simple. A few classic English dishes include Yorkshire pudding (a cake cooked in meat fat), kidney pie (a pot pie-like dish made of kidneys, covered with pastry), and bangers and mash (thick sausages served with mashed potatoes). The favorite hot beverage in England is tea.

Teacher's Note: A recipe for Yorkshire pudding is listed in the Fine Arts section of this chapter. Make it with your student and share a tasty treat, along with conversation.

If your student is interested, you can expand this lesson to include discussion of English sports: football (what we refer to as soccer), cricket (similar to baseball) and rugby (which resembles our football). You may also include lessons surrounding the land regions, religions, industry, etc.

Science: How Airplanes Fly*

The Wright brothers performed an amazing feat. With hard work and dedication, they created and flew the world's first airplane. But how do planes actually fly? Has your student ever flown in an airplane? Did he ever wonder how such a large, heavy machine gets into and stays in the air? Everyone probably has, at one point or another. Take this opportunity to introduce the four basic elements required for a plane to fly.

To understand how a plane flies, it is vital to discuss another topic first: air. Air is all around us. We breathe and smell air. We taste air. It presses against our bodies and our homes. We watch it move tree branches. Air is not weightless. It has weight and pressure. When you hold your hand out the car window and feel it blow back, you're feeling air's weight!

There are four basic principles that affect a plane in the air. They are **thrust**, **lift**, **drag** and **weight**. **Thrust** is the word we use to describe the propeller's action on the front of the plane. The propeller, moved by the engine's power, pulls the plane forward. This is called thrust.

Lift is created by the wings of the plane. An aircraft's wings are shaped in a very specific way, often called the aerofoil design. The wings are flat on the bottom and curved on top, sloping backwards. As the air rushes past the wings, it flows easily over the curved top portion, creating less air pressure on top of the wing. As the air flows beneath the wing (the flat portion), it creates strong air pressure, causing the wing to lift up. With the plane balanced and pulled through the air by thrust, the air pressure beneath the wing forces the plane up. This is called lift.

As the plane is flying through the air, some air pressure pushes against the plane. This is called **drag**. Different planes have different shapes and each shape creates various amounts of drag. The speed of the plane can also change drag.

Finally, we come to the principle of **weight**. Weight is the force of gravity pulling down on the plane, toward the ground. It helps to balance the plane during

24

flight. The heavier the plane, the stronger the engine required—but the more stable the aircraft becomes.

If your student wants to experience what lift feels like, take him for a ride in the car (a relatively isolated road is best for this experiment). As the car reaches speeds of 10-20 miles per hour, have your student extend his arm out the window, keeping his hand and fingers straight. Encourage him to tilt his hand backward and forward. Without holding his arm rigid and stiff (fighting the wind), see if he can find the angle at which his hand must be held in order for the air to flow evenly and keep his arm lifted. Without struggle, he should be able to keep his arm extended and held up by air, without being pushed back. This kind of balance is what aircraft designers achieve with planes' wings.

If your student has more questions about planes and flight, you can encourage him to explore related topics such as rudders, tail planes, ailerons, elevators, engines, pitching, rolling, landing, etc.

Language Arts: Writing and Discussion Question

The Wright brothers invented the first heavier-than-air, powered airplane. What do you think the difference is between invention and discovery? Do they differ? How do they work together? Explain.

Language Arts: Vocabulary*

Teacher's Note: Between the Teacher's Notes and the activity sheets at the end of this unit, you'll find a Vocabulary Sorting Exercise (instead of vocabulary crossword puzzles that are used in some other units). Your student can use this exercise to keep track of the vocabulary words in this unit.

abdicate   To officially give up power or authority to someone else.

duty   The right thing to do; something you ought to do; obligation.

Fine Arts: Your Own Model Airplane

Neil made a simple balsa wood airplane from a kit. A logical art project for this chapter is a model airplane kit, perhaps something similar to the one Neil's mother purchased for him.

Find your student a simple kit if he wants to try his skills at model building. Depending on your student's age, expertise, and interest level, you might choose a balsa wood kit (very easy and inexpensive) or a more detailed plastic or metal model kit from a hobby shop.

Fine Arts: Designing a Book Cover

Draw your student's attention to the cover of the book that Neil is holding in this chapter. It clearly states the title of the book, and you can see below it where the author's name is usually located. Then there is a picture of the Wright brothers' plane.

Encourage your student to look at the cover of the book we are using in this unit. It gives the title of the series (Childhood of Famous Americans). There is the title of the story (*Neil Armstrong: Young Flyer*). There is also a large, color illustration featuring Neil as a young boy, holding a model plane with a *Saturn V* rocket in the background and Neil's landing on the moon. At the bottom, you see the author's name (Montrew Dunham) and the illustrator's name (Meryl Henderson).

What does your student think of this cover? Designing book covers is a difficult job. What does your student think the function of a book cover is? The two main functions are to attract the reader and to inform the reader. What else can he think of?

Search with your student through his own bookshelves and look at various book covers. Which ones catch his eye? Why? Which covers does he dislike? Why?

For a delightful fine arts project, have your student design a book cover. He can design a cover for an imaginary book or for a story he has written, or he can redesign a book cover he doesn't care for. Again, encourage him to take into account the two main functions—to inform and to attract. When the project is completed, talk with your student about his choices.

It is interesting to note that most authors have no control over their book cover designs. Instead, they release the manuscript to their publisher, who then works with a design company or with an in-house book designer. Would your student rather leave the designing to someone else, or have control over it? Why or why not?

Fine Arts: Cooking—Yorkshire Pudding

In our lesson about England, we discussed classic English recipes. Here is a recipe for a famous dish: Yorkshire Pudding. Traditionally, it was cooked along with a roast (in the drippings). We have updated this recipe to exclude the need for an entire piece of meat. Cook according to the directions and you will have a delicious sampling of English cuisine.

Yorkshire Pudding
(Have all ingredients at room temperature)
1 cup flour
1/2 tsp. salt
1/2 cup milk
1/2 cup water
2 eggs
1/4 cup butter or meat drippings

Break the eggs into a bowl and whisk them until they are light and fluffy; set aside. In another bowl, mix together the flour and salt. Make a small well in the center of the flour mixture and pour in the milk and water. Mix well and then combine this mixture with the beaten eggs. Continue stirring the mixture until large bubbles rise to the surface. Cover and chill for at least one hour. Beat again for a minute or so and then let rest at room temperature.

Preheat your oven to 400° F. Put butter (or meat drippings) in a 9"x13" ovenproof baking dish. Heat in the oven until the butter is melted and the pan is hot. With supervision, your student can now pour the batter into the pan. It should be approximately 1/2" high in the pan. Bake for 20 minutes. Reduce heat to 350° F. and cook for 10 more minutes. Serve immediately.

Yorkshire Pudding can be enjoyed with roast beef or steak (using the drippings as a sauce) or it can enjoyed with honey and butter, more like popovers. Make a cup of tea to serve along with the pudding, and think English!

Life Skills: A Sense of Duty

In our story and our studies, we have discussed King Edward VIII and the circumstances under which he left the throne of England. Neil discusses these topics with his father. Our author tells us that the King's voice is soft as he speaks of his sense of duty to his country.

What does your student think those words mean? What is **duty**? The dictionary tells us it means: "a thing that is right to do; what a person ought to do; obligation." King Edward VIII certainly felt it was the right thing to do to lead his country as king, but he knew he couldn't carry out his duty with a whole heart if he was forced to live without the woman he loved. Do only kings have a sense of duty? What does your student think about the issue? In relating to others, most people feel a sense of duty. When your student agrees to take out the trash each week as a part of his chores, he feels a sense of duty. He knows that faithfulness to the chore helps his family. He has an obligation to his parents.

When has your student felt a sense of duty? Perhaps caring for a sibling has sparked this feeling, or defending a friend in a specific situation. Talk with your student about times in which he felt a sense of duty and what he did.

Life Skills: What Makes Some Decisions Difficult

King Edward VIII had a very big decision to make. He needed to decide whether he would rather marry the woman he loved and leave England and his crown, or remain in England as king and remain single or marry someone else. It must have been a very difficult decision.

What makes some decisions more difficult than others? If you are standing at the ice cream shop and you're trying to decide between chocolate and strawberry, the decision may seem hard but it really isn't, is it? But if your parents are deciding whether or not they should move to a different state, that is probably a harder decision. Why?

Some decisions have greater impact than others do. They affect more people in a bigger way. There may be greater consequences or risks involved. All of these factors may work to make the decision more difficult.

What are things you can do to help yourself make difficult decisions? First, you can make a list of pros and cons. Here you write good things that could happen if you decide a certain way and bad things that could happen. Then, look carefully at the list. In this way you can see, in black and white, what might occur.

Next, you can ask others for their opinion. Perhaps someone you know has faced a similar situation and can give you advice. If you know someone who is older or more experienced, he may have greater wisdom in general. By taking what they think into account, you can avoid mistakes you might otherwise have made.

Finally, you can take your time. When you face a difficult decision, you don't always have to rush with your final response. Instead, think about it. Decide, but only when you are sure!

You will face difficult decisions, no matter how old you are or if you are king or not. Learning to handle people and decisions wisely is an important part of maturing!

Chapter 3—A Special Trip

Teacher Summary

Neil's school year ends with great success. His grades are excellent and he is reading nearly two grade levels above his own grade. At the beginning of the summer, his parents take Neil and his siblings for a week-long visit to his grandparents' house. Neil is excited. His grandparents live in the country on a farm, where there are always enjoyable things to do.

What we will cover in this chapter:

Language Arts: Synonyms, Antonyms and Homonyms*
Language Arts: Metaphors and Similes
Language Arts: Writing and Discussion Question
Language Arts: Vocabulary
Life Skills: Being Content

Language Arts: Synonyms, Antonyms and Homonyms

Draw your student's attention to the first line of the chapter: "The pretty teacher stood in the front of the classroom." This lesson will address and teach your student about three important parts of vocabulary and speech: synonyms, antonyms and homonyms.

Our author chose the word "pretty" to describe the teacher. Ask your student to think of three more words that mean "pretty." He might choose beautiful, lovely, attractive, etc. Your student has just compiled a list of synonyms.

Synonyms are words which mean the same (or nearly the same) thing. You may wish to come up with a few more words and have your student list synonyms for each. For example:

• *good*: moral, right, upright, righteous, correct
• *angry*: mad, upset, irate, furious
• *simple*: clear, plain, understandable, uncluttered

Your student has probably used a dictionary before. You may use a dictionary when you know a word but want its definition. Has your student ever used a thesaurus? A thesaurus is used when you know the definition (what you want the word to mean) but you need a different word! For example, if you need a word that means fear (but you don't want to use that word), you can look up the word "fear" in a thesaurus and find a list of words which mean the same (or nearly the same) thing—synonyms! If you looked up the word "fear," you might find these words listed: timidity, anxiety, misgiving, suspicion, apprehension, etc. Get a thesaurus and look through it with your student. You can also look at the thesaurus provided with many word processing programs.

A good thesaurus will go further than simply listing synonyms. It may also list some words that mean the opposite of what you are looking up. For example, if you want to know what the opposite of fear is, you can look in a thesaurus and you might find the word "courage." When a word is the opposite of another word it is called an **antonym**. Can your student think of some antonyms of "pretty?" (Some examples could be ugly, unattractive, odd, etc.)

Finally, introduce your student to the third principle of vocabulary for this lesson—**homonyms**. Can your student guess what a homonym is? Homonyms are words that are either spelled the same or pronounced the same but which mean entirely different things. For example:

• *mail*: letters delivered to your house; or
• *mail*: a suit of armor; or
• *male*: a boy
• *be*: a state of being; or
• *bee*: an insect
• *mean*: being cruel; or
• *mean*: the average or middle

Learning what each word means and the differences between synonyms, antonyms and homonyms will help your student understand the English language more fully, which will assist him in communicating more effectively.

Language Arts: Metaphors and Similes

Teacher's Note: Although your student may have covered this topic in previous Five in a Row volumes, it is always good to review poetic and literary devices.

Our author, Montrew Dunham, describes a sunset in this way, "The sun, which was setting in the west, was a flaming orange ball..." This is an accurate description of the sun, isn't it? It is a ball of flaming gaseous material and it looks orange when it goes down.

What if our author had written: "The sun, which was setting in the west, was a scoop of orange sherbet?" It might be a similar description, but we would know the sun wasn't actually a scoop of sherbet. That is what is called a **metaphor**. A metaphor is a poetic device, used in both prose and poetry. When we *compare* one thing to something else, the comparison is called a **simile**. When we say one thing *is* something else, it is called a metaphor. The following examples show the difference:

The sun was *like* a scoop of orange sherbet, setting in the west.—*Simile*
The sun *was* a scoop of orange sherbet, setting in the west.—*Metaphor*

Encourage your student to try writing some metaphors. If he has trouble thinking up individual sentences, give him some jumping-off points, and let him fill in the blanks. For example:

The blade of grass... (was a sharp knife, was a cool hand, was a finger that tickled.)

The blond hair... (was golden straw, was spun honey, was a halo.)

Encourage your student to look for metaphors and similes as he reads.

Language Arts: Writing and Discussion Question

As Neil falls asleep at his grandparents' house, the only sound he hears is the chirp of crickets. When you go to bed tonight, listen for a few minutes and write down all the sounds you can hear. (Your student might need to step outside for part of this activity.) Then write a description of the sounds you heard. Could you hear crickets at all? What other sounds were inside or outside of your house?

Language Arts: Vocabulary

synonyms   Two words which mean the same thing.

antonyms   Two words which mean the opposite.

homonyms   Two words which are spelled the same, or pronounced the same but which have different meanings.

metaphor   A poetic device writers use to compare two things; it is a direct comparison.

simile   A poetic device writers use to compare two things; it is an indirect comparison (using like or as)

contentment   Being satisfied and at peace.

Life Skills: Being Content

In this chapter, we find out the Armstrong family will be moving again soon. It must have been difficult for Neil's mother to frequently have to set up a home in a different house, make new friends with the neighbors and enroll the children in different schools. Draw your student's attention to where she says, "This will be our sixth move...But Stephen has a good job, and moving is a part of the job. Besides, we always enjoy where we live."

Neil's mother is an excellent example of being content. Instead of thinking about the negative aspects of moving six times, she focuses on the positive. She finds things to enjoy about each place they move to. What a lesson for all of us!

How would your student describe being content? It means being happy, at peace, pleased with what is around us. What are some things your student can think of that people can do to help themselves be more content? What are things he does?

Chapter 4—Great-Grandfather Koetter

Teacher Summary

Neil and his family continue to have fun on the farm. Neil and his siblings find many things to do, including riding their grandparents' pony. One day, Neil's grandmother tells him an interesting story about his great-grandfather Koetter's trip across the Atlantic in the 1860s. Great-Grandfather Koetter came to America via Castle Garden. Neil loves learning about his family history, and thinks about his great-grandfather's journeys after his grandmother's story is over.

What we will cover in this chapter:

Social Studies: History and Geography - Prussia and Germany: An Introduction
Social Studies: History and Geography: Castle Garden and Ellis Island*
Science: Where Does Rubber Come From?
Language Arts: Creative Writing - Beginning with One Item
Language Arts: Writing and Discussion Question
Language Arts: Vocabulary
Fine Arts: Drawing from Memory vs. Drawing from Life
Life Skills: Helping Others - Seeing Needs

History and Geography: Prussia and Germany - An Introduction

Neil's great-grandfather, Fritz Koetter, came to America from Germany. Neil's grandmother tells him Great-Grandfather Koetter did not want to serve in the Prussian army, so he decided to cross the Atlantic Ocean and come to a new country.

What does your student know about Germany and Prussia? Take this opportunity to discuss with your student stories and facts about these two areas. If your student has had lessons in this area, then quickly review what you've covered and then try to bring new aspects to your lesson. If this is an introduction to the subject, then give your student a brief overview. Encourage him to do more research on the topics that particularly interest him.

To begin, share with your student a little of Prussia's history. Prussia, as a nation, no longer exists today. The current countries that made up the former Prussia include Lithuania, Poland, and parts of Russia and Germany. Prussia was a very strong and powerful nation for hundreds of years. In 1871, the Prussian King (King Wilhelm I) united several different Germanic states and formed the German Empire. He became the emperor or **kaiser**. Prussia became known around the world for its military way of life. Developing, strengthening and maintaining a rigid army was the most important aspect of Prussian life. The most respected, highly paid aristocrats in the land were the Prussian army generals. They each owned massive estates and had workers (serfs) who tended the farms and were forced to be in the army. Every family was personally linked to the military in some fashion. Ask your student what he thinks that would be like. Would he enjoy being in a rich family living on an estate? How would he feel if he were a serf, forced to work the land and serve in battle? What would it be like to live in a society of "classes?"

Despite these strong military foundations, the Prussian army was defeated during World War I, and became less and less strong. After World War II, in 1947, most of the countries forming Prussia were divided into smaller districts.

Today, much of the land once considered to be part of Prussia, or the German Empire, is now called Germany. Until October 3, 1990, Germany was divided into two halves, East and West Germany. Now it is one unified country, with Berlin as the capital and largest city.

Draw your student's attention to where our author tells us that many German settlers came to America to escape being forced to join the army. They wanted to lead peaceful lives. Even after much of the Prussian military idealism broke down, Germany still remained as a very strict, military society. People who wished to remain at peace and not enter the army were left no choice but to move. Neil's great-grandfather was one of many German immigrants to the United States. When German families arrived in America, they tended to settle in the same location as other families from that country. In Great-Grandfather Koetter's case, he and many other German families settled in Ohio.

If your student is interested in learning more about Prussia or Germany, encourage him to find some books at the library on either subject. It might be fun to create a map of Germany or the former Prussian Empire. Your student can explore other related topics such as the Seven Years' War, the Berlin Wall, Frederick the Great, the Augsburg Confession and the Franco-Prussian War.

32

History and Geography: Castle Garden and Ellis Island*

In this chapter we learn that Great-Grandfather Koetter came into America through an immigration station at Castle Garden. Castle Garden was located at the tip of Manhattan Island in New York. Locate a good United States map and point out Manhattan to your student. It is small, isn't it? Before Castle Garden was an immigration station, it was a fort and then a concert hall. By the 1890s so many immigrants were coming through, the United States government recognized that Castle Garden was too small to handle them. It was then they opened a new immigration center in New York Harbor, and called it Ellis Island. From 1892 through the 1920s, over 12 million people came through Ellis Island and settled in America!

Has your student ever studied Ellis Island? If you are able, try to locate the book entitled *If Your Name Was Changed at Ellis Island* by Ellen Levine. This book offers children a perfect peek at the fascinating subject of immigration.

The American government wanted people to be able to come to America, and millions of people came through Ellis Island. America was founded as a haven for immigrants who were searching for religious and financial freedom. With so many people coming all at once, the U.S. government had to have an organized system.

When immigrants arrived, they were immediately checked over by health officials. Ask your student why he thinks this was done. What if an immigrant had a highly contagious disease or was carrying a foreign germ or lice? It could spread in this country. To protect the citizens who were already in America,

the government didn't allow the very sick or ailing to stay. They were sent back to their own countries. Can you imagine how disappointing that must have been? Certain doctors also conducted mental tests. They wanted to make sure that immigrants were sane and well. However, many people were sent back to their own country falsely. When they said certain things or did certain things, the doctors thought they were mentally ill. However, many times it was just cultural differences the doctors observed. It is now suspected that tens of thousands of immigrants were mistakenly sent back to their native lands.

After immigrants were checked for health and mental wellness, inspectors made sure each person had the appropriate paperwork and identification cards. If one was able to pass all the tests, examinations and questions, he was sent to the train stations to head into America. Some immigrants were detained longer at Ellis Island, but most were able to leave within one day.

You may wish to discuss the following topics further with your student: immigration, prejudice, multiculturalism, pioneers, etc.

Science: Where Does Rubber Come From?

Neil works on a model airplane that operates on a rubberband motor. Does your student know where rubber comes from? Introduce your student to this fascinating area of science.

To begin, have your student make a list of all the things he can think of, around his house and in the world, which are made from or contain rubber. If he gets stuck, spark his memory with a few suggestions like tires, gloves, mattresses, erasers, tennis shoes, balloons, rubber boots, carpet-backing, tennis balls, mud flaps, fire hoses, conveyor belts, etc.

Obviously, our lives are filled with rubber-based products, but what exactly is rubber? Where did it come from?

Rubber was first brought to Europe by Christopher Columbus. On his second trip to the New World, in 1496, he went to Haiti and came back with a little ball that bounced! It was made from the gum of a tree found in Central and South America. It was new to the Europeans, but the South American people had been working with this amazing substance for centuries.

Further expeditions to the New World brought back more rubber, but by the time it got to Europe it was hard and difficult to work with. People couldn't understand what kinds of things could be made from this substance. Joseph Priestly, a European chemist, first called the natural gum rubber because he found it could rub out pencil marks.

Rubber, in its natural state, is the resin or gum of a tree. The scientific name of the plant is Hevea brasiliensis, but it is commonly known as a rubber tree. Just as people tap maple trees for sap to make pancake syrup, so people tap rubber trees and collect liquid called **latex**. Rubber trees must be at least six years old before they can be tapped. Rubber plantations or estates are found mainly in Thailand, Malaysia and Indonesia. There are a few plantations in South America.

For awhile, Europeans didn't understand the amazing properties of rubber, but soon they invented a machine called a **masticator**. This machine warmed and heated the rubber that was being brought back from South America and Southeast Asia. When rubber (then hard and brittle) was heated, it became soft and pliable again. Suddenly, scientists began finding all sorts of uses for it. The first products using rubber were made in 1823 and were called macintoshes, the first waterproof coats. But there was still a problem!

In the summer, rubber boots got soft and sticky. And in the winter they got dry and brittle. The rubber was too sensitive to temperatures. In 1839, an American scientist named Charles Goodyear (as in Goodyear tires) discovered that if rubber were mixed with a little sulfur (a yellow powder), then it wasn't as affected by temperature changes. This principle became known as **vulcanization**. He also figured out that if rubber was vulcanized while it was in a mold, then after it cooled the rubber would stay in that shape indefinitely!

By the 1920s, scientists knew how important rubber was. Thousands of items were being made every day out of the miracle product. But scientists also understood that only so much natural rubber could be grown and gathered at any one time. It was expensive. There must be a way to make a synthetic or man-made version. By World War II, synthetic rubber was produced in mass quantities.

Today, there are many types of synthetic rubbers produced. They have names like butadiene rubber, styrene-butadiene rubber, neoprene, polysulfide rubbers, butyl rubber, and silicones. Each type of rubber has special purposes and uses. Even with these new types of rubber, however, the two main ways of forming it are still used—mastication and vulcanization.

Rubber is an amazing part of our world. Did your student guess it came from a tree?

Language Arts: Creative Writing - Beginning with One Item

Read with your student the paragraph that begins: "Neil went through the screen door into the summer kitchen." This paragraph goes on to describe the summer kitchen, Neil's grandmother, making bread, the table she's working on, etc.

Sometimes, a wonderful, descriptive paragraph in a story begins with just one item—a summer kitchen, for instance.

For a creative writing exercise, give your student a list of single items. It could be as simple as the following:

- pencil
- doorknob
- shoe
- rock
- spoon
- garden
- rocking horse

Now, have your student select one item. Have him write the word at the top of a piece of paper. Now, tell him to let his imagination run wild. Without forming a story line, plot or even sentences, your student can begin listing further descriptions and details of his selected object. Prompt him with questions such as: Who uses the object? What color is it? How old is it? Where is it located? Who was the last person to use it? Who was the first person to use it? Here are two examples, using the same noun:

spoon
silver
shiny
engraved
used by an old woman
her name is Aunt Matilda
the spoon was from England
very expensive

spoon
wooden
worn
splitting down the handle
held by a child
moving through vegetable soup
the only meal the family can afford
even the potatoes are cut small

As you can see, suddenly, from a single object your student can begin framing a lovely tale. Once your student's list has grown fairly long, then he can begin to write the story. He can begin to fill in the missing pieces around his list of creative observations and voila!—a story is formed.

If your student enjoys the above exercise, encourage him to try it with different objects or people. If he challenges and disciplines himself to think with imagination, creative writing will become easier and easier.

Language Art: Writing and Discussion Question

Our author writes, "Neil could run and play and do whatever he wanted." But he couldn't really do whatever he wanted, could he? Freedom always has some restrictions. Why is that? How would you describe freedom?

Language Arts: Vocabulary

kaiser   An old title for the rulers of Germany.

masticator   A machine which heats and softens rubber.

vulcanization   The process through which rubber is combined with other chemicals.

latex   An emulsion which holds small rubber particles; what is tapped from rubber trees.

Fine Arts: Drawing from Memory vs. Drawing from Life

In the evening the fireflies (also called lightning bugs) are out. Does your student know what a firefly looks like? Have him describe it to you. There are generally two ways a picture happens when an artist draws. Either the artist is looking directly at an object, person or photograph, or he draws from memory—recording with his paintbrush or pencil what he sees in his mind. Both ways artists work are wonderful, but they are different.

Have your student paint or draw a picture of a firefly. He can spend as much time on it as he wishes. When he is done, find a photograph of a firefly in a dictionary or encyclopedia. Does your student think his drawing looks similar? It probably does, but it may not have the details and exact proportions it might have had if he had been looking at a real firefly or photograph of one. (If you live in an area where there are no fireflies and your student has never seen one, you can choose a different insect for this activity.)

It's important for artists to remember this principle. If your student wants to draw a very realistic, detailed and accurate picture of something, he should try to look at the real object! But if he wants to create a picture using his imagination and memory, which is a bit more fanciful, then encourage him to do so.

Life Skills: Helping Others - Seeing Needs

After a wonderful meal of fried chicken, the children clean up the lunch area. Neil tries to drag the heavy picnic basket into the house, but it is too heavy. His mother sees him and she helps.

Draw your student's attention to this wonderful display of helping someone else. Neil sees a need: the lunch basket should be put away. Without grumbling, he tries to help his mother. A part of being a good person and neighbor is seeing the needs of others and helping without even being asked.

Encourage your student to be helpful whenever possible. Even if a task can't be completed, friends and family will be excited that the attempt was made. People feel cared for when they see you trying to help.

Chapter 5—The Wolf Patrol

Teacher Summary

Neil gets settled into his new school and does very well. Soon he is reading nearly three grade levels above his grade. Neil still loves planes and flight. He finds a couple of friends who are interested in those topics, too. Neil soon finds that he needs more money to pay for his plane kits, so he gets a job mowing the grass at an area cemetery.

U.S. involvement in World War II begins that winter with the bombing of Pearl Harbor, and Neil finds it difficult to understand why the war is happening. To help keep the boys' spirits up, and to provide fun activities, Neil's father and another man start a Boy Scout troop. Soon Neil and his friends are happily working on becoming Tenderfoot Scouts.

What we will cover in this chapter:

Social Studies: History and Geography - Pearl Harbor
Social Studies: Geography - The Pacific Islands
Science: Research Doesn't Have to Be Boring
Language Arts: Writing and Discussion Question
Language Arts: Vocabulary
Fine Arts: Making Maps*
Life Skills: Creativity in Scarcity

Social Studies: History and Geography - Pearl Harbor

Neil was a young man during a very difficult time in America—World War II. The United States' involvement in the war began with an event that is often simply called "Pearl Harbor." (If your student studied *Helen Keller* in FIAR Vol. 7, he probably studied World War II. Review what he remembers from that lesson and build on that knowledge with this one, which concentrates on one particular event and its repercussions for U.S. citizens.)

Teacher's Note: You may wish to define for your student the word **harbor**. It is any sheltered body of water where ships can dock. Most harbors are sheltered by the strips of land surrounding them, which protect ships from high winds and waves.

Pearl Harbor is a U.S. naval base in Hawaii. On December 7, 1941, Japanese bombers swooped down and began dropping bombs and torpedoes on U.S. ships. Japanese dive-bombers also bombed the planes lined up on various U.S. airfields including Wheeler Field, Hickam Field and others. The first bomb fell a few minutes before 8 a.m. and the assault was continuous until 8:25 a.m. Just as the U.S. soldiers thought it was over, another wave of attacks came through. All in all, the attacks lasted over two hours. Four major ships were sunk and thousands of American soldiers died. Only 100 Japanese airmen were killed or wounded.

Pearl Harbor Memorial

The next morning, President Franklin Delano Roosevelt addressed Congress with the following words: "Yesterday, December 7, 1941—a date which will live in infamy—the United States of America was suddenly and deliberately attacked..." His speech was only six minutes long, and within one hour every person in Congress but one voted to declare war on Japan.

What does your student think of when he hears the word "war?" What are the feelings that arise within him? War is a frightening, threatening thing. At first, the war didn't affect Neil and his friends much. They knew older boys who were being sent away to fight, but their lives remained normal.

Rationing occurred. Does your student know what the word ration means? To ration something means to deal it out in specific portions. When the portion runs out, no more is available until the next ration. Many things were rationed during World War II, mainly gasoline and food items. Meat, butter, sugar, cooking oil, coffee, canned foods, even shoes were all rationed to help the war effort. Feeding the troops abroad was top priority and some of the food manufacturing plants were being used for other wartime projects. So food was rationed at home where each family received a book of ration stamps. Each rationed item was worth a certain number of stamps. If you went to the store to buy meat, it didn't matter how much money you had. You could only buy the meat if you had the correct number of stamps. When you had used your stamps, you had to wait until more stamps were issued.

World War II also meant rations on gasoline in the United States. This ration was required for two reasons. First, it helped to conserve a valuable energy source. The United States Armed Forces needed a lot of fuel to power the tanks, planes, Jeeps and ships being used in the war. Factories needed fuel to run the heavy machinery used to manufacture weapons and vehicles. There just weren't many fuel sources left for citizens to use. Gasoline was also rationed because the rubber supply from Asia had been cut off. Because rubber is needed to make tires, each and every tire now had to last as long as possible. If the gasoline was rationed, people couldn't drive their cars as much and their tires lasted much longer.

In order to keep track of the gasoline ration, the government assigned each personal vehicle a lettered sticker. Most families, who simply used driving for pleasure (such as the Armstrong family) were assigned a letter A. This meant they could use three gallons of gasoline a week. Professional drivers and workers who found driving a necessity (doctors, police officers, etc.) were issued E stickers. This meant they could use unlimited amounts of gasoline.

To illustrate this principle for your student, develop some rations for use around your house. Perhaps each shower can only last three minutes, or only four ice cubes can be used for a beverage each day. Even if the rations aren't realistic, they will give your student a sense of what it feels like to be restricted. You may even enjoy creating some ration stamps with your student. You can make it a family project. Each member of the family might need three stamps in order to drink a soda, watch a television program, etc.

The attack on Pearl Harbor introduced the United States to a war that forever changed the face of America. Suddenly, the world seemed smaller and it was easier to see how all the countries influenced each other. Encourage your student to study this war further, if it is of interest, in order to gain a better understanding of this amazing historic event.

Social Studies: Geography – The Pacific Islands

Hawaii (including Pearl Harbor) is located in a huge body of water called the Pacific Ocean. Locate the Pacific Ocean on a detailed world map or globe. Does your student notice the many islands scattered across the ocean? These are known as the Pacific Islands.

The Pacific Islands is the name given to the thousands of islands located in the Pacific Ocean. They are also sometimes referred to as Oceania. Amazingly, it is not known exactly how many islands there are! Most scientists agree there are between 20,000 and 30,000, but no one knows for sure. Some islands are thousands of miles across, while others are just tiny piles of sand rising above the surface of the waves.

New Guinea is the largest island in Oceania, with New Zealand's two main islands being second and third. Can your student locate these three islands on a map or globe?

The Pacific Islands can be divided into three sections: Melanesia, Micronesia, and Polynesia. Encourage your student to look at those words. Can he guess what each might mean? What about the prefixes mela-, micro- and poly-?

Melanesia is sometimes referred to as the Black Islands. (Mela- comes from the word melanin, which is a pigment in the skin that is brown or blackish.) These islands include Fiji and New Guinea. The native people of Melanesia generally have very dark brown skin.

Micronesia is made up of many tiny islands. (Micro- means small.) Micronesia includes Guam and the Caroline Islands. Most of Micronesia, however, is composed of very tiny reefs and islands—many without specific names.

Polynesia is made up of many islands. (Poly- means more than one.) It is the largest section of islands in the Pacific and stretches over many thousands of miles.

To help your student remember these distinctions, it might be helpful for him to make a simple chart. He can draw illustrations of mela-, micro- and poly-.

The Pacific Islands are fascinating in their differences. Some islands are inhabited by hundreds or thousands of people, while others are completely uninhabited. The beaches range from white sand to rocky coral and black volcanic (lava) sand stretches. New Zealand and the Hawaiian islands differ the most from the rest of Oceania. New Zealand is an entirely independent nation, with a modern economy and a large percentage of citizens of European ancestry. Hawaii is a state of the United States and has a modern culture and economy.

Another amazing fact to share with your student is that while the world has more than 7,000 languages, over 1,500 of them are spoken in the Pacific Islands!

If your student is interested in learning more about the Pacific Islands, he can select one specific island to study in more depth. He can research and learn about related topics such as coral, the Pacific Ocean, volcanoes and the United Nations Trust Territory (1947 to 1996).

Science: Research Doesn't Have to Be Boring

Ask your student what he thinks of when he hears the word research. Some students are convinced that research for a project must be boring—poring through countless journals and thick books filled with difficult information and reams of facts. Sometimes, that is what research is about. But it doesn't always have to be.

Show your student the paragraph in our book which reads:

"Neil did well in his new school. He read more and more about planes and flying. He read magazines about airplanes, and he kept a scrapbook, cutting out pictures of planes and saving them in it."

Does your student know that Neil was doing research? Research isn't always gathering information for a certain project or research paper. If you love horses or model cars, and you are always reading about the topic and saving information or pictures, then you are doing research!

Encourage your student to employ a technique to compile and save information on a topic he is greatly interested in, as Neil did. He could create a scrapbook like Neil, or he could use a folder (a physical folder or a folder on a computer) to hold all of the information he finds. He'll enjoy adding to his collection of information and pictures and reviewing it occasionally for years to come.

Language Arts: Writing and Discussion Question

In this chapter we learn the Boy Scout motto: "Be Prepared." What do you think a motto for your family might be? Why?

Language Arts: Vocabulary

scale   Drawing an area to a specific size and indicating the ratio.

symbol   A specific item used to represent something else.

Melanesia   A subregion of islands in Oceania; sometimes called the "black islands."

Micronesia   A subregion of Oceania consisting of about 2,000 small islands.

Polynesia   A subregion of Oceania; includes several large islands.

Pearl Harbor   The U.S. Naval base in Hawaii.

cartography   The science and study of making maps.

Fine Arts: Making Maps*

Neil and his friends like to practice their map skills. **Cartography** (the science and study of making maps) is an important profession. Your student can practice being a cartographer and making simple maps by learning a few basic principles.

Most maps include the following three things: a scale, symbols and a legend (or key). **Scale** means drawing an area to a specific size and indicating the ratio. You can draw any size area any size you wish. Think about a world map. The entire world fits on a small piece of paper! You can decide to use whatever scale you choose, but always remember to be consistent. Your student should choose a scale to use on a project like mapping his backyard. One helpful scale might involve using paces. Each step of his foot in front of the next is one pace. After he paces off the yard, he can create a scale such as ten paces to the inch.

Symbols are small pictures or designs that communicate to the viewer what is pictured on a map. It is easier to use a symbol for something than to draw the entire building or item. It saves space! Legends (or keys) are usually located in a bottom corner of a map and they tell the viewer what each symbol stands for and what the scale of the map is.

To begin making a map, your student can gather the following materials: plain drawing paper (or thicker paper for painting), pencil, felt-tip pens or markers, and colored pencils. If your student loves to paint, watercolors can be used as well.

Your student can begin with something as simple as a map of his backyard or bedroom, or try something more difficult like his neighborhood (perhaps a three-block radius).

Most maps are oriented so that the direction north is at the top. If your student needs help identifying north, you can get a compass for him and help him.

If your student enjoys creating a map of his neighborhood, he can try creating a map to buried treasure. First, have your student develop a plan, locate some treasure, bury the treasure and then create a basic map using a scale of paces or feet. Next, he can create an authentic-looking old treasure map by folding the paper he will be using in small squares. Unfold the paper and paint it with brewed tea. Allow the paper to dry and then your student can begin to record the symbols, trails and legend. This is an excellent activity to do with (or for) friends or siblings.

Making maps, either realistically or using fantasy, is a fun learning activity for children of all ages!

Life Skills: Creativity in Scarcity

Even though meat and food items were being rationed, Neil's mother always provided healthy, delicious meals. Talk with your student about what scarcity is like. Has he ever worked on a project and needed a specific item, only to discover it wasn't available? Did he give up or did he look for an alternative? Sometimes, when we have the very least, then we are forced to be more creative. When you think something won't work, suddenly you're able to find a different way of solving the problem. Sometimes, it may be even better than the old way!

Encourage your student to be creative when experiencing scarcity, instead of discouraged. Learning and practicing contentment is an important part of growing up!

Chapter 6—Camping Out

Teacher Summary

Neil and his friends Bud and Kotchko decide to go on a campout. After gaining permission, the boys gather their own materials, food items and bedrolls.

Excitement grows among them as they realize they will be able to complete badges in cooking, camping and hiking all in one event! By working together and planning well, the boys have a wonderful trip.

What we will cover in this chapter:

Science: Constellations*
Science: Types of Campfires
Language Arts: Writing and Discussion Question
Fine Arts: Making Knots
Fine Arts: Cooking Outside
Life Skills: Compromise

Science: Constellations*

When Neil, Bud and Kotchko finish dinner, the evening is already dark. The boys start looking at the heavens and recognize the Big Dipper and the North Star. Has your student ever learned about constellations? Can he easily identify a few basic ones? The Big Dipper and Little Dipper are actually called star groups (parts of larger constellations); Orion and Casseopia are constellations. Stargazing is a relaxing, ancient pastime. It can be enjoyed with the naked eye or a telescope, with one person or the entire family!

A constellation (kahn stell LAY shun) is the term scientists use to describe a group of stars which are visible in the night sky. The heavens are divided into 88 constellations. Each one is unique. In ancient times, mythology was combined with astronomy and each constellation was given a different name, depending upon what the design of stars resembled. For example, the constellation Orion is named for the mythological character Orion the Hunter. If you look at the constellation Orion, you can see the three stars that form his belt, the stars which make up his

shoulders and feet and then a string of stars which make up a sword hanging from his belt.

The North Star is an easily visible star that is positioned nearly directly above the North Pole. It is also called Polaris. This star makes up the tip of the handle in the constellation Little Dipper. There is also the Big Dipper, which consists of seven different stars.

Because of the rotation of the earth, different constellations are visible during the early evening hours at different times of the year. In the U.S., for example, Orion can be spotted in the fall and winter sky. The Big Dipper is located to the east of the Little Dipper in January, but then is located to the west of it in July.

If your student is interested in learning more about constellations, encourage him to find a good book on the topic and then get to gazing! (*Find the Constellations* by H. A. Rey is one of many good books.) Nothing teaches more about constellations than simply looking at a clear night yourself. Become familiar with the skies. If your student is having a hard time seeing the stars because of city light pollution, then wait for a clear night and drive away from the city a little bit to get a clearer view.

Science: Types of Campfires

Neil and the boys are trying to decide which kind of fire to build. They settle on a "hunter's fireplace." Did your student know there are different types of campfires with different uses? Share with your student a few of the major types of campfires: hunter's fire, keyhole fire, star fire and Swedish fire lay.

To begin the discussion, explain the two main rules for making a campfire: (1) locate a site of packed dirt or rock and (2) remove debris (leaves, sticks, trash, etc.,) at least three feet from the site on all sides.

The boys decided to build a **hunter's fire**. Two large green logs placed one to two feet from one another in a parallel manner form this fireplace. A fire is built between the logs and a cooking pot can be placed over the coals, on the green logs. This kind of fireplace is practical for cooking and boiling water.

A **keyhole fire** is formed with rocks. A narrow channel of rocks is placed on a dirt patch and then off the channel is a round circle of rocks. The design resembles an old-fashioned keyhole. This kind of fireplace is ideal for light and cooking. A fire is built in the circle of rocks. Once hot coals have formed (when the fire has burned down a bit and ash is forming), then they are pushed carefully up into the narrow channel of rocks and the cooking pot is placed over them.

A **star fire** (or Indian fire) is formed by five logs all pointing into a center point. This kind of fire is good for light and helps if logs are scarce.

Finally, there is the **Swedish fire lay**. You build a small fire and then lay three hand-hewed log planks toward one another over the fire to form a little tent. A cooking pot is set on top of the three planks. This type of fire is useful for cooking and is also a space saver.

Have fun learning more about campfires with your student. Perhaps you can try one out on your next camping trip!

Language Arts: Writing and Discussion Question

The boys were quick to get their parents' permission and that of Mr. Reber to camp in his woods. What do you think might have happened if they hadn't gained Mr. Reber's permission? Write a descriptive passage telling the story that might have been.

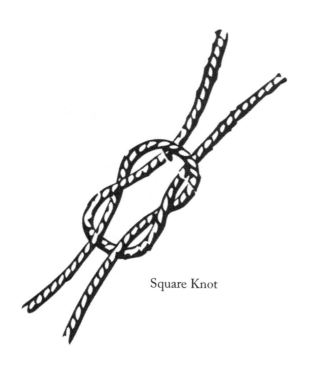

Square Knot

Fine Arts: Making Knots

The boys like working on their knot badge. Has your student ever studied knots? Knot tying is a fun and historic activity that your student can work on anywhere—as long as he has a little rope.

The Egyptians were the first to make and use rope, as long ago as 3500 B.C., and knots were devised to use with the rope. Although ropework and knots have been necessary in many occupations, they probably had the greatest impact in the days of large sailing ships. With their miles of rigging and the many needs aboard ship, enormous numbers of knots were needed in order to keep the ships afloat.

Three terms are commonly associated with rope tying: knot, bend and hitch. A **knot** is formed with one rope. A **bend** is used when two or more ropes are joined. A **hitch** is used to describe a rope being attached to a post or pole.

If your student studies the art of knot-tying in any depth, he will encounter terms such as splicing, lashing, whipping, sheepshank, dogshank, granny knot and overhand knot.

The most basic of all knots is the overhand knot—a simple twist. This is also referred to as a type of stopper knot. Think with your student for a moment. If you wanted to prevent a rope from pulling through your hand or a hole, then you will need a knot bigger than the hole. Knots that provide that kind of stopper action are called stopper knots.

If your student is interested in creating beautiful and useful knots, then get him a piece of rope (nylon ropes work well and don't hurt the hands) and a beginner's book, and then set him loose. Soon he'll be "tied up" with fun! (If your library has a copy of the classic book, *The Ashley Book of Knots* by Clifford Ashley, your student will be amazed at the more than 3,900 different knots shown, as well as the history that goes along with them!)

Fine Arts: Cooking Outside

Has your student ever noticed that everything tastes better when it's cooked and eaten outside? Maybe it's because of the hard work that must be done in order to enjoy it, or perhaps it's the fresh air. Food prepared outdoors is certainly delicious.

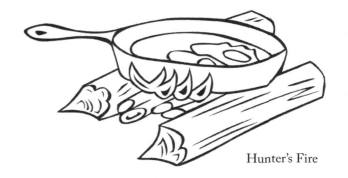

Hunter's Fire

Neil and his buddies cooked over a hunter's fire. If your student is not quite that adventurous, or if you live in an area where building campfires is prohibited (check with local police or fire authorities), then why not try an alternative grill-type cooking? The following instructions are for a fun "Tin Can Grill.'

Teacher's Note: Even for older children, this activity requires supervision. If you are working with younger students, then do the metal cutting for them. Supervise all students around hot coals!

Tin Can Grill

This is an inexpensive, creative way to make a delicious meal outside. It works well in small spaces like patios, too! You will need the following:

a large aluminum can—coffee cans work well
metal cutters
safety gloves
heavy aluminum foil
charcoal
lighter fluid
matches
a small grill rack

Using safety gloves, begin by cutting with metal cutters down the sides of the aluminum can in 2" strips. Cut only to about two inches from the bottom. After each strip has been cut, carefully fan it out (strips will be very sharp). When you are finished, you should have approximately ten strips of metal flared out to create a shallow basket of metal. Carefully fill the bottom of the can with dirt. Line and cover the entire can with heavy foil. You have created a shallow, bowl-shaped grill.

Place the charcoal on top of the foil and lay the grill rack on top of the covered metal strips. It is important that the rack be at least four inches above the coals. By adjusting the metal strips up or down, creating this correct space is relatively easy.

Light the coals. When they have burned for awhile and turn white with ash, then the student can place whatever he wants to grill on the rack and watch it cook! Hot dogs are delicious, but so are beef kabobs or even just marshmallows made into s'mores! Have fun eating outside and share your new grilling idea with a friend.

Life Skills: Compromise

Neil and Kotchko have a discussion regarding who will build the fire. Both boys are anxious to try their skill, but they solve the problem this way. Neil says, "What if I build it today and you build it in the morning for breakfast?"

Learning how and when to suggest a compromise is an important life skill. There are many areas where it would be wrong to compromise one's beliefs. But, in general, learning to work out conflicts and find ways where both conflicting parties are satisfied is an important part of maturity.

In an actual compromise, neither party gets all of what he wants, but rather, each party gets some of what he wants and the conflict ends. When Neil suggests that one boy make the fire one day and the other the next (when both boys want to do it both days), and when his friend agrees, the boys have reached a compromise.

Talk with your student about times you remember when you had to reach a compromise to end a conflict. Can your student think of a time when he has done the same? How was the decision made?

Chapter 7—A Scout's Pace

Teacher Summary

The boys continue the fun on their campout. Neil, Bud and Kotchko each take a nature walk and record the special plants and birds they recognize. The rest of the summer is peaceful. In the fall, Neil gets a new job at Neumeister's Bakery. He makes over 110 dozen doughnuts every night! Neil is happy when he's working, but he enjoys making his model airplanes even more.

What we will cover in this chapter:

Social Studies: Career Path - Chef or Baker
Science: Where Stars Go in the Daytime
Science: Principles of Digestion*
Language Arts: Personification
Language Arts: Writing and Discussion Question
Language Arts: Vocabulary
Fine Arts: Drawing a Scene

Social Studies: Career Path - Chef or Baker

Neil's job at the cemetery mowing grass was over at the end of the summer. Neil soon found a new job at Neumeister's Bakery. Does your student enjoy being in the kitchen? Does he like both the mathematical aspects of measuring and mixing, as well as the fun parts of creating delicious baked goods and foods? Either a chef or a baker is a wonderful career for your student to explore.

Professional chefs and bakers are hard working people! They train rigorously at academies and apprenticeship programs. Some chefs begin training when they graduate from high school and remain in training programs for two to five years.

Students who want to become a chef or a baker usually begin in the same classes for the first year or so. These classes include basic food preparation, nutrition, accounting, garde manger (gar mon ZHAY, a class in the preparation of salads, hors d'oeuvres and other cold foods), butchery, pastry classes, menu design and management. After these beginning classes, students can generally branch off into specialties. Some choose restaurant management or chef school. Those who want to become bakers (often referred to as pastry chefs) may attend pastry school.

If your student is interested in becoming a chef, then he must be prepared to work long hours. He must also be ready to work with a team. No professional kitchen produces food with only one person. Chefs work together to provide delicious and beautiful meals for their patrons.

Pastry chefs (bakers) often work more independently. A hotel or restaurant with three chefs and 15 cooks may only have two pastry chefs. Pastry chefs work very early in the morning, so your student needs to make sure he likes rising early. The early baking ensures a supply of fresh-baked goods for the opening hours. Bakeries are often producing goods as early as 4 a.m.

If your student is interested in pursuing a degree or certification in culinary arts, he can contact his local community college or university for program information. For now, however, he can work on honing his kitchen skills at home. He can learn new recipes, read books on baking or cooking, try out new techniques and practice safe kitchen skills (washing hands, avoiding cross-contamination, carefully handling knives, etc.). These skills can all work toward preparing your student for a fulfilling career as a chef or baker.

Science: Where Stars Go in the Daytime

In the morning at the campsite, Neil is thinking about how many stars he had seen the night before. Now that day has dawned, he can't see any stars in the sky. Where do they go during the daytime? Has your student ever wondered about this? The answer involves a knowledge of the solar system and the rotation of the earth around the sun.

In reality, the answer to the question, "Where do stars go in the daytime?" is very simple. They don't go anywhere. Stars and planets are always above us in the heavens. Does your student know that the sun is a star? It is, indeed. In fact, it is the nearest star to our planet.

To understand why stars aren't visible during the day, it is important to explain to your student a few facts about the sun. First, the sun is nearly 400 times larger than our moon. It doesn't look much larger, however, because it is over 93 million miles from Earth. The sun is vital to Earth. Without the light and heat generated by this "nearby" star, life on Earth would be nonexistent. Our planet would be as lifeless and barren as the other planets.

When the sun comes up in the morning (in the east), the brilliance of its light outshines that of all the other stars. The stars appear to have vanished, but they are simply being outshone. As the earth turns (once every 24 hours), the sun appears to set in the west. As it goes down, the other stars are suddenly quite bright against the dark sky.

To illustrate this for your student, go into a room (preferably one with no windows) and take a small flashlight with you. With the light turned off, shine the flashlight on the ceiling. Now, with your student watching, flip the light switch. The flashlight beam seems significantly weaker now, doesn't it? Is it really a weaker light? No, it is not. This illustration is similar to what happens with the stars and our sun.

Science: Principles of Digestion*

Neil fixes the boys a wonderful breakfast. There is so much delicious food! Does your student ever wonder what happens to his food after it has been consumed? Where does it all go? How does his body use it? Ask your student what he thinks happens to his food.

When a person eats food, his body uses the food to build strong bones, hard teeth and solid muscles. We also get energy from our food. Before the body can get this energy, it must break the food down and turn it into a liquid. Even the liquid we drink, like milk and soda, must be changed slightly. In brief, digestion is the word we use to describe the system that effects these changes.

Digestion breaks the food we eat into very tiny pieces. The first part of digestion begins with chewing. How many times does your student chew each mouthful of food? Does he chew it 10 times, 20 times, or more?

To graphically demonstrate chewing to break down food, get a raw piece of carrot or celery and a plate, and sit with your student at the table. Have your student take a bite and chew the food 10 times. Now comes the fun part. Instruct him to spit the mouthful out on the plate. He can take another bite and chew it 30 times, again spitting it onto the plate next to the first pile. Do this three more times in increments of 50 chews, 75 chews and 100 chews. The more times your student chews, the smaller the pieces become and the less his stomach will have to work when he swallows food. As small as those pieces were at 100 chews, the stomach makes them even smaller with the next process of digestion.

When food is swallowed, the throat squeezes together and forces the food down into the **esophagus**, a tube leading to the stomach. Have your student put his hand on his throat and feel the muscles constrict when he swallows.

When the food gets to the esophagus, it is again pushed by muscles and forced into the **stomach**. The stomach muscle stretches wide or small depending upon how much is eaten. In the stomach, food is smashed even smaller yet again, by muscles squeezing and by special fluids in the stomach. These fluids are a kind of **acid** and they help break the food down into smaller and smaller pieces.

After something is eaten, say a hamburger, it will probably be in the stomach for at least five hours. Some foods that are harder to digest stay longer. When foods leave the stomach, they are the consistency of thick soup! Everything has been mashed into millions and millions of tiny pieces. Can they get any smaller?

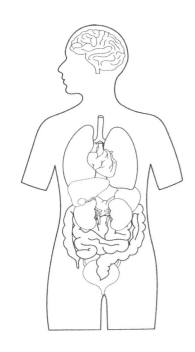

When food leaves the stomach, it moves into the part of the digestive system called the intestines. First, it goes through the section of intestine called the **small intestine** and then it goes into the **large intestine**. Intestines are nearly 21 feet long, but they are coiled inside the body like a rope. Once food has been squeezed in the intestines for awhile, it is in the form of molecules. Molecules are so small that they can't be seen without a microscope.

The food is now small enough for the body to use! The walls of the intestines allow molecules of food to pass through them via small blood and lymph vessels. The body then sends the molecules wherever they are needed. Not all the food can be used, however. The rest of the matter goes to the large intestine and then is eliminated when you go to the bathroom. From the time the first bite of a meal is taken to when it exits the body can be as long as 36 hours! The body works hard to provide good digestion.

Language Arts: Personification

As Neil wakes up and steps out of his tent, he hears the sounds of nature around him. Our author writes, "He saw a plump gray rabbit scamper across the clearing as a blue jay scolded from the oak tree."

What does the word scold mean? It means to blame with angry words. Ask your student if a bird can really use angry words? No, it cannot. A bird's call may sound angry, but it isn't really using words. Our author has used a literary device called **personification**. He gives a non-human thing human characteristics. Even though that blue jay isn't really talking, it is easy to imagine the way it sounds by that description.

Personification can be used to enliven descriptions for both non-human and non-living things. For example:

The tree was solemn.

The rock stubbornly refused to move.

Encourage your student to employ this new literary device in either a new writing exercise or by including it in a project on which he is already working.

Language Arts: Writing and Discussion Question

Neil experiences a dream where he is floating in the air. Have you ever had a dream where you were floating or flying? Talk about it. If not, what is the strangest dream that you've ever experienced?

Language Arts: Vocabulary

digestion   The breakdown of food in the body.

saliva   The liquid the mouth produces to aid in food breakdown.

esophagus   The muscular tube which leads from the throat to the stomach.

acid   The liquids present in the stomach which aid in food breakdown.

personification   A literary device where human characteristics are given to non-human things.

Fine Arts: Drawing a Scene

When your student draws pictures, does he generally draw one specific item, like a tree or flower, for instance? Does he sometimes employ several objects to create a scene? A delightful way to draw is to create a complete scene. Use chapter 7 in this book about Neil to lead your student to draw a scene.

Encourage your student to reread and to make notes about the various descriptions of the boys' campsite and fireplace and about Neil's breakfast preparations. Armed with the notes, his own imagination and some art supplies, he can then draw the scene.

He can use watercolors, crayons, colored pencils or even pastels. He can include all the boys in the picture, if he wishes. What color is Bud's hair? How tall is Kotchko? What is Neil doing in the picture—cracking eggs? Is he setting the pots on the fire? Have fun recreating our author's words in picture form.

Chapter 8—Winners and Losers

Teacher Summary

Neil and his friends, Bud and Kotchko, decide to enter projects in their school's science fair. Bud and Kotchko work on a project together, a photoelectric cell. But Neil decides to work on his own project—a small handcrafted steam turbine engine. Neil works hard on his project and it turns out wonderfully. Bud and Kotchko's photoelectric cell does not work at all, so they hurriedly throw together a new science project on the day before the fair—a small homemade camera. Neil is secretly sure he will win, but in the end his little turbine doesn't work at the very critical moment of judging. Neil isn't sure why. Soon he realizes the problem, but it is too late. The judges won't look at his project again and his friends gain the higher prize.

After the summer, the Armstrong family moves to Wapakoneta, Ohio. Neil begins at Blume High School, which has a very fine science and math program. Neil is right at home.

What we will cover in this chapter:

Social Studies: History - Steam Engines
Science: Science Fair Projects
Science: Conduction, Convection and Radiation*
Language Arts: Writing and Discussion Question
Language Arts: Vocabulary
Life Skills: Dealing with Envy

Social Studies: History - Steam Engines

Neil's science fair project is a small steam turbine. Use this opportunity to share with your student some information regarding the history of steam power.

For centuries, the power of steam to move a machine has been known. In fact, the first description of a steam engine was made by a scientist named Hero in A.D. 60 Egypt. His little device proved that steam can move stationary objects, but it didn't prove very practical. It wasn't until the 1600s (over 1,500 years later) that the first successful steam engines began to be made.

Every steam engine in the world has what is called a boiler. A boiler is a large metal container that holds water. Water is heated by either a furnace or reactors. When it heats up, it turns into steam (water vapor). The vapor takes up much more room than water's liquid form and it soon builds up pressure. This pressure is power that can be channeled in two main ways: to spin a turbine (wheel) or to push a piston back and forth.

During the 1700s, steam engines were made to be bigger, faster and more dependable. Their power made modern industry possible. Suddenly, factories went up everywhere and clothing, goods and machinery could be manufactured at a fast, economical pace.

To show the power of steam to your student, make or purchase a small pinwheel. Boil a kettle of water and let it generate a good strong stream of steam coming out of its spout. With your supervision, let your student hold the pinwheel near the steam. He can watch the pinwheel turn and see how steam can power machines.

Science: Science Fair Projects

Teacher's Note: It is strongly encouraged that you do this lesson with your student. The experience will be invaluable, educational and quite memorable.

Neil and his friends took part in a great educational and fun event—a science fair! Even if your student is in a class of one, he can still have a great time creating a science fair project and presenting it to friends and relatives.

Developing and presenting a science fair project teaches your student a variety of lessons: doing research, writing a proposal, gathering supplies, recording data, fixing problems, designing graphs and charts, oral presentation skills and much, much more! This lesson will give you and your student information on how to organize, conduct and present a science project.

To begin, your student needs to choose a topic. Here are three criteria your student should use when deciding:

1. What am I interested in?

2. Is this experiment at my level? Not too difficult and not too easy?

3. Will it be interesting to others when I present it?

Your student can get ideas for science projects online or in library books (many books are filled with science project ideas!). Your student may also come up with good ideas by following his own curiosity.

Next, your student needs to write a formal proposal for his experiment. The proposal can be as simple as a one-paragraph description for a younger student, or as big as a few pages describing the hypotheses, theories, plans and expected outcomes, for an older student. This paper should be kept so the student can use the information throughout the experiment.

Your student should gather the necessary materials and start the experiment. Make sure your student records all the raw data in a notebook.

Throughout the project (some projects may take several weeks), your student should also gather outside information and background information to include in his research report. When his experiment is over, he should begin assimilating his data into charts or graphs. He can use poster board, markers, construction paper, pie charts or computer programs to show his results. He should also write out his research report including background information, description of the experiment, any further explanations needed, results and conclusions. As always, this lesson can be made simple or complex, based on your student's needs. The important points are the same, regardless of the length of the report or the difficulty of the experiment.

Next, your student should design a visual backdrop for his experiment and practice his oral presentation (where he explains his experiment and findings). The backdrop for science experiments is most often a three-sided panel that can stand up behind the experiment display. Talk with your student about the importance of designing an effective visual backdrop. It should be simple. Too much information will confuse the viewer. It should be colorful, visually appealing, and it should clearly tell the story of your student's experiment (including a title, the topic and the experiment description and conclusions).

Finally, it is time to present his science fair project. Be sure your student understands that the important parts of this project were to learn something new and to have fun!

Here is a list of all the points mentioned above for your student's benefit:

1. Choose a topic
2. Write a proposal
3. Gather materials, start experiment and record raw data
4. Gather outside information

5. Assimilate information and create charts and graphs
6. Write research report
7. Create visual backdrop and formulate oral presentation
8. Present the project

Encourage your student to tackle a science fair project! You will learn along with him—guaranteed!

Science: Conduction, Convection and Radiation*

Neil explains to his little brother Dean how the steam will be created: "I'm going to light it [a candle] and it will heat the water in this little pan." Ask your student if he knows how the water inside the pan will become heated. The candle flame is hot, but how does that affect the water? Eventually, the pan will get hot from the flame and then it makes the water heat up, right? That is called conduction. Take this moment with your student to discuss with him the three main ways heat is transferred: conduction, convection, and radiation.

Conduction is set up when a warm object touches a cooler object. Heat will go directly to the cooler object by means of conduction. Certain metals or materials conduct heat better than others do. Copper, for example, is an excellent conductive material, while plastic is not. Copper is often used for cooking pots and pans.

Get a glass and fill it with very warm water. Have your student put a metal spoon and a plastic spoon in the water. Wait 30 seconds. Pull out the spoons and touch them. Which feels hotter?

The metal spoon conducted heat from the water into its metal, molecule by molecule. Plastics and other materials that do not conduct heat well are called insulators.

Convection occurs when a warm object sits in cool air. Heat from the object warms the air around the object and that air rises. As the warm air moves up, more cool air drops down and is warmed. The newly warmed air rises, and so forth. This process is called convection. Remind your student of this important science principle: warm air rises and cool air falls! Convection works with gases (like air) and liquids.

54

Have your student place a glass pan on the stove, half on the burner and half off the burner. Fill the pan with water and put a few drops of food coloring in it. Now turn on the burner. Watch the liquid rise on the warm side and drop on the cool side. This shows convection!

Finally, heat can travel by **radiation**. In the processes of both conduction and convection, heat is transmitted by moving molecules. Heat can also travel where matter does not exist. For example, if you sit outside in the sunlight, you will get warm, even though the sun is over 93 million miles away!

If you set two thermometers outside, one in the shade and one in the sunlight, which will get warmer? The thermometer in the sun will show a higher temperature because of the sun's radiating heat.

Enjoy this lesson and these experiments—they will help your student become familiar with these important scientific principles.

Language Arts: Writing and Discussion Question

Neil's project didn't work when he needed it most. The judges weren't impressed and he did not get a superior mark. If this happened to you, how would it make you feel? Have you ever been in a competition where you didn't do as well as your friends? What happened?

Language Arts: Vocabulary

conduction   The process of one object serving as a channel to carry heat to another.

convection   The transference of heat by the circulation or movement of the heated parts of a liquid or gas.

radiation   The giving off and spreading out of rays of heat, light or electricity.

Life Skills: Dealing with Envy

Kotchko gets a little envious of Neil's project. He knows it's better than the photoelectric cell he and Bud are working on. Later in the chapter, we see Neil become a little envious when his project doesn't do as well as his friends' science experiment. Ask your student what he thinks jealousy or envy is.

Everyone sometimes feels a little jealous of someone else. When you envy someone else, you wish you could be like him, or that you could have something he has. It isn't that the other person is so much better, but that you're unsure of or feeling sorry for yourself. When you feel envious, it is important to remember two things: you are fine just the way you are; and you should be glad you know successful, interesting people. If you are confident in yourself and thankful for others, then you really should not be jealous! Encourage each other today to be more confident and grateful!

Chapter 9—Another New School

Teacher Summary

Neil quickly makes new friends at his new school, Blume High. He likes the town, Wapakoneta, because it's friendly and close to his grandparents' farm. Neil finds two new mentors at his new school—a terrific math and science teacher named Grover Crites, and a local astronomer named Jacob Zint. Mr. Zint has a wonderful observatory built on top of his garage. Neil and his friends go there often to look at the stars and talk to Mr. Zint.

Neil's activities in school grow. He enjoys scouting,

the Boys' Club and music. One day, his teacher, Mr. Crites, talks to Neil's parents. He tells them how smart and disciplined Neil has become. He shares with them Neil's desire to go to college. The Armstrongs are happy, but a little worried about how they will pay for it.

In the spring of 1945, the Armstrong family, along with the rest of America, is thrilled to celebrate V-E Day (Victory in Europe Day). The war is nearly over!

What we will cover in this chapter:

Social Studies: History - President Truman*
Science: Galaxies and Our Solar System
Language Arts: Writing and Discussion Questions
Language Arts: Vocabulary
Fine Arts: Make Your Own Musical Instruments

History and Geography: President Truman*

On April 12, 1945, President Franklin Roosevelt died unexpectedly and the Vice President, Harry Truman, stepped into office. Truman had only been the Vice President for 83 days when he became President. Shortly thereafter, America's involvement with World War II came to a close.

Harry S. Truman was born on May 8, 1884, in a small town called Lamar, Missouri. He was the eldest of three children. Although he had very loving parents, Harry's childhood wasn't all that happy. By the time he was only six years old, his family had moved three times. His father had poor luck as a farmer. He kept moving, hoping things would get better. On the third move, the family settled down in a town called Independence, Missouri. The family did better financially, but poor Harry was very lonely.

Sometimes moving makes developing friendships difficult. Harry didn't have any friends in Independence, and because of very poor eyesight he had to wear thick glasses. Later in life, President Truman said: "I was so carefully cautioned by the eye doctor about breaking my glasses and injuring my eyes, that I was very afraid to join in the rough-and-tumble games in the school yard and back lots. My time was spent in reading, and by the time I was 13 or 14 years old I had read all the books in the Independence Public Library, and our old Bible three times through."

President Harry S. Truman

Discuss with your student that even during sad or adverse times, people can make something wonderful happen if they have a positive attitude. Harry Truman was a lonely child, but he found friends in books. Imagine how all that reading helped him when he became President!

When he reached high school, Harry enjoyed his experience more. He had gained confidence. He and some friends formed a club called the Waldo Street Gang. The group of boys and girls went swimming, ice skating and played organized sports. It was in the Waldo Street Gang that Harry met his future wife, Bess Wallace. He said that he thought she was great because she could "whistle between her teeth" and she enjoyed sports.

Even though Harry did wonderfully in school, he wasn't the top student. That honor went to Harry's best friend, Charlie Ross. (Charlie Ross later became President Truman's Press Secretary.)

At graduation, the school's English teacher, Miss Brown, kissed Charlie Ross, her best student. Harry asked if he could have a kiss. Miss Brown told him he'd get one when he did something great to deserve it. Years later, Harry called his old teacher from Washington. He said, "Miss Brown, this is the President of the United States. Do I get that kiss now?"

During his young adult life, Harry Truman served bravely in World War I. His men loved him and when he returned to Independence in 1922, he became a judge. He was very successful in public office. People liked his honesty and his hometown attitude. In 1934, he was elected to the United States Senate.

Truman worked diligently as a senator. During World War II he saw many problems with wasteful defense spending in America. He was made chairman of a group to investigate the poor management that became known as the Truman Committee. In all, Truman and his fellow senators saved the American people over 15 billion dollars and increased weapons production. People were thrilled! It was because of his success with the Truman Committee that Harry Truman was selected to run with President Franklin Roosevelt as Vice President. In 1944, the formerly shy young boy without any friends was elected Vice President of the United States of America. After just 83 days, he was sworn in as President when President Roosevelt died suddenly of a cerebral hemorrhage.

Be sure to include a few of the important moments in the presidency of Harry Truman in your discussion with your student. Topics might include:

The A-bomb (1945): On August 6, 1945, President Harry Truman gave the command for United States Air Force pilots to drop an atomic bomb on the Japanese city of Hiroshima. On August 9, a second atomic bomb was dropped on the Japanese city of Nagasaki. Although many people today disagree with the use of nuclear weapons, Truman's historic decision did end World War II. By September 2, 1945, it was over.

The Truman Doctrine (1947): After WWII, President Truman understood the importance of keeping communism from growing. He promised American aid to free nations trying to stop communist propaganda or trying to resist sabotage. This idea became a welcome relief to many nations, and became known as the Truman Doctrine.

The Fair Deal (1949): President Franklin Roosevelt had worked on programs he called the New Deal. President Truman decided to call his reform programs, The Fair Deal. These programs worked diligently to help provide every American citizen with civil rights, housing, social security and aid for education, all provided through federal dollars.

If your student's interest has been sparked by your discussion, encourage him to locate more information on Harry S. Truman at the library or online. You might also want to discuss with your student some related topics, including Japan's history, the atomic bomb, communism, nuclear weapons, federal relief, etc.

When you have finished this unit, remind your student what he learned about Harry Truman in the beginning. A young, near-sighted, shy boy who didn't have any friends found his joy in books. He gained confidence, and became a great leader. Never underestimate the power of an education and never assume someone won't be successful!

Science: Galaxies and Our Solar System

Neil and his friends enjoy spending time with Mr. Zint and looking through his telescopes. Studying and gazing at the heavens is an old science. When we look up through a telescope, what are the things we're actually seeing? What is up there?

To begin this discussion with your student, it is important to talk about what we mean when we say space, outer space, atmosphere, galaxies and the solar system. Before you can study something, it helps to see the bigger picture.

First, talk with your student about **air**. Air surrounds us every day. It surrounds our bodies, our homes and, of course, is in the sky. Scientists call the air that surrounds the earth its atmosphere. As you leave the earth, the air (or atmosphere) gets thinner and thinner. It has less and less oxygen. No one knows where the defining line is between our atmosphere and **outer space**, but most scientists say it is approximately 60 miles away from Earth. Outer space isn't completely empty. Dust and other types of particles float there.

Teacher's Note: It will help your student if, as you discuss these terms, you have him draw a picture or diagram of each term and its definition. For example, he could draw a picture of the earth and label its atmosphere. He can draw a circle around it marked "60 miles up" and then label the space around that, "outer space."

Jupiter, the largest planet in our solar system

A **galaxy** is a system (or grouping) of billions of stars, dust and gas, held together by gravity. Instead of spinning away from one another in all directions, gravitational pull holds stars and particles together in one section. There are many, many galaxies. Some are small and some are very large. Astronomers have been taking pictures of millions of galaxies by telescopes equipped with special cameras. Scientists estimate that there are over 100 billion galaxies, each with billions of stars, in our universe. When there are several galaxies in one general area, it is called a cluster.

Take a moment to review with your student what you have learned so far: Our earth is surrounded by air (atmosphere). As you get farther away from the earth, the air gets thinner and it is called outer space. Throughout outer space there are billions of galaxies. A galaxy is a group of stars and dust held together by gravity.

Within various galaxies are stars and planets. Our planet, Earth, is located in a group of planets called our **solar system**. Our solar system consists of a large star (the sun); nine planets (including Earth); satellites (or moons) which surround the planets; asteroids; meteoroids; dust and gases.

Teacher's Note: Your student can decide which areas of the solar system he would most like to study. The rest of this lesson will center around the planets, moons and the sun. Discussions based on other topics are strongly encouraged for the older student.

The word *planet* comes from a Greek word, meaning "to wander." Planets don't exactly wander, but they do move, in relation to our view ofthe stars. In our solar system, we have nine planets. (Currently, Pluto is considered a dwarf planet. Pluto's changed planet status could be a topic of research for your interested student!) Going outward from the sun, they are Mercury, Venus, Earth, Mars, Jupiter, Saturn, Uranus, Neptune and the dwarf planet Pluto. Our sun and the stars are balls of gases. Planets are solid, or have solid cores. The stars and our sun produce their own heat. The planets in our solar system are heated by light energy from the sun.

Share with your student this amazing fact: if you put all the planets together, they would still weigh less than a hundredth as much as the sun. Jupiter is the largest planet and Pluto is the smallest.

The planets in our solar system move around the sun in the same direction. A famous astronomer from Germany, Johannes Kepler, studied the planets and published articles about their movement in the early 1600s. Kepler's work is still the basis for much of what we know today about the movement of the planets.

Some evening, take your student outdoors and look up into the night sky. It may be difficult to tell the difference between a star and a planet, but look closely. Planets shine more brightly than stars. A planet will also shine more steadily; stars seem to twinkle.

If your student wants to work on a project, why not make a mobile or model of our solar system? Your student can hang various Styrofoam or *papier-mâché* balls on strings from a coat hanger. He can paint or color each one. With a small flag (made from a toothpick and paper), he can label each planet. He can include a sun and our moon, as well.

Language Arts: Writing and Discussion Questions

1. Neil had to make new friends at his new school. It's often scary to make new friends. Why might this be true? Discuss.

2. President Harry S. Truman made the decision to end World War II by using a nuclear weapon, the atom bomb. This decision killed hundreds of thousands of people in Japan, but may have saved just as many lives by stopping the war. What do you think of his decision?

Language Arts: Vocabulary

air   The mixture of gases which surround the earth; atmosphere.

outer space   The point at which the atmosphere is thinned significantly; the space beyond the earth's atmosphere.

galaxy   A group of billions of stars and other matter held together by gravity forming one system.

solar system   The earth's sun and all the planets, satellites and matter which revolve around it.

Fine Arts: Make Your Own Musical Instruments

Besides being interested in math, science and scouting, Neil also loved music! He even learned to play the baritone horn and enjoyed playing in a jazz quartet. If your student has always wanted to learn more about musical instruments, or if he is already an accomplished musician just looking for some fun, take some time and learn to make your own musical instruments!

Here is a list of a few musical instruments your student can make, along with simple instructions:

Maracas (Maracas are a popular form of rattle used throughout Latin America, Spain and Europe.)

You can make maracas from a variety of things around the house. Take a small pint-sized) ice cream carton (the round kind with a lid). Fill it with a few spoon-

fuls of dry beans or small pieces of macaroni. Cover the top with wax paper. Secure the paper with a rubber band around the rim. Shake it! Let your child design and construct his own idea for a maraca as well. He can make one for each hand.

Drums

You can make a drum by using a coffee can. Cut a circle of heavy paper (like a grocery sack) a few inches larger than the can opening. Cover the open top of the can with the paper. Wet the edges down and fold them into pleats along the sides of the opening. With someone helping, your student can pull each piece taut and tape. Wrap tape firmly around all the edges to secure. The student can decorate the sides of the drum with construction paper or paint.

Sand Blocks

Take small blocks of wood (they should be equal in size and easily held in the student's hand) and cover each with a piece of sandpaper. Glue the edges of the sandpaper to the top of the wood and then secure carefully with tacks. Now the blocks can be rubbed together to a beat!

For more information and great ideas on making your own instruments, go to your local library or search online.

Chapter 10—Flying Lessons

Teacher Summary

Neil is determined to fly. He tells his parents he is interested in taking flying lessons. The lessons will cost nine dollars an hour. His parents tell him if he will pay for them, then he may have their permission to take them. They cannot afford to help. Neil knows it will take him a long time to save enough money, but he is sure it is what he wants to do. Neil works each day at Rhine and Brading's Pharmacy for 40 cents an hour. It takes Neil one solid year to earn enough money to obtain his pilot's license. On August 6, 1946, Neil is given his pilot's license. His parents are very proud.

Shortly after obtaining his license, Neil and his father see a plane crash. Unfortunately, one of Neil's friends is the pilot and he dies. Neil is solemn for some time after that, but he soon regains his resolve to continue flying. He also continues to work hard to pay for college. One day, a letter comes from the U.S. Navy. Neil has received a full Navy scholarship to the college of his choice! Mr. and Mrs. Armstrong are proud and relieved that their son will be able to pursue his dream and attend a good school.

What we will cover in this chapter:

Social Studies: Career Path - Pilot
Language Arts: Summarizing Information
Language Arts: Writing and Discussion Questions*
Life Skills: Determination
Life Skills: Dealing with Death

Social Studies: Career Path - Pilot

Neil is a pilot! Is your student interested in planes? Does he talk about what it would be like to fly? There are many popular and exciting careers in commercial aviation.

If your student wants to become an airline pilot, he must first obtain a student pilot certificate. To get this certificate, he must be at least 16 years old and pass a simple physical examination. Next, a student pilot must successfully complete a series of lessons in flight instructions. These instructions include classes on ground, dual-instruction (the instructor flies the plane and talks with the student, then the student flies and only talks to the instructor) and solo flight (the student flies the plane by himself). All in all, nearly 40 hours of flight time are required for a pilot's license. When these lessons are completed, the student must pass a written exam and a flight exam and then his pilot's license is granted. Flight lessons differ in cost, but they can be found at schools, colleges and local flying clubs.

Jobs in aviation include air taxi services, business light planes and major commercial airlines. Different certificates and examinations are required for each type of job.

If your student is interested in learning more about becoming a pilot someday, why not contact a local flying group or a small airport in or near your town? Your student can gain valuable information by simply observing the operation of a small airport.

Language Arts: Summarizing Information

Learning to summarize information is a critical skill. This chapter provides a good opportunity for your student to try his hand at summarizing. Many things happen in chapter 10. Here is a basic list of the events, in order:

Neil asks about flying lessons.
Neil begins working to pay his own way through flight school.
Neil obtains his pilot's license on his 16th birthday.
Neil's friend from school is killed in a plane crash.
Neil applies halfheartedly for a Navy college scholarship.
Neil is granted a full scholarship to college from the U.S. Navy.
Neil tells his mother.
Neil's mother drops a jar of blackberries on her toe, in surprise!

Talk with your student a little bit about what a summary is. Explain that a summary of information is a group of main points from a story or article. You may wish to use a classic fairy tale your child is familiar with to demonstrate. For example, in "Goldilocks and the Three Bears," the main events are:

Goldilocks arrives at the Bears' home. She tries several bowls of porridge. She tries several different chairs. She tries several different beds and falls asleep in the smallest one. The bear family comes home. Everyone is surprised, and Goldilocks runs out of the house.

Encourage your student to try to summarize chapter 10 without rereading it. He can look back later to see what he left out.

Continue working on summarizing information with your student throughout the school year. Read passages of stories or articles aloud. See if he can repeat back to you the main points of each.

Learning these skills now will help your student immensely in high school, college and throughout his life.

Language Arts: Writing and Discussion Questions*

1. Have you ever had a friend or close relative die? What were the feelings you felt? How did you get through that time?

2. Describe a goal or dream you have and what you think it might take to accomplish it.

Life Skills: Determination

Neil Armstrong is a determined young man! Even though his parents cannot help him pay for flying lessons, he is sure he wants them—even if he has to pay for them himself. Talk with your student about how long it must have taken Neil to save enough money for his lessons. We can calculate that it took Neil nearly 23 hours of work to pay for every one hour of flight instruction! Remember that he could only work after school!

Has your student ever exhibited amazing determination? Talk about that time and discuss reasons for tenacity. When people make up their minds to do things, distraction comes easily sometimes. Work gets too hard, and suddenly the goal may not look as good as at first. Practicing determination in daily life helps make disciplined, happier individuals. We'll achieve more of our goals, just like Neil!

Life Skills: Dealing with Death

Neil is confronted with the death of his fellow classmate in chapter 10. Depending upon how old your student is, this may or may not be a good time to discuss dealing with death. If you feel that it is, then take this opportunity to gently talk with your student about feelings and concerns they may have with death. Perhaps they've lost a loved one or friend. Even talking about the death of a pet can be an open door to further discussions. You may wish to share some personal experiences of your own regarding this topic, such as how you felt when someone died, and how you worked through your grief. Grief is an important part of the healing process. Knowing that it is okay and healthy to cry and be sad helps you to feel more relaxed during this difficult time.

When we lose someone to death, we may feel many different feelings all at once. It's normal to sometimes forget that a person has died and think about that person as if he were still around. Sometimes people find it hard to eat or sleep. A grieving person might not be interested in seeing friends or playing outside for awhile. That is understandable.

In time, we accept that the person is really gone, and realize life is still moving along. We move on, too. After awhile, we'll even remember what laughing is like and enjoy life again. Photographs, letters and family videos can help remind us of our loved one. Talking about them helps, too.

Death is a part of life, but it's helpful to know that we're not alone. There will always be people around who love and care for us.

Chapter 11—Airplanes to Astronauts

Teacher Summary

Neil decides to attend Purdue University and enters their aeronautical engineering program. The classes are tough but he really enjoys them. After only a year and a half, the U.S. Navy sends Neil to Pensacola, Florida for flight training. The Korean War has begun and the Navy needs Neil in active duty. At 20 years of age, Neil leaves for Korea. He fights bravely and successfully completes 78 combat missions. He is also awarded three air medals for outstanding service during the war. Neil's family is glad and relieved to have him home, and he continues at college.

It is at Purdue that Neil meets a girl named Jan Shearon. Jan and Neil begin dating. They are married after Neil's graduation. Neil takes a job at Edwards Air Force Base in California, near the San Gabriel Mountains.

Neil's new job gives him many opportunities to fly new and exciting aircraft. He isn't just a pilot anymore, but also works as an engineer and researcher. Soon Neil is flying rocket-propelled aircraft, and is working on problems that face the Mercury astronauts. Neil develops a growing interest in outer space.

What we will cover in this chapter:

Social Studies: History and Geography - The Korean War
Social Studies: History - NASA*
Language Arts: Creative Writing - Showing vs. Telling
Language Arts: Writing and Discussion Question
Language Arts: Vocabulary
Life Skills: Bravery

Social Studies: History and Geography - The Korean War

Neil flies bravely with Fighter Squadron 51 during the Korean War. This would be a good opportunity to discuss the Korean War with your student. The Korean War could be a subject for an entire unit study, or you can choose to simply concentrate on a few main points. Encourage your student to understand the main causes of the war and how it affected the United States.

To begin, explain to your student that the United States was not involved when the Korean War began. The war began on June 25, 1950, when soldiers from North Korea invaded South Korea. North Korea is a communist country. South Korea is a democratic country. For your student's understanding, in very basic terms, the Korean War was fought because both sides wanted to control the entire country.

After North Korean troops invaded South Korea, the United Nations demanded that they halt. It was an invasion that violated international peace rules. But North Korea didn't stop, and so the United Nations (U.N.) asked other nations to give military aid to South Korea. The U.N. asked other countries to share food, supplies, military equipment and, of course, troops. Although 41 countries sent supplies and food, the United States of America supplied nearly 90% of the troops sent to South Korea. American soldiers, like Neil Armstrong, were expected to help as fast as they could.

Neil and the other pilots' involvement in the Korean War was quite historic. The Korean War was the first war to include battles between jet aircraft. The Soviet Union, also a communist country, supplied North Korea with MIG-15 jets. Suddenly, air battles (tradi-

tionally called dogfights) became a critical part of the war. Dogfights were dangerous battles, and the United States lost nearly 2,000 planes during the war.

The Korean War was a very bloody war. Over one million Korean civilians were killed and several million were injured and left homeless.

The Korean War was ended on July 27, 1953, when North Korea finally agreed to sign a peace agreement with the United Nations. It is interesting to note, however, that a permanent peace agreement between South Korea and North Korea has never been signed! United States military forces still remain in South Korea today, to enforce peace and discourage fighting. In many ways, the Korean War has never ended.

If your student is interested in learning more about the Korean War or related topics, areas for him to explore might include the United Nations, General Douglas MacArthur, the Truce Talks, MIG Alley and the 38th Parallel.

Help your student locate North and South Korea on a map or globe. Talk with him about what it would be like to be sent there at age 20 to fight in many battles. Neil and many other young men were brave to go and fight for the freedom of South Korea.

Social Studies: History - NASA*

While Neil is looking for a job after the war, he considers going to work for the National Advisory Committee on Aeronautics. In 1958, this committee became known as the National Aeronautics and Space Administration, or NASA.

Because of its vital work for our nation, it is important for your student to have a working understanding of this administration. If your student is interested in space or space exploration, he may find learning more about NASA very fulfilling.

Explain to your student that NASA is a United States government agency. NASA's main aim is to conduct and coordinate the research of flight within and beyond the earth's atmosphere. NASA isn't just one building with employees. NASA employs thousands of scientists, pilots, engineers and technicians at 10 different locations, called field centers. A few such locations your student may have heard of include: the Kennedy Space Center, Armstrong Flight Research Center, Goddard Space Flight Center and the Johnson Space Center.

Some of the work NASA does while studying outer space involves sending people on space flights. For example, Neil Armstrong was the first man to walk on the moon. That was a manned space flight. Other work, however, involves unmanned space flights. These include sending things like artificial satellites and space probes into space to collect data and information for research. This data may be used to gather information about the earth's atmosphere and weather patterns.

NASA is an important United States government agency. To learn more about this fascinating administration, search online or contact your local library.

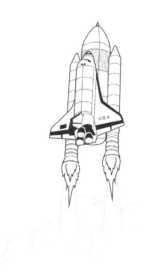

The U.S. Space Shuttle was used for 135 missions from 1981-2011

Language Arts: Creative Writing - Showing vs. Telling

Reread this paragraph near the end of the chapter with your student:

"From the Armstrongs' house far up in the mountains, through her binoculars, Jan could see the X-15 aircraft drop away from the B-52 mother airship and go into flight. And on its return she could see the dust rise down in the valley as the X-15 landed on the 25-mile-long dry lake bed at Edwards."

Ask your student what he thinks this paragraph says about Neil's wife. Why would the author include it? Discuss with your student that the paragraph shows that Jan is a caring wife. She probably worries about Neil and his dangerous job as a test pilot and engineer. Jan is also interested in what Neil's work involves. She doesn't just watch when he lands safely, but she watches his release in the air, as well. Perhaps Jan tries to see Neil throughout the flight.

Good authors show us things about characters in their stories, instead of telling us. For example, the author could have written this paragraph like this:

"Jan Armstrong loved her husband and was interested in knowing about his work."

The previous sentence tells us much of the same information, but doesn't demonstrate it. Stories are much more interesting when we see characters doing things to show their character and thoughts, instead of just having those things told to us.

Encourage your student to try this technique in stories he writes. He can even practice this technique with the following exercise.

Here are two examples of given facts. Write a few sentences *showing* the facts, not just telling them.

1. Jane loved her kitten.

(Example: Jane sat quietly petting her purring kitten. She nuzzled the little animal's soft body against her cheek and kissed her gently on the head.)

2. Bobby was nervous while taking the difficult test.

(Example: Bobby sat tensely at his desk, staring wide-eyed at the test in front of him. The pencil he held slipped slightly as his palms started to sweat. He quickly marked number 12 and then feverishly moved on, with his head bent low to his paper.)

Your student will improve his writing and delight his readers if he learns the valuable skill of showing, not telling, his writing.

Language Arts: Writing and Discussion Question

When Neil leaves for the Korean War, we read:

"Grandmother Korspeter was delighted to spend time with Neil. She was always very cheerful. She thought, though, about her father who had left Germany and come to this country to get away from the wars. And now Neil was going off to fight in one."

What do you think about this? Would it be hard for Neil's grandmother to watch him go off to war? Why or why not? Explain.

Language Arts: Vocabulary

NASA: National Aeronautics and Space Administration.

Life Skills: Bravery

Neil received three different medals for outstanding service during the Korean War. He exhibited bravery. What is bravery? Can anyone be brave? What is required in order to be brave? Does it take a war for someone to be brave?

Being brave can be as simple as walking into a new group of people you don't know and being the first one to say hello. A person could conquer a personal fear, such as playing in a recital or climbing up a ladder. Tell your student about a time when you felt particularly brave, or perhaps a time when you did not. Ask him to give examples also.

Chapter 12—Successes and Failures

Teacher Summary

Neil Armstrong becomes the first civilian to become an astronaut. He is accepted by NASA on September 17, 1962, and is named to the backup crew for *Gemini 5*. Within just four years, Neil is named command pilot for *Gemini 8*.

Neil and his copilot, David Scott, exhibit bravery and skill as they maneuver the docking of *Gemini 8* with an unmanned satellite, the Agena. Although there are some close calls, Neil's skill at manually controlling the thrusters saves the mission and protects his and his copilot's lives.

Neil's part in the success of *Gemini 8* catches the attention of the NASA officials who choose the crews for missions to the moon. Neil stays busy working on other lunar projects, but NASA is already considering him for commander-in-chief of the crew of *Apollo 11*—possibly the first crew to set foot on the moon.

Teacher's Note: This chapter includes an exciting account of Neil Armstrong's close call with death when he tries to land an LLRV at Ellington Air Force Base on May 6, 1968. You might want to also watch the video created by the Discovery Channel in 1994 called *One Giant Leap*. It includes actual footage of Neil's parachute exit from the LLRV and the explosion of the spacecraft shortly thereafter. Fascinating footage of the moon landing and other *Apollo* missions are also included, as well as interviews with Buzz and Joan Aldrin. Your student will be amazed to see the things he has been reading about!

What we will cover in this chapter:

Science: Air and Sound Travel*
Language Arts: Creative Writing Exercise - Use of Imagination
Language Arts: Writing and Discussion Question
Language Arts: Vocabulary
Life Skills: Teamwork

Science: Air and Sound Travel*

Look back with your student where the author writes, "They felt a solid contact as they closed the final few inches and latched the two vehicles together. There was a soft thump in the cockpit when the *Agena* docked, but outside in space there was only silence."

Ask your student what the author means by this description. Why wasn't there any sound in space, but only in the cockpit? What is his guess?

Take this opportunity to discuss with your student some important facts about sound and how it travels.

Sound travels in wavelike frequencies as it moves through the air or some other substance (e.g., water, walls, etc.). To hear a sound, sound waves must be traveling in a substance. Ask the student why then, can sounds not be heard in space?

Remind your student of the lesson covered in chapter 9 of this study, regarding outer space and the atmosphere. Approximately 60 miles away from the earth's surface, the air begins to get thinner and thinner and becomes "outer space." Outer space is almost entirely void. Although there are some dust particles and an occasional meteoroid, it is virtually empty. There is no air or other significant substance. If outer space lacks substance, air or any other medium, then how would that affect sound? Without substance, sound waves have nothing to bounce off of and then back to our ears. A sound wave is produced but there is no way for it to travel. Outer space is an utterly silent place. Even giant, noisy spacecraft propulsion engines can't be heard in outer space.

Ask your student why Neal and David could hear the soft "thump" inside the spacecraft? Within *Gemini 8*, there was air. The sound they heard reverberated from the walls of the spacecraft, through the air, and to their ears. Remind your student that sound waves must pass through a substance in order for the waves to have something to compress and expand.

Language Arts: Creative Writing Exercise - Use of Imagination

The last two pages of our chapter are devoted to an exciting account of Neil's close call with the LLRV at Ellington Air Force Base. Although the author does a good job describing the events and Neil's actions, he doesn't include many of Neil's thoughts. Our book is a nonfiction work. It is a true story, and who could know what Neil was thinking?

Ask your student to pretend, for a moment, that he is Neil. What might he have been thinking? Encourage your student to try a creative writing exercise using this prompt from our chapter: "Neil Armstrong was in the final stage of his landing." While writing in the first person—"I was in the final stage of landing when suddenly..."—your student can write a few paragraphs or more as if he were Neil. With each situation (spinning and backfiring, rolling over to the right, black smoke billowing out, hitting the ejection button, parachuting out, looking back and seeing the destruction), what is Neil thinking? Of whom is he thinking? What does he think when it's over?

This kind of creative writing exercise will help your student by stretching his imagination and forcing him to think of different angles. He isn't responsible for the plot, only the subplot.

Language Arts: Writing and Discussion Question

The title of our chapter is "Successes and Failures." What is something you've done recently that didn't go well? What is something successful you've done recently? Discuss the details.

Language Arts: Vocabulary
(These words are all found in Chapter 12.)

orbit   The path an object takes around a planet.

thrusters   Jet propulsion rockets.

roll   Spin in one direction.

re-entry   The process of a spacecraft returning into Earth's atmosphere.

splashdown   The landing of a spacecraft in water.

docking   Touching and connecting with another spacecraft or satellite.

lunar   Having to do with the moon.

Life Skills: Teamwork

Neil's accomplishments are amazing, aren't they? However, nothing he accomplishes is his achievement alone. Many, many people work hard to help him and his crews. Each of the engineers, technicians, flight commanders and mechanics who work on spacecraft is a vitally important part of his team.

Teamwork is essential for reaching certain goals. Learning to work with others is an important part of maturing and becoming an adult. It is also important to recognize the help others give you and to thank each of them.

Talk with your student about his own family. Most families work in many ways like a team. Different people in the family have different jobs and everyone pitches in to keep the house clean, the yard looking good and everybody fed. What part does your student play? How do the others in his family help him?

Encourage your student to thank those around him who help and enrich his life. We are all part of a team in some way!

Chapter 13—Preparations

Teacher Summary

Neil Armstrong has been chosen for the *Apollo 11* mission to the moon! Along with Edwin "Buzz" Aldrin and Mike Collins, Neil will work hard to prepare for his space flight.

The three men will fly to space in a massive *Saturn 5* rocket. For months they train extensively to prepare for every possible scenario. They practice in flight simulators and full-scale replicas of the command module and the lunar module. Each man spends over 400 hours simulating real situations.

Finally, on July 10, 1969, the master clock in Firing Room One begins ticking. The real countdown has begun. Neil says in a press conference: "...we're willing and ready to attempt to achieve our national goal..." of putting a man on the moon!

What we will cover in this chapter:

Teacher's Note: In case you haven't used or noticed it yet, this chapter would be a good time to begin referring to the glossary of "space vocabulary" provided at the end of *Neil Armstrong: Young Flyer.*

Social Studies: History - Sir Isaac Newton
Science: Gravity Experiment
Science: The Moon*
Language Arts: Writing and Discussion Question
Language Arts: Vocabulary

History: Sir Isaac Newton

Many of the skills required for the astronauts in our chapter are related to dealing with the one-sixth gravity of the moon (compared to Earth's gravity). For example, we see Neil, Buzz and Mike experience near-weightlessness during sudden dips in a KC-135 airplane.

In order for your student to understand these training drills, it is helpful if he has a beginning understanding of gravity and of the man who discovered its principles—Sir Isaac Newton.

Sir Isaac Newton is considered one of the greatest names in the history of human thought. He was born at Woolsthorpe, Lincolnshire (England) on Christmas Day, 1642. He went to school and helped his mother with her farm. (His father had died when he was very young.) Newton was always interested in mathematics, science and inventions. In fact, he never did all that well in grade school because he spent too much time working on his science projects. He attended Trinity College at Cambridge and graduated in 1665. No one thought he was very special, but considered him an average student. However, when

Sir Isaac Newton

he returned to Cambridge in 1669, he was a professor of mathematics.

In 1687, Newton's life changed forever. His discoveries in gravitation and motion, which up to this point had been unknown to the world, were published in a book called *Philosophiae Naturalis Principia Mathematica* (*Mathematical Principles of Natural Philosophy*). Newton's friend, English astronomer Edmond Halley, had begged him to publish the book. Halley knew how important the findings were. Newton finally agreed and suddenly the world knew the name Isaac Newton. Queen Anne knighted Newton in 1705, giving him the title "Sir." He died in 1727; his body is buried in Westminster Abbey in England. Friends of Newton said he was very modest and humble. Discuss with your student this quote of Newton's, from shortly before his death:

"I do not know what I may appear to the world, but to myself I seem to have been only like a boy playing on the seashore, and diverting myself in now and then finding a smoother pebble or a prettier shell than ordinary, whilst the great ocean of truth lay all undiscovered before me."

Share with your student Newton's three main scientific inventions and discoveries. (Please note: these are by no means the total of Newton's work in science.)

1) Calculus
2) Principles of light and color
3) Theories of gravitation

By discovering and developing **calculus**, Newton created a new branch of mathematics. Calculus helps mathematicians solve for unknown quantities. It is similar to algebra, but more in-depth. Astronauts like Neil Armstrong use calculus every day to help them find out distances between planets, satellites and more. Aeronautical engineers use calculus to help them design airplanes. It allows them to find out what forces affect planes during flight and solve many other practical problems. (Remember that Neil Armstrong majored in aeronautical engineering in college and worked as an aeronautical engineer at Edwards Air Force Base.)

Teacher's Note: Independently from Newton, a German philosopher named Gottfried Leibniz also discovered the fundamental theorem of calculus. Together, these two men are considered the founders of calculus.

Newton's discoveries in **light and color** are perhaps even more astounding than his work in mathematics. Newton discovered that all color is included in sunlight. He found that by using a prism, he could separate the beams of color and study each independently. Purchase a small prism and show your student what Newton saw.

Newton also figured out why everything appears to be colored. Everything in the world absorbs or reflects certain colors in the sunlight around it. If you look at grass in the sun, it appears green. This is because the grass reflects the green light in the sun and absorbs most of the other colors. If you took a patch of grass and shone a red light (or any color light not containing green) it wouldn't look green. This is why, to see the truest color of an object, it should be placed in "natural" light, or sunlight.

Finally, Newton's most amazing discoveries are probably in regard to **gravity**. Newton discovered that the reason objects are pulled toward the earth (which is also why we can stand up and why a dropped penny falls to the ground), is the same reason that the moon stays in its orbit. Newton came to understand that there was a universal gravitational "pull" or force that draws bodies in the universe together. This force is always pulling objects toward the center of the earth. The amount of force depends on two things: (1) the amount of matter in the objects being attracted and (2) the distance between the bodies.

To help illustrate these principles to your student, get out one large and one small canned item. Ask your student which one weighs more. It should be an easy answer: the larger can. But why is it heavier? The larger can contains more matter or substance. The greater the matter, the greater the earth's gravitational pull on the object. We call the earth's pull the weight of the object. Therefore, the larger can weighs more because it has more mass and is being pulled harder by the earth.

Another famous scientist, Albert Einstein, said that the ideas Newton uncovered "...are even today still guiding our thinking in physics."

So why isn't there any gravity on the moon? Well, actually there is some gravity, just not as much as on Earth. Remind your student of what he learned about the earth's gravitational forces, in relation to an object's mass. The moon weighs almost 81 times less than the earth. The moon's mass is less than the earth's mass, so its gravitational pull is less than that of the earth's pull. In round numbers, the moon's gravitational pull is one-sixth that of Earth's. If a child weighs 60 pounds on Earth, he would only weigh 10 pounds on the moon. Learning to walk, move and conduct experiments at one-sixth your weight is difficult. This is one reason why Neil, Buzz and Mike had to train so rigorously.

If your student is interested in learning more about these topics, he can get more information at his local library on gravity, light, color, calculus and Sir Isaac Newton.

Sir Isaac Newton made incredible discoveries and we should be thankful for his tenacious curiosity and drive!

Science: Gravity Experiment

Your student can learn more about gravity by conducting this simple experiment at home:

Straight, No Matter What

You need:
10" piece of string
paper clip (or safety pin)
ruler (or use a stick roughly 12" in length)
two hardback books which are the same size

Tie the paper clip on one end of the string, and the other end of the string tightly to the ruler. Set the books on end several inches apart and lay the ruler on top of the books. Have your student observe which way the string is hanging and where the paper clip is positioned. Now, your student can lift one side of the ruler up in the air a few inches. Again, where is the paper clip positioned?

This experiment will show your student that regardless of how the ruler is positioned, the paper clip always pulls the string straight down. Why? The earth's gravitational force always pulls an object toward the center of the earth. It wouldn't matter where you were in the world, or at what angle you were holding the ruler. The paper clip will always pull the string down toward the center of the earth.

Science: The Moon

In this chapter, Neil and his two other crewmembers are intently focused on one thing: going to the moon.

In this lesson, your student can learn (or review) answers to the following questions:

• What is the moon made of?
• What does the moon look like close-up?
• What makes the moon shine?
• What is the shape of the moon's orbit?
• What does the moon have to do with oceans and tides?

If your student is a visual learner, it may help him to draw illustrations for each of these questions and answers. Your student can also take a ball of clay and form his own moon, carefully molding craters and **maria** (flat plains, previously regarded as "seas") on its surface.

The moon is made of bits of rock, glass and sand. We have learned much more about the moon's composition since U.S. astronauts, like Neil, have been able to bring back samples. Moon rocks are made mostly of materials that include aluminum, calcium, iron and magnesium. Sand covers many of the moon's maria. The sand, when put under a microscope, is often just microscopic glass balls.

The moon's surface is covered with many dips and concave places called **craters**. These craters were formed by the moon being hit by meteoroids, which are solid objects traveling through space. Because of the moon's lack of atmosphere, even the smallest meteoroids form craters. The moon is covered by billions of these small pits, but it also has several very large craters. One in particular, Copernicus (named for the astronomer), is nearly 50 miles wide.

Teacher's Note: Nicolaus Copernicus (kuh PER ni kus) was a Polish astronomer who developed the idea that the earth is a moving planet. He is considered by most to be the founder of modern astronomy. Copernicus would make an excellent subject for your student to use for a report or oral presentation.

The moon's surface also includes wide, flat plains called maria. When one looks at the moon with a naked eye or through a telescope, the maria appear dark. Galileo called these dark flat patches "maria," which means "seas" in Latin. Galileo must have thought maria were water-covered portions of rock. Instead, they are simply low plains.

Teacher's Note: Galileo was an Italian astronomer and he was the first to effectively use a refracting telescope to gain new information about the planets and the moon. Galileo would make an excellent outside study topic for your student. A simple but profound book on Galileo is called *Starry Messenger* by Peter Sis. Look for it at your library.

Although the moon is the brightest object in the night sky, it does not give off any light of its own. When we see the moon "shine" we are merely seeing the moon reflecting the light of the sun. Sometimes the moon looks full and sometimes it appears to be a thin sliver. The moon never actually changes shape. It appears to change because different parts of it are being lighted by the sun. When the moon appears to be getting larger, we say the moon is **waxing**. When it appears to be getting smaller, we say it is **waning**.

The earth orbits the sun and the moon orbits the earth. But the moon doesn't orbit the earth in a regular circle. Instead, its orbit is an oval, which scientists call "elliptical." Because the moon moves in an oval path, it is not always the same distance from the earth. When the moon is closest to us, we call it the moon's **perigee**. When it is farthest, we say it is the moon's **apogee**.

What does your student know about **tides** and the moon? If your student lives by an ocean, then he is probably quite familiar with high tide and low tide. If not, explain to your student that every place along the seashore (all over the world) has two high tides and two low tides daily. A tide is the rise or fall of ocean waters on the shore.

Teacher's Note: In reality, the gravitational forces of the sun and moon affect every body of water on the earth. It is only where ocean and continents meet that the effects of tides are noticeable. Lake Superior experiences high and low tides daily but the difference is only that of two inches. Other even smaller bodies of water, like ponds, experience nearly indistinguishable tides.

Just as the earth's gravitational pull affects the moon's rotation and keeps it in orbit, so the moon's gravity pulls on the earth. These forces affect the earth and its large bodies of water. The moon's gravity pulls the water that is directly below the moon. On the other side of the earth, the moon's gravity is pulling the earth away from the water. These forces form bulges in the ocean that create low and high tides. As the earth moves, these tidal bulges travel from east to west. Although they occur at different times, the seashore will always have two high tides and two low tides in each 24-hour day.

Language Arts: Writing and Discussion Question

Neil, Buzz and Mike have worked seemingly endless hours in preparing for their mission to the moon. What is something you want to do someday that you would devote this much work toward?

Language Arts: Vocabulary

calculus   A branch of mathematics which helps mathematicians solve for unknown quantities.

maria   The low plains on the moon which look dark from Earth; the Latin word for seas.

crater   A bowl-shaped dip in the moon's surface, created by meteoroids striking the moon.

waxing   Growing gradually larger (referring to the period in the moon's phases when it appears to be getting larger).

waning   Growing gradually less in extent (referring to the period in the moon's phases when it appears to be getting smaller).

perigee   The point at which the moon is closest to the earth.

apogee   The point at which the moon is farthest from the earth

tide   The rise and fall of ocean waters.

Chapter 14—The First Man on the Moon

Teacher Summary

It is July 16, 1969, and Neil, Buzz and Mike are finally on their way to the moon. From their spacecraft, the *Columbia*, Neil and his fellow astronauts telecast pictures from space. By July 20, they are approaching the moon and getting the lunar landing module, the *Eagle*, ready. Finally, after months of preparation, Neil steps onto the surface of the moon, becoming the first man to ever walk on its surface. Buzz follows him and together they report back to Earth what they are seeing and how things are going. They talk to the American people, the President, take pictures and gather many samples. In a little over two hours, their job is done and they get back into the lunar module.

What we will cover in this chapter:

Social Studies: History - Mike Collins: Command Module Pilot
Social Studies: History - Edwin "Buzz" Aldrin: Lunar Module Pilot
Social Studies: Geography - Capes*
Science: Rockets
Language Arts: Conducting and Writing an Interview
Language Arts: Writing and Discussion Question
Language Arts: Vocabulary

Social Studies: History - Mike Collins: Command Module Pilot

Our story is titled *Neil Armstrong: Young Flyer*. It is, indeed, a biography on the life of the first man on the moon. In this chapter, however, we get to know the other crewmembers on *Apollo 11*: they are Buzz Aldrin and Mike Collins. In our story, obviously, the emphasis is on Neil. It would be interesting for your student, however, if you took some time to share a little background information on Mike Collins as well. Even though he is the least well-known of these three history-making astronauts, his story is, in many ways, just as interesting as Neil's.

Michael Collins (1930-2021) was born in Rome, Italy, but he wasn't Italian. His father was in the United States Army and was stationed in Rome. Mike grew up wanting to be like his dad, and followed in his footsteps. He attended the United States Military Academy in 1952 and became an Air Force officer. In less than 10 years, he realized he wanted to fly farther than the earth's atmosphere. He was a skilled test pilot (just like Neil) and joined NASA as an astronaut in 1963.

In 1966, Collins co-piloted the *Gemini 10* mission into space. By the time *Apollo 11* came around, Mike was married and had three children.

Many people, including your student, might think Mike was disappointed he wasn't able to walk on the moon, with Neil and Buzz. After all, he was so close! It's hard to imagine going all that way and not being able to walk around a little bit, isn't it? On the contrary, he was just thrilled to be included on the mission. Collins was supposed to have flown on an earlier *Apollo* mission, but because of a back injury, NASA wouldn't let him go. For a while, it was doubtful he'd fly again at all. However, the injury healed and the opportunity for the *Apollo 11* mission came up. Collins was quoted as saying he was just happy to be in space again and along for such a historic moment. He knew his job was an important one, and he would not have missed the chance to go along.

Collins' job during the *Apollo 11* flight was a critical one. As the command module pilot, it was his job to direct the command module, release the *Eagle*, dock with the *Eagle*, and communicate with the flight commanders back on Earth. In many ways, Collins had the most intimidating job of all. He was required to keep track of everything, all by himself, while Neil and Buzz collected samples and conducted tests on the surface of the moon.

When the *Eagle* docked with *Columbia*, Collins was said to have grabbed Aldrin's head and kissed him as he floated back in through the hatch. Collins was relieved that Neil and Buzz had safely returned from the moon's surface and that everything had gone so smoothly.

If your student is interested in reading more about Mike Collins, or books that he has written, here are some recommendations:

Carrying the Fire: An Astronaut's Journeys by Michael Collins
Liftoff! by Michael Collins
The Far Side of the Moon by Alex Iruine
Flying to the Moon and Other Strange Places by Michael Collins

Social Studies: History - Edwin "Buzz" Aldrin: Lunar Module Pilot

Here are a few interesting facts about Buzz Aldrin, *Apollo 11's* lunar module pilot and the second man on the moon.

Buzz's father was a military man, much like Mike Collins' father had been. He had been a colonel in the United States Army Air Corps. He was also a personal friend of Orville Wright and Charles Lindbergh! With these connections, aviation was certainly in Buzz's family blood.

Teacher's Note: If your student did the lesson about the Wright brothers in chapter 2, he will remember the amazing tales of Kitty Hawk and the first planes. You may also wish to find a book or two on Charles Lindbergh and include him in your study of this unit.

Aldrin had been in space before *Apollo 11*, on the space mission *Gemini 12*. At the time, he held the record for the longest walk in space. Like Collins, at the time of *Apollo 11*, Aldrin was married and had three children.

Share with your student one other fun fact: the maiden name of Aldrin's mother was Marian Moon.

Social Studies: Geography - Capes*

Neil and his crew await blastoff at Launch Pad 39A at Cape Kennedy. Does your student know what a cape is?

Teacher's Note: Until 1963, Cape Kennedy was called Cape Canaveral. At that time, it was renamed for President John F. Kennedy, who had set the national goal of landing a man on the moon. The name was changed back to Cape Canaveral in 1973.

Share with your student about this unusual geographical formation and where a cape can be found. A **cape** is a body of land that juts out prominently into a lake, sea or ocean. Capes are often found at the edges of islands and continents. Your student might be interested to learn that there are three other words people use to mean cape: headland, promontory and point. The water around a cape is often choppy and difficult to navigate.

There are two ways a cape can be formed. One is by erosion. Waves of water wash away a piece of the coastline, leaving a strip of land extending prominently. The land that is left is generally hard, dense rock such as volcanic material. Examples of capes made from erosion are Heceta Head and Cape Foulweather, both found on the Oregon coastline.

The second way capes can be formed is by deposits forming from waves that dump sand and other particles in a specific spot. After many years, the deposits become land. Cape Canaveral (also referred to as Cape Kennedy; see the previous Teacher's Note) is a cape formed by this second method.

Perhaps one of the most famous capes in the world is Cape Horn, found at the tip of South America. The waters surrounding the cape are legendary for being extremely hazardous and rough. Today, most sailors use the Panama Canal instead of "rounding the cape."

Capes are an interesting geological formation and a nice additional study topic for your student!

Science: Rockets

In this chapter, we read about the ignition of *Saturn 5's* enormous first-stage engines. The *Saturn 5* is a giant rocket. Does your student know anything about rockets? Here is a great opportunity to share with your student some beginning facts of rocketry science.

Explain to your student that a **rocket**, in its simplest form, is a container that holds gas, under pressure. When a small opening in one of the chambers is opened, it allows some of the gas to escape. As it escapes, it provides thrust, which propels the rocket in the opposite direction.

To illustrate this principle for your student, have him blow a small balloon full of air. Instead of tying a knot in the balloon, have him pinch the end closed. Now release the balloon. What does he observe? As the air is released, the balloon is thrust in the opposite direction. The balloon will probably swoop around in various directions because there isn't anything attached to it to stabilize its flight. If your student thinks of the balloon as the chamber and his breath escaping out as the fuel, then he can look at a balloon as a primitive rocket.

Teacher's Note: You might mention to your student that the real science of modern rocketry began shortly after the publication of Sir Isaac Newton's *Principia*. It was because of Newton's laws of motion, that many scientists began to understand why rockets work. Because of Newton's discoveries, scientists were able to begin experimenting with and developing more successful rockets. This makes a nice connection for your student from the chapter 13 lessons on Newton!

In rockets, the gas pressure isn't produced by our lungs, but instead by burning fuel called **propellants**. In modern rockets, these propellants can be either solid or liquid.

For your student to understand the difference between solid and liquid propellants, explain that a propellant is more than a fuel. A rocket propellant is both a fuel (the thing which burns) and an oxidizer (oxygen), which must be present for the burning to take place. (If you have FIAR Vol. 7, then you may want to refer to chapter 6 in the unit study on *Skylark*. There is a complete lesson on the chemical and scientific background of fire.)

A **solid-fuel** rocket has the fuel and oxidizer (propellant) already combined. To take off, the rocket needs only to be ignited, and once it has been ignited you can't stop it. A **liquid-fuel** rocket has chilled propellants (chilled gases which have become liquid) inside, located in separate chambers (one for fuel and one for an oxidizer). When a rocket engine is fired, the fuel and oxidizer are mixed together and combustion takes place. With modern liquid rockets, once the engine has fired the fuel and oxidizers can be adjusted, thus adjusting the speed of the rocket.

The *Saturn 5* rocket that propelled the astronauts into space was powered by a three-stage liquid-fueled rocket system. At this point, if your student is interested, it might be helpful to explain the difference between this type of rocket system and what your student may know about the recently used space shuttles.

Space shuttles, used by NASA from 1981 to 2011, were reusable spacecraft. They were propelled into space by means of rockets, and they landed the way an airplane does. Shuttles were thrust into the air by both solid-fueled and liquid-fueled rockets. The solid-fueled rockets were clamped to the sides of the shuttle. When it was time to launch, the liquid rockets inside the shuttle began firing up. When they reached full power, the solid rockets on the sides were ignited and unclamped. These solid rockets thrust the shuttle very high,

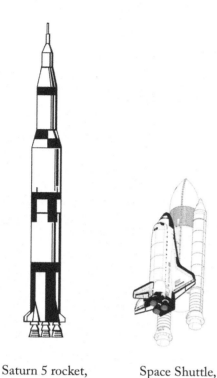

Saturn 5 rocket,
used from 1967-1973

Space Shuttle,
used from 1981-2011

very quickly. Then they fell away into the ocean. The liquid rockets, which could be controlled, continued thrusting the shuttle higher and higher.

Your student can learn more about rockets and thrust by conducting some simple experiments at home, using materials from around the house.

I. Rocket Staging

Materials:
2 long balloons
1 paper or Styrofoam cup, with the bottom cut out
1 plastic straw, cut into four equal lengths
a clothespin
masking tape
30-60 feet of heavy thread or fishing line
2 supports (e.g., trees or poles, 30'-60' apart)

Directions:

1. Slide the four pieces of straw onto the line and tie the ends of the line to supports.

2. Place one balloon inside the open bottom of the cup and inflate it.

3. While holding on to the neck of the inflated balloon, insert the end of the second balloon and inflate this balloon also. When the second balloon expands into the cup, the nozzle of the first balloon should be squeezed shut. Pinch the nozzle on the second balloon with a clothespin.

4. Tape the balloons to the straws.

5. When all is ready, count down from 10 and launch your two-stage rocket by releasing the nozzle of the second balloon. When that balloon is finished thrusting, the first balloon (the second stage) will automatically "fire" and make the rocket travel farther along the string.

Your student can experiment and try this same idea several different ways. He can even measure the length his rocket travels and then try to beat his best distance each time.

II. "Pop" Bottle

Materials:
1/3 cup water
clear plastic 2-liter soda pop bottle
rubber stopper that fits the neck
2 Tbs. baking soda
a few Tbs. vinegar
a few layers of tissue paper
several short lengths of dowel rods or round,
    smooth pencils

Directions:

1. Place water and vinegar inside the bottle.

2. Wrap baking soda in a few layers of tissue paper.

3. Lay the dowel rods in a straight row along a flat surface.

4. Drop the wrapped baking soda into the water and cork the bottle. (**Important:** Make sure the stopper is snug, but do not ram it in too tightly. If you do, the bottle could explode. The stopper needs to be able to pop out.)

5. Lay the bottle on the dowel rods and stand to the side. Be prepared to clean up any water that gets spilled from the bottle.

Talk with your student about why these experiments work and different ways they could be conducted. Have fun learning more about rockets, fuels, and other related science topics!

Language Arts: Conducting and Writing an Interview

Watching Neil walk on the moon was an amazing moment in the lives of millions of people around the world. Perhaps your student's grandparent, other relative, neighbor or older friend remember this event. Here is a great opportunity for your student to practice conducting and writing an interview.

Encourage your student to locate someone he knows who remembers watching this historic moment on television. Your student has done his background research for this interview by doing this unit study. Now, he can write down some questions he would like to ask the person. For example:

• Where were you when Neil Armstrong walked on the moon?
• How old were you?
• What were you doing?
• What did you think when you saw Neil standing there?
• What were people talking about after it was over?
• How did you feel?
• Did it change the way you thought about yourself, America, etc.?

After your student has conducted, and possibly recorded, his interview, then he can compile his notes and write the interview. It can be short (a paragraph) or several pages, depending upon his age and ability level.

This can be a great way of drawing this unit study to a close, because it will give your student valuable writing practice and it will give him a human perspective on these awesome events.

Language Arts: Writing and Discussion Question

Mike Collins went with Neil and Buzz, but he never stepped foot on the moon. His job was to fly the command module. He went, knowing he wouldn't step out of the spacecraft. We know how he felt about that, but how might *you* feel? Why?

Language Arts: Vocabulary

cape A body of land which juts out prominently into a lake, sea or ocean; headland, promontory, point.

rocket A container which holds gas under pressure; the rocket is thrust forward when the chamber is opened.

solid fuel Propellant for a rocket which contains both the fuel and oxidizer together in one unit.

liquid fuel Propellant for a rocket which contains the fuel and oxidizer in separate chambers.

propellant The fuel and oxidizer which can be combined and ignited to thrust a rocket forward.

Chapter 15—A Hero's Welcome Home

Teacher Summary

The mission is complete! Neil Armstrong and his crew have completed their goal of walking on the moon, and they are coming home. When they come back to Earth, they are put into a time of quarantine, to make sure they don't have any germs from the moon. Soon, however, they are back with their families and the celebrations begin.

Neil, Buzz, Mike and their wives begin a three-month tour of the world, visiting countries and talking about their trip to the moon. Parades greet them in various towns and parties are everywhere. President Nixon presents each of the astronauts with the Presidential Medal of Freedom, the nation's highest honor.

After the *Apollo 11* mission, Neil works in the NASA Office of Advanced Research for two years. Then he becomes a professor of aerospace and engineering at the University of Cincinnati. (Neil Armstrong died on August 25, 2012.)

What we will cover in this chapter:

Social Studies: Geography - Explore a New Country*
Language Arts: Space Terms
Language Arts: Writing and Discussion Question
Life Skills: Reaching Your Goals

Social Studies: Geography - Explore a New Country*

In this chapter, we see an exhaustive list of the countries Neil, Buzz, Mike and their wives visited after their famous mission was complete. Has your student heard of all of these countries? Here is the list:

Mexico, Columbia, Argentina, Brazil, Spain, France, The Netherlands, Belgium, Germany, England, Vatican City, Italy, Yugoslavia, Turkey, India, Bangladesh, Pakistan, Thailand, Australia, Guam, Korea and Japan

Take this opportunity to let your student explore a new country. He can pick any country he wishes from the chapter and explore it (or you can allow him to choose any other country in the world). He can find out where the country is located, the country's anthem, its flag, the population, cuisine, the economy, the history of the country, etc. For example, if your student were to pick Italy as his topic, then he might find out the following:

Italy is a peninsula that juts out into the Mediterranean Sea.
It is shaped like a boot.
Northern Italy is a richer region with large, modern cities like Milan and Turin.
Southern Italy is a poorer region, with farming communities like Sicily.
Rome is the capital of Italy.
The currency is the euro, but used to be the lira.
The official language is Italian.
The main exports include wine, olive oil and fashion.

Your student's imagination can run with this lesson. He can create a notebook, poster or scrapbook to collect his research and facts. He can take a small box and cover the top and sides with paper. Then he can glue printed pictures which relate to that country on the top and sides. He can make a three-dimensional clay map of the country he is studying, or he can cook a meal for his family using that country's native cuisine.

This lesson will broaden your student's awareness of a new geographical region and another culture. Take this opportunity to explore all of the geography books that your local library has to offer for today's students. Look for books on the particular country that your student has chosen, as well as general books or atlases on countries of the world. Many of these references will have beautiful pictures, helpful graphs and tables, fascinating information and fun facts.

Language Arts: Space Terms

Have you and your student read through the list of space vocabulary located at the end of *Neil Armstrong: Young Flyer*? Now is the time to read or review these terms and talk about any that are still confusing. Your student will feel smarter, more accomplished and will have fun when he can use terms like satellite and lunar module with ease!

Language Arts: Writing and Discussion Question

What a homecoming the astronauts received! If you were Neil, do you think you'd want to travel around the world, or would you rather go back to your own home when you returned from space? Why?

Life Skills: Reaching Your Goals

Neil Armstrong's life is an example of what people can accomplish when they have goals. At the end of our story, we read that Neil said, "any goal can be reached, if first you identify what your goal is and then work together to reach that goal."

Think back, with your student, about the Neil we read about in chapters 1, 2 and 3. Even when he was very young, he longed to pilot an airplane. He always knew what his goals were. Those goals changed a little bit over the course of his life, but they always centered on flying. As Neil said, those goals were reached by working together with others, not just alone.

Neil Armstrong can be a wonderful role model for your student, even if your student doesn't want to become an astronaut. Neil's life demonstrates a focused and happy pursuit of a dream. He never gave up, but instead worked hard every day, in order to be successful.

What is a goal your student would love to achieve? It doesn't have to be a career. Perhaps learning to swim or planting a successful garden are goals your student has. What can your student learn from Neil? He needs to be able to articulate his goal (because it's hard to achieve something you're fuzzy on). He needs to work with others, in order to be successful. The next time your student is frustrated and isn't sure he'll be able to complete a goal, remind him of Neil!

Use this page to jot down relevant info you've found for this
Five in a Row chapter book, including favorite lessons, go-along
resources, field trips, and family memories.

NEIL ARMSTRONG: YOUNG FLYER

Dates studied: _____

Student: _____

Favorite Lesson Topics:

Social Studies:
_____
_____
_____

Science:
_____
_____
_____

Language Arts:
_____
_____
_____

Fine Arts:
_____
_____
_____

Life Skills:
_____
_____
_____

Relevant Library Resources: Books, DVDs, Audio Books

_____
_____
_____
_____
_____
_____
_____

Websites or Video Links:

_____
_____
_____
_____
_____
_____
_____

Related Field Trip Opportunities:
_____
_____
_____

Favorite Quote or Memory During Study:
_____
_____
_____

86

Neil Armstrong: Young Flyer - Directions for Vocabulary Words

Language Arts: **Vocabulary Sorting Exercise**

In some previous FIAR chapter book units, vocabulary words have been made into crossword puzzles for you to complete. For this unit, though, you will create a flashcard or small piece of paper for each vocabulary word. Write the word on the front of the piece of paper or flashcard and its definition on the back.

Once your vocabulary words for a chapter are written you will then begin a sorting exercise with them. You may choose to sort only the new words for each chapter or add new words to words from the previous chapter(s).

You'll need four pieces of 8.5" x 11" paper. On each you will write a category name on the top or bottom of the paper. There are four basic categories given, but you can also change the categories and resort your words into new categories of your own choosing (such as quiet/loud, good/bad, soft/hard, big/small). You can even resort the words with the same four categories (in this case you will move each word into a different category). Start with the four categories (words written at the top of the paper): **easy**, **difficult**, **stationary**, and **moving**.

The categories are random words that require some thought and reasoning of each vocabulary word and its definition to decide a best fit. The "reasoning" required helps you think through the meaning of the word, which will help you remember the word. There are no right or wrong answers.

For example, *abdicate*: to officially give up power or authority to someone else (a vocabulary word from chapter 2), could be categorized into the category **difficult** because it would be a hard decision to hand over power or authority to someone else. Or, you could sort it into the category **moving** because the authority is moving from one person to another.

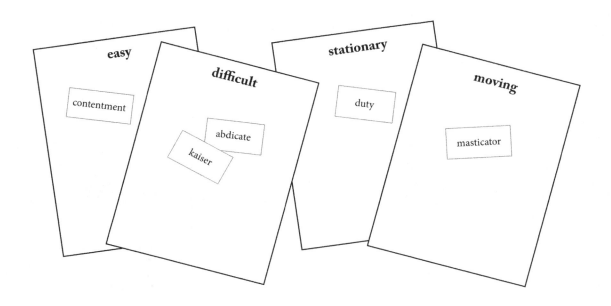

Name:

Date:

History: **Timeline of Neil Armstrong's Childhood: 1930s**

The lesson **History: Our Story's Time Frame: 1936** introduces many topics of study for exploring the history surrounding the decade in which Neil Armstrong was raised. People, events and dates are mentioned within the lesson and provided as topics of additional research.

The timeline below spans Neil Armstrong's first decade of life (1930-1940). Mark any people or events that you research or learn about throughout this chapter. Include printed images if desired and use hash marks along the timeline to represent specific dates and mark accordingly.

1940

1930

88

Neil Armstrong: Young Flyer - Chapter 2

Name:

Date:

Science: **Forces of Flight**

After completing the **Science: How Airplanes Fly** lesson, you will have discussed the four basic principles that affect a plane in the air. Look at the image below and label the four principles as shown on the diagram based on what you learned in the lesson.

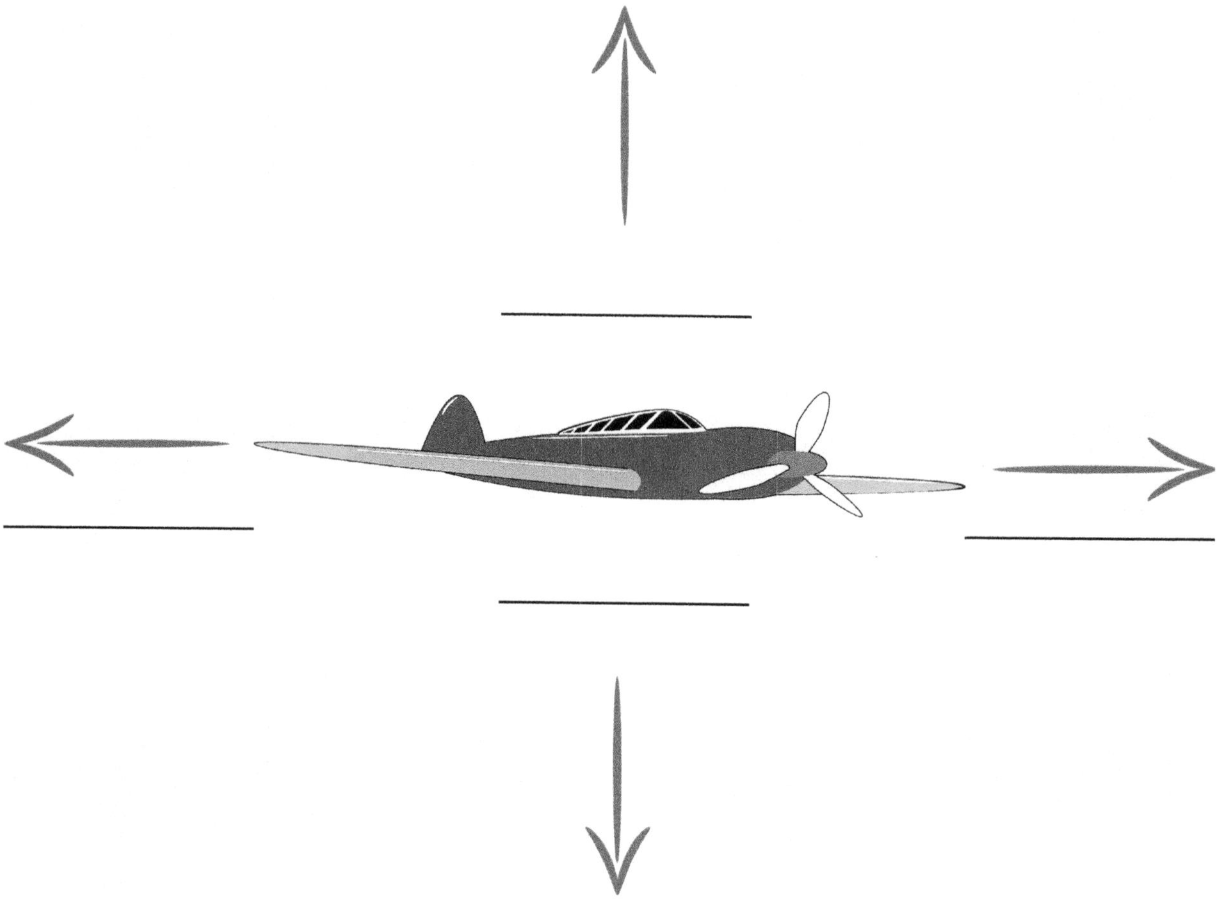

Search online or look in library books to find answers to these questions:

What increases lift when flying? ______________________________

____

What design features can reduce (friction) drag on an airplane? ______________

____

____

Name:

Date:

Language Arts: **Synonyms, Antonyms and Homonyms**

Complete the chart below with examples from the **Language Arts: Synonyms, Antonyms and Homonyms** lesson. Think of the new words to add to each column, such as pear/pair/pare, rain/rein/reign, whether/weather (homonyms), or other examples of synonyms or antonyms for vague words like nice, sad, easy, bad, etc. You can also list the synonyms that you chose for the word "pretty" in the space provided bleow.

Synonyms	Antonyms	Homonyms

90

Synonyms for pretty:

_____

_____

_____

Name:

Date:

History and Geography: **Ellis Island**

Virtual 🖥 FIELD TRIP

Chapter 4 introduces the topic of immigration and an introduction to Ellis Island. Search online for "Ellis Island virtual tour." Take notes below, and include any information that you find particularly interesting. Print and paste an image from your virtual tour into the frame above.

Name:

Date:

Fine Arts: **Making Maps**

The lesson **Fine Arts: Making Maps** suggests you try your hand at map making. To learn a bit more about maps and give you more inspiration to work with, we suggest searching online for "map making books" or "how to draw maps". Spend time reading the books or researching more online before embarking on your map making journey. Take notes in the space provided below of any tips, ideas, or methods of map creation that you want to include on your map.

Go-along book for map making:
Disney Maps: A Magical Atlas of the Movies We Know and Love by Disney

92

Ideas to incorporate with my map:

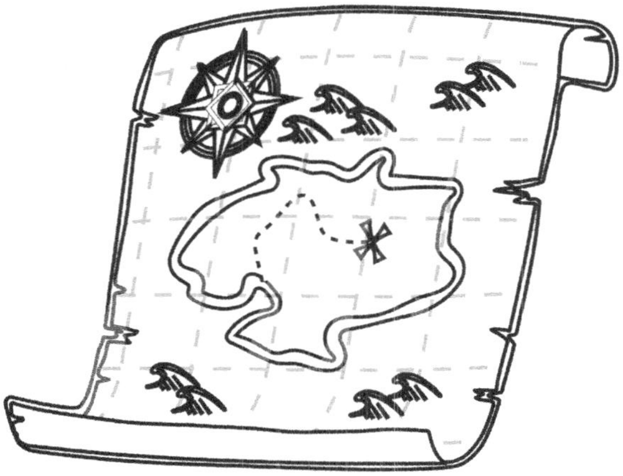

Name:

Date:

Science: **Constellations**

After completing the **Science: Constellations** lesson, search online or find astronomy resource books from the library and choose three different constellations to draw into the frames below. Write the name of the constellation and where and when it's visible into the spaces provided.

Go-along books for constellation research include:

Find the Constellations by H. A. Rey

Constellations by F. S. Kim

Constellations: The Story of Space Told Through the 88 Known Star Patterns in the Night Sky
    by Govert Schilling

Constellation:

Visible (location and season):

Constellation:

Visible (location and season):

Constellation:

Visible (location and season):

Name:

Date:

Science: **Anatomy of Digestion**

After completing the **Science: Principles of Digestion** lesson, you can use what you learned along with the resource book recommendations below or an online search to label the parts of the body associated with digestion.

An few excellent resource books are:

The Digestive System by Jennifer Prior
The Digestive System by Christine Taylor-Butler
How Food Travels In The Body: Digestive System by Biology Books for Kids

94

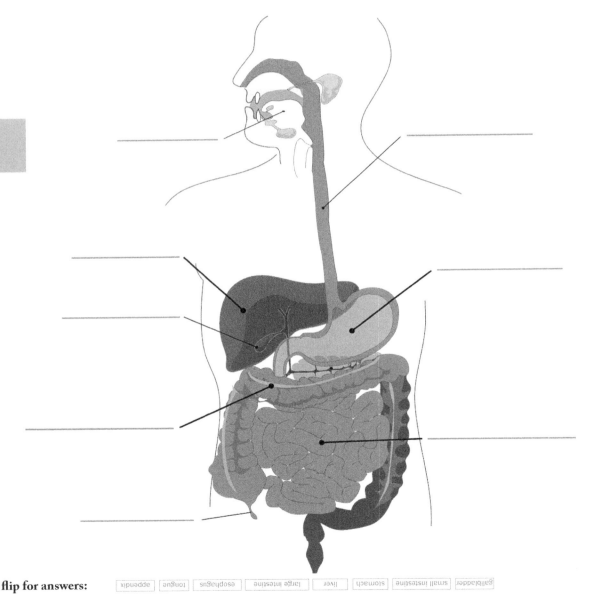

flip for answers: appendix tongue esophagus large intestine liver stomach small intestine gallbladder

Name:

Date:

Science: **Heat Transfer**

After completing the **Science: Conduction, Convection and Radiation** lesson, you will have a basic idea of how these three forms of heat transfer. Fill in the blanks below (choose which type of heat transfer is occuring) using your knowlege of conduction, convection and radiation. If you are unsure of an answer, seach online, "what type of heat transfer is ..." and fill in the blank.

1. Cooking an egg in in a hot pan _____

2. Ironing a sheet _____

3. Adding cold cream to your hot coffee _____

4. Baking cookies inside an oven _____

5. The sun warming your driveway _____

6. Drying your hair with a blowdryer _____

7. Boiling water in a pan on the stove _____

8. Sun rays warming a swimming pool _____

9. Snowflakes melting on your hand _____

10. A microwave heating food _____

11. A candle under a warming dish (to keep food warm) _____

12. Hot air balloon _____

Radiation	**Convection**	**Conduction**
5, 8, 10	4, 6, 7, 12	1, 2, 3, 7, 9, 11

Name:

Date:

History: **Biography - Who Am I?**

Harry S. Truman was the thirty-third president of the United States of America. Once you've completed the **History: President Truman** lesson, research Harry Truman to learn more about his life and his influence on America. You can search online or use books from the library.

A go-along book that you could read is: *Harry S. Truman* (Childhood of Famous Americans series) by George E. Stanley

Print and paste an image of Harry S. Truman into the frame.
Write information gathered through your research into the spaces below.

96

Name: _____

Lived: _____

Known for: _____

_____

_____

_____

_____

_____

Connections to story: _____

_____

_____

_____

_____

_____

Name:

Date:

Language Arts: **Writing and Discussion Question**

The second Writing and Discussion Question for this chapter asks you to describe a goal or dream you have and what you think it might take to accomplish it. In the space below, identify one "dream" you have (just as Neil had a dream to be a pilot), add your own drawing or printed illustration that represents your dream, and write about how you might take steps to achieve this dream someday.

My goal/dream: _____

_____

_____

_____

_____

_____

Name:

Date:

Science: **Biography - Who Am I?**

Once you've completed the **History: NASA** lesson, there are many books you could read and people that you could study to learn more about astronauts or the history of NASA. Here are two books you can choose from to dig deeper and learn more. There is also a movie based on the book *Hidden Figures* (which is based on a true story).

Two go-along books:

Hidden Figures: Young Readers' Edition
    by Margot Lee Shetterly

Chasing Space: Young Readers' Edition
    by Leland Melvin

Name: _____

98

Print and paste an image of someone from the book you choose into the frame (write their name below the frame). Write information gathered through your research into the spaces below.

Name: _____

Lived: _____

Known for: _____

_____

_____

_____

_____

_____

Connections to story: _____

_____

_____

_____

_____

_____

Name:

Date:

Science: **Sound Waves**

After completing the **Science: Air and Sound Travel** lesson, you know that sound travels in wavelike frequencies as it moves through the air or some other substance. Sound is made up of two basic qualitites: pitch and volume.

Pitch is based on how high or low a sound is and is related to the frequency of the soundwaves. A higher frequency of vibration will produce a higher pitch sound and a slower frequency will produce a lower pitch sound. This can be easily demonstrated or observed on a guitar where the highest (E) string has a higher frequency of vibration than the lowest (E) string: therefore the high E produces a higher pitch, while the low E creates a lower pitch.

Volume is how loud or soft/quiet a sound is. Volume can be determined by pressure or intensity (the harder you hit a drum, the louder it sounds). Sound waves travel higher and lower in relation to the mid-line the louder the sound is. The waves stay closer to the mid-line in height when the sound is softer.

Based on this information look at the sound waves below and label them as **high pitch** or **low** pitch and **loud** volume or **soft** volume.

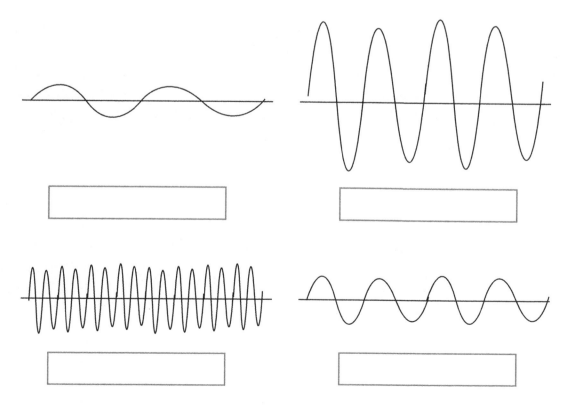

Name:

Date:

Science: **Earth's Moon**

100

Virtual 🖥 FIELD TRIP

In the lesson, **Science: The Moon**, you learned many interesting facts about the moon. If a picture is worth a thousand words, then perhaps a virtual tour is worth a million words. Go to https://moon.nasa.gov/resources/168/tour-of-the-moon-4k/ for a *virtual tour* of the Moon. Or, search online for, "NASA tour of the moon." Take notes below, and include any information that you find particularly interesting. Take a screenshot during the virtual tour and paste an image into the frame above (or search online for an image of the moon to print and paste).

_____

_____

_____

_____

_____

_____

Name:

Date:

Social Studies: **Geography - Capes**

After reading the **Social Studies: Geography - Capes** lesson, use an atlas or world map, as well as online research, to locate and label the following ten capes found around the world:

☐ Cape Horn (South America)
☐ Cape of Good Hope (Africa)
☐ Cape Cod (U.S.)
☐ Cape Leeuwin (Australia)
☐ Cape Hatteras (U.S.)

☐ Cape Morris Jessup (Greenland)
☐ Cape Canaveral (U.S.)
☐ Cape Reinga (New Zealand)
☐ Cape Agulhas (Africa)
☐ Cape Roca (Europe)

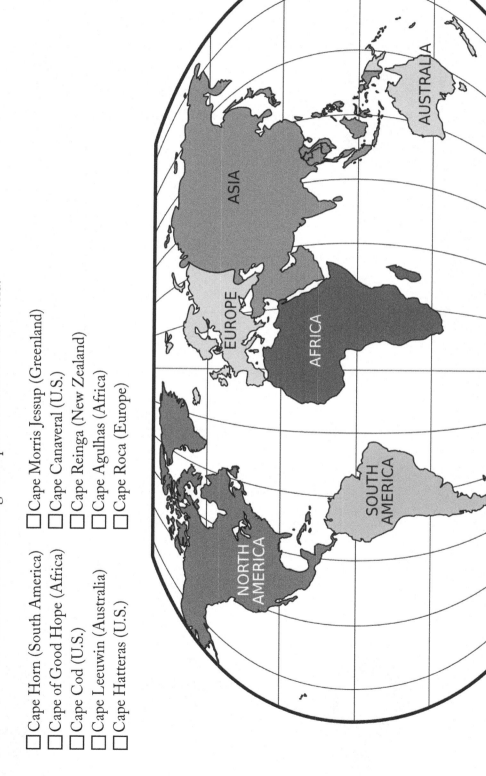

Name:

Date:

Geography: **Explore a New Country**

Once you've completed the geography lesson, **Geography: Explore a New Country** you can use the page below to start your research project, recording your choice of country and what you learn about it. Use this as a cover page for your project, adding blank pages after as needed for additional information and images.

102

I explored: _____

Capital: _____

Official Language: _____

Currency: _____

Main Exports: _____

Population: _____

image of country

flag of country

Marie Curie and the Discovery of Radium

Title: *Marie Curie and the Discovery of Radium*
Author: Ann E. Steinke
Copyright: 1987

Chapter 1—Small Beginnings

Teacher Summary

In the first chapter, we meet the young Marie Curie. When she was born, her name was Manya Sklodowska—her family calls her Manya. The Sklodowska family lives in Poland. Manya's mother is a principal at a school for girls. Her father is a professor of mathematics and physics.

The Sklodowska family is poor, and with five children they need extra help. They live in an apartment within the school where Mr. Sklodowska teaches. Manya's parents raise their children with a great sense of pride in their Polish heritage. At this point in history, Poland was ruled by Russia, Austria and Germany. Shortly before, the Poles had tried to revolt, but it failed. Manya is taught all about Polish history even though it isn't allowed to be taught in schools. And Manya, as her family will soon discover, is very bright and learns it as quickly as they can teach her.

Teacher's Note: This biography, a part of the Solutions: Profiles in Science for Young People series, includes two helpful sections. In the back of the book, you will find both a glossary of terms and a list of topic discussion questions. These questions will not be used to replace the Five in a Row Writing and Discussion Questions, but some are included in addition to the discussion questions when they correspond with a chapter study.

Also, your student may notice that the last name of Manya's family is spelled two different ways in this chapter. The copyright page of the book clarifies this discrepancy with this statement: "In this book the feminine version of the Polish name Sklodowski is spelled with an a, instead of an i. This is the custom in that country." The concept of gender-based suffixes on words and names will probably be foreign to your student. Explain that this is a grammatical rule that many languages employ. Words are considered either feminine or masculine. English does not make use of this convention. Your student might want to discover which languages do use this convention.

What we will cover in this chapter:

Social Studies: History - Exploring our Timeline: The Late 1800s*
Social Studies: Geography - Poland
Science: Tuberculosis
Science: Geology - Malachite
Science: Barometers
Science: A Brief Introduction to Physics
Fine Arts: Being a Good Storyteller
Life Skills: Doing What Needs to be Done

Social Studies: History - Exploring our Timeline: The Late 1800s*

Our main character, Manya, was born in Poland in 1867. Take this first chapter as an opportunity to explore our story's time period with your student. Her

understanding of what the world was like for Manya will be enriched if she sees what was happening at the same time around the world.

Find a book or a video that talks about the 19th century or the late 1800s. You can even make this timeline exploration an online treasure hunt for your student. Give your student three subjects on pieces of paper: sports, literature and music perhaps. Now set your watch for a short length of time (10-15 minutes) and let your student hunt for events that occurred in those topic areas during the 19th century. For an older student, you may even wish to give her a specific decade. For example, she might find:

Sports—In 1869, the first college football game took place between Rutgers and Princeton in America.

Music—Johannes Brahms, the famous German composer, spent much of the 1860s touring as a concert pianist.

Literature—In England, Lewis Carroll released his work, *Alice's Adventures in Wonderland* in 1865.

This kind of hunt gives your student a chance to research things for herself. It gives her information to assimilate into a timeline and it makes it fun!

Social Studies: Geography - Poland

Poland is a country that has an interesting and important history. Throughout this unit your student will be looking at different aspects of Poland, and the surrounding countries: Russia, Austria and Germany.

Take this time to give your student a brief introduction to Marie Curie's homeland. First, find Poland on a map. It is large country located due east of Germany,

Poland

in Central Europe on the shores of the Baltic Sea. The name Poland comes from the word Plane, which was the name of a Slavic tribe of people who lived in that region hundreds of years before. Plane means "flat or without hills." Poland has very few hills, and is covered with beautiful grassy plains. There are, however, steep mountains which frame the country on its southern edge. The northern side of the country has many small, lovely lakes that form toward the Baltic Sea.

Emphasize Poland's rich cultural heritage to your student. Poland has wonderful customs of folk songs, dancing, music and literature. Dances like the mazurka and the polonaise were not only popular in Poland, but influenced other countries as well. The great composer Frederic Chopin based much of his music on these dances and forms. You might want to show you student a video of these dances, which are usually performed in colorful, traditional costumes.

Poland also has a varied political history. At one time, the Polish people were powerful and ruled an empire that encompassed much of Central Europe (from the late 1300s through the mid-1500s). However, foreign countries slowly chipped away at Poland. By the late 1700s, Poland had been conquered and divided up by Austria, Prussia and Russia. (Your student may have learned about Prussia in Chapter 4 of the *Neil Armstrong* unit in this volume.) Your student may also be interested to know that it was not until 1989 that noncommunists came to power in Poland and lifted all the restrictions off the people.

Geographically, Poland is divided into seven different land regions. Look with your student online or in an atlas and point out each of these regions:

1. The Coastal Lowlands—Located along the Baltic coast of northwestern Poland. These coasts naturally form important harbors used for trade and industry.

2. The Baltic Lakes Region—This area covers most of northern Poland and is dotted with thousands of small lakes. Although few people live there, it is a popular holiday destination.

3. The Central Plains—This region stretches across the mid-section of Poland. These low plains are fertile farmland and also hold the three largest cities: Warsaw, Poznan and Wroclaw.

4. The Polish Uplands—Consisting of small, rolling hills and plateaus, this region is rich farmland and mineral mining country.

106

5. The Carpathian Forelands—This land is a strip between the Vistula and San Rivers in southeastern Poland.

6. The Sudeten Mountains—Bordering southwestern Poland, forests cover most of these mountains.

7. The Western Carpathian Mountains—This mountain range forms the southern rim of Poland. This region has several national parks and beautiful villages.

Your student will also see on a map of Poland the many waterways, including the longest river—the Vistula. Chapter 2 will give your student a closer look at this important river.

Poland is a country that fought its way back from very difficult circumstances. Much like her country, the life of Marie Curie is one of overcoming obstacles and succeeding, in spite of them.

Science: Tuberculosis

Poor Manya! Her mother, Mrs. Sklodowska, is very sick. Our author describes Mrs. Sklodowska's illness as tuberculosis. Your student may have heard of this illness before. In America today, people rarely hear about tuberculosis. Because of our research and understanding of prevention and treatment, thankfully, few people have to deal with this difficult disease. In other regions of the world, developing nations like those in Africa still face this plague and have few drugs to use in the fight.

Explain to your student that tuberculosis [too BUR cue LOW sis] is a bacteria-born infection that affects the lungs. Patients with tuberculosis (also called TB) cough a lot and produce sputum (a combination of spit and phlegm). Because TB is contagious, Mrs.

Sklodowska was right to try to keep distant from her family. How sad, however, to be unable to hug or kiss her children!

Certain powerful drugs have been developed today to help people overcome TB infections. There are vaccines, but they aren't always effective. Instead, doctors use skin tests, x-rays and laboratory tests to detect an infection in a person. Then, through drug treatment and rest, the patient generally gets better quickly. Tell your student to remember that x-rays are used to detect and monitor TB. This will be of interest as we learn more about what Marie Curie does later in life!

Science: Geology - Malachite

This chapter offers an opportunity for your student to explore a quick geology lesson. The Sklodowski's clock is made of a green mineral called **malachite** [MAL a kite].

Malachite is made of copper oxide, carbon dioxide and water. As the mineral forms, it makes layers. The layers are all green, but are different shades, from light apple green to dark forest green.

Malachite has been used mainly as an ornamental stone. Just like the Sklodowski's clock, many pieces of decoration and jewelry are created from pieces of malachite. During Biblical times, the high priests of Israel wore breastplates that included sacred stones—including malachite. Look online or in a rocks and minerals reference book and find a picture of malachite for your student to see.

Science: Barometers

Little Manya likes to look at her father's science equipment and instruments. Draw your student's attention to where Manya examines her father's barometer.

A barometer is an instrument used to measure atmospheric pressure. Specifically, barometers measure the weight of air pushing down on Earth. Your student can feel and see air pressure by conducting a simple experiment.

Get a clean or new toilet plunger. Have your student press the plunger onto a hard floor. Now, have your student try to pull it up. What happens? The plunger is difficult to pull up for two reasons. First, the air inside the cup was pushed out when it was forced down on the floor. And second, the air pressure around the cup on the outside is pushing down on the cup on the floor. It's holding it down.

Air pressure is important to weather because a change in the air pressure generally indicates a change in the weather pattern and temperature. For the most part, low air pressure means warm temperatures and high air pressure means cooler temperatures.

Meteorologists use barometers to measure air pressure and notice its changes. There are two kinds of barometers: mercury and **aneroid**. The first kind of barometer was invented by an Italian physicist, Evangelista Torricelli, in 1644. Barometers work on a simple principle, but they can be complex to operate and read. In brief, a mercury barometer consists of a glass tube of mercury with a bowl at the bottom. As the air pressure changes, the mercury in the tube is forced up or down, and a scale beside the tube shows the scientist the inches or millimeters of change.

Your student can make a simple barometer of her own, using items found around the house. You will need a wide-mouthed jar, a piece of balloon rubber (cut to fit across the mouth of the jar), a rubber band, a plastic drinking straw, a straight pin and a piece of lined paper.

Fasten the section of balloon over the mouth of the jar and secure it with the rubber band. Glue one end of the drinking straw to the stretched balloon (about halfway across the mouth, extending out). Glue the pin to the other end of the straw. Tape a piece of lined paper to the wall and set your barometer close enough to the paper that the pin touches one of the lines. Have your student mark carefully with a pen or highlighter where the pin is resting. What happens? Over the course of an hour or more, air pressure will continue to push the balloon down and the straw/pin will move, according to the changes.

Science: A Brief Introduction to Physics

Manya's father teaches physics, and she enjoys looking at his **physics apparatus**. Although physics is a complex realm of science to explain in full, your student can certainly understand the basic topics that physics includes and what physicists do every day.

Physics is a branch of science that involves matter and energy. Physicists want to understand what matter is, how it changes and why it changes. They also look at energy—how it's produced, channeled and used in nature and technology. If your student wants to know what physics is in a nutshell, just remember two words—matter and energy.

The word physics comes from a Greek word that means "natural things." Because matter and energy are what make up our universe, the study of physics affects all other realms of science. A physicist's observations can influence and assist astronomers, biologists, chemists, geologists and more. Remind your student of the lessons about Isaac Newton during the unit on *Neil Armstrong: Young Flyer*. Isaac Newton was a physicist; he studied the laws of motion and its affect on the earth.

Physics is generally divided into two main divisions: classical and modern. Classical physics deals with mechanics, heat, sound, electricity and light. Modern physics looks at atoms, nuclear science, particles, solids and fluids.

If your student enjoys math and science, doing experiments in physics will excite, educate and inspire her. An excellent resource to use throughout this unit is Janice VanCleave's *Physics for Every Kid*. Janice VanCleave, as in all her books, has compiled excellent, easy physics experiments for your student to try on her own.

Language Arts: Writing and Discussion Question

Mrs. Sklodowska works hard to help her family by making shoes, even though she is ill. What is something you do to help your friends or family, even though you don't care for it? How does it make you feel? Write about it.

Language Arts: Vocabulary

malachite   A green mineral.

physics   The science and study of matter and energy.

physics apparatus   The equipment used in the study of physics.

aneroid   Using no liquid (the opposite of a mercury barometer).

Fine Arts: Being a Good Storyteller

Adults and children alike love to hear an exciting tale told by a gifted storyteller. Manya particularly enjoys listening to her sister Zosia tell stories.

For some children, the skill of storytelling comes easily. For others who are shyer, it may be difficult. Everyone, however, can learn to improve their dramatic storytelling abilities and better entertain their audiences. This lesson will help your student develop confidence, dramatic ability and sharpen her storytelling skills.

Your student may enjoy listening to a family member, grandparent or older friend tell her stories about when she was young. She may like to listen to real-life stories, or fictional tales—tall tales, fairy tales, etc. What makes a good storyteller? What do you need to think about as you prepare to tell a good story? What makes a story exciting to listen to? What kind of stories does your student like to hear?

There are three basic components your student should consider: the storyteller, the story and the audience.

As the storyteller, your student should try to use her voice, hands, posture and facial expressions to help her convey the story's ideas. The way a story is told is called the delivery. Every person has a different delivery, but there are a few things to keep in mind, no matter what your style is like. Remind your student to avoid speaking too fast. If the audience misses parts of the story they won't be able to follow and will get frustrated. Don't speak too softly, either. Speak distinctly—enunciate. Sometimes people don't even realize they speak softly, too fast or slur their words. If your student wants to know if she suffers from any of these common speech problems, have her record herself telling a story and listen to it. This can be a helpful way of noticing things we sometimes don't realize we're doing.

The story your student chooses to tell should be appropriate to her audience and a story that she enjoys herself. It may come from a personal or family incident. It may be a folk or fairy tale. It may even be something she created. Whatever the story, your student should make sure her audience will enjoy it. Here are some exercises your student can do to help her understand this point:

1. Find a story that you enjoy and then analyze (think about) why you like it. What appeals to you?

2. Think of a particular audience group (e.g., your siblings, your grandparents, a group of your peers, the professional sports team in your area, etc.) and then find a story you think they would enjoy. Why would it appeal to them?

3. Think of a personal anecdote (experience) and use it as the basis for a story. Now change the story to appeal to two different audiences. What would make it more exciting for a child? More exciting for an elderly neighbor?

If your student wants to try her hand at storytelling, assign her the following plan. She should pick a time, place and audience for her presentation. This can be as simple as her family, after dinner, in the living room. Next, she should find a story. It can be a personal or fictional tale.

Encourage your student to prepare her presentation by writing the story out. She doesn't have to write it out word for word, but it should include the main sequence of events. Afterward, have her go back and circle important words or phrases—items that are critical to the plot, description or conclusion of the story. Anything she feels she should be sure to remember correctly. She may even want to indicate with arrows or lines where she will pause for dramatic effect. Or use specific facial expressions she thinks will help the story be understood.

Your student should then practice telling the story to herself. Remind your student that she learns the story better each time she tells it—even if it's only to herself. The story will become more natural and she will have more confidence. Great storytellers often say they have to "live with a story" to tell it correctly.

Finally, host the presentation. And remind your student to relax, breathe, smile and have fun! If your student enjoys this lesson, then she may wish to try doing several stories in one sitting or to embellish a story with props, music or moments of audience participation.

Life Skills: Doing What Needs to be Done

Mrs. Sklodowska is ill. She is forced to quit her job, and the family struggles to make ends meet. To help save money, Manya's mother works diligently to make the family's shoes. The work is hard, but she knows she is helping her husband and children.

Discuss with your student Mrs. Sklodowska's sacrificial actions. She has a sense of duty and does what needs to be done. Talk about how difficult it must have been for her to work that hard while she was ill. Learning to think of others and do what needs to be done is a part of becoming a mature, honorable person. Your student can begin working now on being a person others can count on—someone who steps in, even when the situation is difficult, and helps out.

Chapter 2—The Painful Years

Teacher Summary

The Sklodowski family continues to struggle financially, and they are forced to move several times from apartment to apartment. They even bring boarders to live with the family, for extra money. Poor Manya is forced to sleep in the dining room, because there is no extra bedroom for her. Then, more difficulty strikes. Mrs. Sklodowska passes away and so does Zosia, Manya's sister.

Manya continues to be brave and works hard in school. She attends a school where the teachers instruct the children in Polish history. Even though the Russian Empire rules Poland and forbids it, the Polish people know how important learning about their heritage is for their children. Studying in secret, Manya learns all she can about her people and their history.

What we will cover in this chapter:

Social Studies: History - Russian Rulers: The Czars and Empresses
Social Studies: Geography - The French Riviera*
Social Studies: History and Geography - Appreciating and Enjoying Polish Culture
Language Arts: Writing and Discussion Questions
Life Skills: Developing Better Concentration

Social Studies: History - Russian Rulers: The Czars and Empresses

Marie Curie grew up during a difficult period of Poland's history. Having been defeated during the late 1700s, Poland's land was divided among Prussia, Austria and Russia. The land to the east (where Marie lived) was taken over by Russia in 1772.

The Russian Empire was strong and cruel. They did not want anyone learning Polish history, or even speaking Polish. Inspectors worked diligently to make sure young Polish children were being taught Russian history and culture only. When Manya is questioned by one of the inspectors in school, she is asked who rules over her. She is required to answer, "His Majesty Alexander II, Czar of All the Russias." At other times, she is asked to recite the list of czars who ruled previously. Take this opportunity to share with your student a little bit about czars and empresses of Russia.

The name **czar** is the title used by the emperors of Russia. Your student may also see it spelled in its alternate form: tzar. The word comes from Caesar, which was the name used by all the emperors of Rome. Explain to your student that a czar is similar to a king, but with even more power. In Russia, each czar had complete ruling power. Some of the czars of Russia used this power in an evil way. They abused and frightened the Russian people into submitting to their empire.

The first czar of Russia was a man named Ivan the Terrible, in 1547. Ivan christened himself czar, and became a maniacal and cruel leader. He was considered insane by many, but he did build the power of the Russian Empire. The czars who followed Ivan were:

Theodore I	1584-1598
Boris Gudunov	1598-1605
Theodore II	1605
False Dimitri	1605-1606
Basil Shuisky	1606-1610

In 1613, the first czar from the Romanov family, Michael Romanov, was crowned. Share with your student that although the czars of Russia had gone through great upheaval and change in just a few years, the Romanovs were popular and strong. They continued to rule Russia for the next 300 years, until czarist rule was abandoned in 1917.

The most famous Romanov leaders were Peter the Great, Catherine the Great and Nicholas I. These Romanov czars (and empresses) ruled Russia with strong leadership. During the reign of Catherine the Great, Russia became a major world power. Throughout the late 1700s, many new schools were begun (mostly for the upper classes), the arts were encouraged (fashion, music and opera) and talk of freedom and social reform was everywhere. The problem, however, was that class structure was still enforced strictly. Very few people were considered middle class during this period. Most were either part of the upper class or poverty-stricken serfs.

Talk with your student about the oppression Manya and other Polish people must have felt under the rule of Russia. How frightening to be forced to submit under a foreign leader! Many historians describe the takeover and partitioning of Poland to Austria, Russia and Prussia as the time when "Poland vanished!" Literally, the country that had been there before, no longer existed. Instead, it became only regions controlled by new conquering leaders, like the czars.

The czars of Russia were powerful, unyielding leaders who controlled their empires with iron hands. Slowly, throughout the centuries, the people under their leadership (the Russians, Poles and other Slavic people) began to rebel against this type of government. Although the Romanovs were the most successful line of czars, at the end of Nicholas II's reign, his entire family was taken out of the palace and imprisoned.

Discuss with your student how this kind of leadership made the Communist Party's ideas so appealing to the people in Central Europe. Communists said everyone should have equal amounts of money, food and land. They told the people that it wasn't right for one small group to command such a large nation. Unfortunately, communism turned out to be just as terrible as the czars' rule—for different reasons.

Social Studies: Geography - The French Riviera*

Mr. Sklodowski desperately wants his wife to get well. During that period of history, people didn't understand the disease tuberculosis. They thought that breathing fresh air and resting would make the disease go away. Sometimes, in mild cases, such vacations did help, but very rarely. This lesson, however, focuses on the geographic region where Mrs. Sklodowska was sent: the Riviera.

Manya's mother is sent to a town in France called Nice. Nice is located on a strip of land called the Riviera. Your student can find the Riviera on a map. It is found on the southwestern border of France, directly on the Mediterranean Sea. Many towns make up this posh resort area, such as Nice (neece), Cannes, St. Tropez, and Antibes.

The Riviera is loved the world over for its wonderful sunshine, soft breezes and beautiful shorelines. The climate is mild, and fresh fruit is abundant—bananas, dates, pomegranates and prickly pears.

Your student might enjoy buying and eating a fresh pomegranate or some dates. Enjoy the wonderful flavors and think about being on the lovely Riviera! Even though it did not make her well, Mrs. Sklodowska no doubt enjoyed her stay.

Social Studies: History and Geography - Appreciating and Enjoying Polish Culture

The Sklodowski family, as well as the rest of Poland, desperately love their heritage and culture! It is painful for Manya to have to learn about her land in secret. Take some time to share with your student how wonderful, diverse and interesting the Polish culture is.

There are many aspects of Polish culture your student might enjoy exploring. Perhaps she would like to learn a few phrases in Polish. By reviewing the following words, you and your student can have fun speaking to each other in Manya's native tongue.

Yes	Tak (tawk)
No	Nie (neeye)
Please	Prosze (PRO-sheh)
Thank you	Dziekuje (DINK-wee)
How are you?	Jak sie masz (yock shee masz)
Good morning	Dzien dobry (gen DO-bri)
Goodbye	Do widzenia (doh veet-ZEN-ya)

Polish people are very hospitable. A Polish saying your student can remember is, "A guest in the house is God in the house."

Polish people, called Poles, are hardworking and put a heavy emphasis on education. Most Poles are Roman Catholic—nearly 93%! Religion is a big part of their lives. During Communist leadership, the Poles were forced to hide their faith. Today, they proudly worship in churches and in their homes. Like religion, traditions and customs mean a lot to Poles. They have a fierce love of all things Polish—just like the Sklodowskis. Perhaps this is because for so long, they were forced to abandon their culture.

The food in Poland includes many soups, fish dishes and bread. Poles also love beets and lots of potatoes! Most Polish meals are very simple, but filling. Here is a recipe for what many consider the Polish national dish, bigos, known in English as hunter's stew.

Bigos

2 lbs. sauerkraut

3 cups shredded cabbage

1 1/2 cups diced onion

1/2 lb. crumbled sausage or ground beef

1 tsp. oil

4 bay leaves

1 clove garlic

salt, pepper and a little tomato paste

Boil the sauerkraut and fresh cabbage separately until tender. Fry the meat in the oil with the onions. Place everything else including the meat, cabbage and sauerkraut into a casserole dish with the seasonings. Cover and bake in a 325° F. oven for 90 minutes, taking bay leaves out after 15 minutes.

This pungent, stew-like dish may or may not be your student's favorite, but it will give her a taste of what Manya may have enjoyed on a cold winter night.

As you continue exploring Poland, show your student the Polish flag, with its simple half-white, half-red design. Poland is a unique and wonderful country. No wonder Manya loved it so!

Language Arts: Writing and Discussion Questions

1. Why do you think Manya was frightened of Mr. Hornberg's questions if she was sure she knew the answers? Write about it.

2. When Marie was a young student in Poland, she had to study Polish secretly. The Russians, who ruled Poland at the time, had made it illegal for schools to teach Polish history. Why do you think the Russians did this? Why did Marie and other Poles disobey this law?

Life Skills: Developing Better Concentration

Manya certainly can concentrate on her books, can't she? Her brothers and sisters can't even distract her with a tower of chairs built around her head.

Although Manya's ability to concentrate may be a little extreme, learning how to apply yourself to reading or doing lessons is an important part of school and life. Talk with your student about concentration. Does she think she does well in this area? What easily distracts her? How long can she sit still or read before her mind wanders? What things does she think would help her concentrate better?

Everyone struggles to maintain focus sometimes, but it is possible to develop better concentration. Try reading in a quiet room, away from distractions. Learn to take notes while you read a report or schoolbook. This can help you stay focused and review what you've read.

Some children, like Manya, have no problem concentrating for long periods of time. For others, however, it is a struggle. Encourage your student to talk about her attention span and what she thinks hurts her ability to concentrate. With practice and the right environment, most people can learn to concentrate better, for longer periods of time.

Chapter 3—Growing Up

Teacher Summary

Manya, along with her siblings, graduates from high school with honors—the gold medal. Tired from all the hard work, Manya takes a year off and spends it with relatives in the country. She has a wonderful time and returns home, ready to work hard and help her family.

She takes a position as a governess and brings in enough rubles every month to help her father, and help send her sister Bronya to medical school in Paris.

Although Manya desperately wants to attend school in Paris as well, she knows that Bronya is older and should go first. It is a sacrificial decision, but one Manya does not regret.

What we will cover in this chapter:

Social Studies: Geography - The Alps and Carpathian Mountains*
Science: Louis Pasteur
Science: Lakes
Language Arts: Writing and Discussion Question
Language Arts: Vocabulary
Fine Arts: Kulig Streamers and Sleigh Bells
Life Skills: Self-Sacrifice
Life Skills: The Power of Education

Social Studies: Geography - The Alps and Carpathian Mountains*

The Alps are considered to be one of the most spectacular geographical regions in the world. The Carpathian Mountains, which Manya particularly loves, are a part of the mountain range that includes the Alps. Your student will enjoy learning about these beautiful mountain ranges.

The Alps are the largest mountain system in Europe. They host snow-capped, majestic peaks and sheltered valleys. Show your student on a good world map (or map of Europe) where the Alps are located. You may also want to view a topographical map, which clearly shows the mountains and lakes in Europe.

The Alps extend across most of south-central Europe in a sweeping arc. They begin near the Mediterranean Sea and form the border between France and Italy. Show your student how the Alps continue northeastward through Italy, Switzerland, Austria and more. The mountain range forms a stunning and strong barrier between central and southern regions of Europe. Throughout history people have rarely tried to cross the Alps, but many areas are used for skiing, recreation and sports. Today, the Alps are easily crossed at certain points by modern rail and highway systems. Many people travel to the Alps to just look and enjoy the scenery.

In general, the Alps have a climate which is cool and wet. Explain to your student that this is called a highland climate. Occasionally, however, strong warm winds blow through the Alps. These winds are called foehns, and cause dangerous avalanches.

Beautiful animals and plants live in the Alps. Plants like fir trees, pine trees, mountain flowers, moss and lichens grow at various elevations. Animals such as antelope, goats, golden eagles and more call this mountain range their home.

The biggest and most famous peaks in the Alps include Mont Blanc, Matterhorn, Monte Rosa and Grossglockner.

Matterhorn, in Switzerland

The wonderful Carpathian Mountains, which Manya so enjoyed, lie on the southern rim of Poland. They are generally lower than most of the Alps. The land in the valleys of the Carpathian Mountains is extremely fertile, and successful farms dot many of the valleys.

A lot of timber is also gathered in the Carpathian Mountains—oak, beech, fir and more fill the forests. Wolves, lynx and bears make their homes in these forests as well.

For a fine arts enrichment project, your student can work on making a relief map of the Alps, a portion of the Alps, the Carpathian Mountains, or even one specific peak.

By using a strong piece of cardboard or wood, your student should create a base large enough to hold her entire model. Now, line the board or wood with paper and draw an outline of the region, base of the peak, etc. Make a simple flour dough by mixing equal parts of flour and salt and moisten with water to playdough consistency. Let your student knead the dough until it's soft, and pat it all over the board, pushing it to the outer lines of her drawing. Continue making the simple dough in small batches until your student has enough to create the peaks or mountain ranges. Your student can pinch, mash and pull the dough up into hills, mountains, valleys, and more. Use toothpicks with paper flags to mark famous mountain summits and other important features. Have these ready and put in before the model dries.

Science: Louis Pasteur

Manya loves science and learning about how things work. At the same time she was learning at the Floating University, many other scientists were making interesting discoveries. Our story mentions Louis Pasteur and his development of a rabies vaccine.

Your student may have covered the lesson on rabies found in our unit on *The Saturdays*, FIAR Vol. 6. Louis Pasteur, the French scientist, developed the first vaccine for rabies, as well as significant research on milk pasteurization (covered in *The Boxcar Children*, FIAR Vol. 5).

There are many wonderful junior biographies on Louis Pasteur and his life. If your student has not studied this important person in science, perhaps now would be a good time to find a book or two at the library.

To get you started, share with your student that Louis Pasteur was born on December 27, 1822, in Dole, France. He became interested in treating rabies when he saw a rabid dog attack some people in his village when he was only eight years old.

After many years of study and research, he developed a drug to prevent rabies in 1884. He worked diligently to help people with the disease, particularly children.

If your student is interested in learning more about Louis Pasteur, here are some more related topics she may wish to explore: microbes, vaccinations, France, disinfectants, pasteurization.

Science: Lakes

Manya enjoys her time in the country. She loves the mountains and a small lake named "The Eye of the Sea," high up in the mountain peaks.

Lakes are large bodies of water surrounded by land. There are lakes in every part of the world. Lakes differ from the seas/oceans because they are entirely encompassed by land. There are many lakes in the world that are so large that people mistakenly call them seas. The Dead Sea, for example, and the Caspian Sea.

The largest and most numerous lakes occur in areas that were once covered by glaciers. During the time glaciers moved and fell, large pieces of mountain were gouged out and then filled with water. Mountain lakes, such as the one Manya enjoyed exploring, tend to be clearer and colder than other lakes.

Remind your student that lakes form in other ways as well. For example, in areas where limestone forms bedrock beneath the soil's surface, the stone can slowly dissolve and form cracks. Those cracks occasionally fall in and form a hole called a sinkhole. Those sinkholes fill with water and much later become lakes. Sinkholes can also form ponds. Share with your student the difference between a lake and a pond. Both are bodies of water surrounded by land. A pond, however, is much smaller and shallow enough that sunlight reaches the bottom. The fish, wildlife and water plants differ between lake and pond because of this depth difference.

Some mountain lakes are fed by rivers and streams. Others, however, are fed by underground streams and springs.

Lakes can be a wonderful source of beauty and practical benefits for the people who live near them. They can be used for recreation (fishing, boating, skiing, etc.), as a water supply, hydroelectric power, and even irrigation.

Language Arts: Writing and Discussion Question

Would you be excited or frightened to be a part of the Floating University? Why?

Language Arts: Vocabulary

lake   A large body of water surrounded by land.

kulig   A festive party and sleigh ride celebrated in Poland.

Fine Arts: Kulig Streamers and Sleigh Bells

Manya enjoys an interesting Polish tradition during her year in the country—a **kulig**. Kuligs are festive, carnival-like dancing celebrations in Poland. They also include wonderful sleigh rides. The sleighs are fixed up so many people can ride on them at a time, similar to hayrides in America. The sleighs are decorated with beautiful streamers and sleigh bells. The sleigh bells are more than decoration; they are are a personal touch by each family. Two or more bells are selected by each family to create their own "sound." The horses and animals learn to recognize their owner's bells.

In addition to the splendid sleighs and bells, people at kuligs dress up and wear ribbon-steamers on their clothes and head wreaths. Manya wears a wheat "crown" on her head with colored ribbons hanging down.

If your student enjoys creating costumes or designing accessories, she may enjoy making her own "kulig" crown. You may also want to have fun finding some bells and making sleigh bells for your family. What sound is going to be your signal?

Life Skills: Self-Sacrifice

Our story brings up many relational issues, including examples of bravery and self-sacrifice. Talk with your student about Manya's unselfish decision to send her sister Bronya to Paris first. How difficult that must have been to put off her own education to help her sister!

When was a time recently when your student acted unselfishly? Was it difficult or easy? Why? Sometimes we want things so badly it is easier to ignore what is the right or noble thing to do. At the time, it may be more painful to let someone else go before us. In the end, however, our characters will be stronger and more mature when we have practiced going last.

Life Skills: The Power of Education

Manya and her peers work hard to learn as much as they can, in spite of their oppressive government. Ask your student why she thinks they concentrate so much on education.

Relate the Polish people's situation to that of black people during slave times in America. Slaves often educated themselves in secret, learning how to read and do mathematics, without their masters knowing. Why do controlling leaders like the Russians and the slave owners suppress education?

Education is a powerful thing. Learning to read and speak correctly is a key to learning about the world around you. The slave owners understood that if their slaves could read, they could look at the newspapers and books of the era, and communicate with each other through writing to fight back against their situation. If a group of people is uneducated, they are more easily controlled. That is an important aspect of all historical studies. The Poles, along with many other oppressed and controlled groups of people, knew that the only way they were ever going to escape Russian control and become their own country again would be through education and enrichment.

Discuss with your student how blessed and fortunate she is to live during a time and in a place where she can study and learn as much as she wants. Helping your mind grow by learning, reading and watching, is as important to a successful life as helping your body grow by eating the right foods and getting exercise.

Chapter 4—The Sacrifice

Teacher Summary

Manya works hard to earn money by teaching children as a governess. In those days in Poland, being a governess wasn't a highly respected position. Manya works for a few different families before finding people she likes and who pay her enough money to save a bit for herself and help support Bronya in France.

Manya works hard for nearly three years and continues to educate herself. She also finds she loves science and mathematics. She tries to read chemistry and physics books, but it is frustrating when she has nowhere to conduct experiments. Manya knows, however, that eventually it will be her turn to attend a university. For now, she must work hard and prepare.

What we will cover in this chapter:

Science: Metric System
Science: Sugar from Beets?

Science: Economics - Poland's Monetary System
Language Arts: Writing and Discussion Question
Language Arts: Vocabulary*
Life Skills: Generosity
Life Skills: Realizing Your Dreams

Science: Metric System

Manya works nearly 100 kilometers from her home. Our author reminds us that 100 kilometers is roughly 62 miles. This explanation provides an excellent jumping off point for a discussion surrounding the metric system. How is it different from the English system?

The two main measuring systems used in the world today are called English and metric. In the United States, we use the English system of measurement. The English measuring system was slowly developed and standardized over 100 years. By the 19th century, however, the standards were mostly set. Britain worked hard to standardize measurements for everything—distance, area, weight, liquids and more. Units such as the gallon, quart, pint, and ounce became understood and implemented. People could talk with one another and when they mentioned an inch, foot or yard they both knew what was being discussed.

Having a well established measuring system helped everyone deal fairly and clearly with one another. The English system, however, can be awkward to use sometimes. For example, an inch is 1/12 of a foot, a foot is 1/3 of a yard, a pint is 1/8 of a gallon, and so forth. The units used in the English system don't seem to be related.

The United States adopted the English system, but in other regions of the world scientists worked at developing another way of measuring things. The metric system is the easiest method of measurement found anywhere on Earth to date. It was created in the 1790s by a group of French scientists, and has the official name of Systeme International d'Unites (International System of Units).

The metric system is so easy to use for two reasons: 1) it operates on the decimal number system, where each unit increases by places of 10; and 2) a person only needs to know a few units to understand all measurements.

Sit with your student and have her list, or tell you, all the units of measurement she can think of from the English system—for example, cup, tablespoon, teaspoon, pint, quart, gallon, inch, foot, yard, acre, mile, square mile, ton, cord, carat, bushel, peck and more. There are so many names and units used in the English system!

The metric system operates on only seven base (basic) units of measurement. They are:

meter	the base unit of length
kilogram	the base unit of mass
second	the base unit for time
kelvin	the base unit for temperature
ampere	the base unit for electricty
mole	the base unit for chemical reactions
candela	the base unit for light

The metric system uses Greek prefixes to add onto these units and denote larger numbers. For example, hecto- means 100 times and kilo- means 1,000 times. Latin prefixes are added to denote smaller numbers: centi- means 1/100, and milli- means 1/1,000.

Encourage your student to begin becoming familiar with metric units by helping her create her own meter stick. Using a 12" ruler that also has millimeters/centimeters on it and a long strip of cardboard, help your student mark on the cardboard 10 decimeters (ten 10-centimeter sections). Now she has a meter stick. Send her off and have her measure things around her room or home in meters—the height of walls, length of the family car, size of her bed, size of the family room in square meters, how tall she is in meters, and so forth.

If she likes this exploration, she may want to try it with other metric units—liters, for example. Using a measuring cup with metric equivalents, your student can figure out how many liters in a glass of milk she drinks in the morning, in a soda can, etc. Also, draw your student's attention to your car's speedometer. All U.S. automobiles show their speed in both miles and kilometers per hour.

Using the metric system can be fun and educational for your student. One day, the United States may completely convert to metric. For most of the world, our units of measurement (the English system) are entirely obsolete. We are the last major country in the world to not use the metric system. Why do you think that is?

Science: Sugar from Beets?

Manya borrows books from a factory near her place of employment. The factory is a **sugar beet** factory—converting sugar beets to sugar. Your student is probably familiar with sugar cane sugar, but does she know that about 35% of all the world's sugar comes from sugar beets?

Sugar beets, grown in the United States mainly in California, Montana, Idaho and Michigan, contain natural sugar in their large, thick roots. Sugar beets grow in temperate, even cool, climates. Sugar cane, on the other hand, grows best in tropical and semitropical climates.

Sugar beets have been grown as food as far back as ancient Babylonia and Egypt. In 1744, Andreas Sigismund, a German chemist, figured out that the sugar extracted from sugar beets was the same kind of sugar that came from sugar cane. He was excited by this discovery, because it meant that sugar could be made in countries other than tropical, warm regions. Countries like Germany, Russia, Poland and others could use his discovery for both industry and trade, but also for sugar for themselves. As soon as they could be built, sugar factories sprang up all over Europe and Russia. Beet sugar wasn't produced in the USA until the 1830s.

During Manya's day, sugar beet factories employed many people and created a successful living for them. Even today, Poland, Ukraine and other Slavic nations still rely on their sugar beet farms and factories for critical income.

Go to the grocery store (perhaps even a health food store) and look at packages of sugar with your student. Find some sugar beet sugar and taste it in comparison with cane sugar. Can she tell the difference?

Science: Economics - Poland's Monetary System

During the time of our story (the late 1800s), the region of Poland Manya lives in was still under Russian control. That region, therefore, operated under Russian economy and with Russian money: rubles.

Share with your student that today, Poland no longer uses rubles as their money. Instead, they use a unit of money called a **zloty**, which dates back to the 14th century. With your student, take a look at the zloty online and see how much it is currently worth in American dollars.

Language Arts: Writing and Discussion Question

Manya believes no one should ever "let one's self be beaten down by persons or events." What are the parts of Manya's life you've learned about where you think she might have felt beaten down?

Language Arts: Vocabulary*

zloty   Main unit of Polish currency.

sugar beet   Second largest source of sugar, second only to cane.

Life Skills: Generosity

This chapter talks a great deal about Manya's generosity toward others, particularly her sister Bronya. Start a dialogue with your student about different aspects of generosity. Sometimes people think of generosity only in terms of material things, i.e., possessions, money, etc.

Being generous, however, can mean much more than that. Truly generous people are lavish with non-material things as well—their time, trust, love, forgiveness, etc. Being quick to forgive and forget when someone hurts your feelings, for example, is one way of being generous.

This lesson can be enriched by an art or language arts exploration. Your student can draw a picture of what generosity means to her, or perhaps write a poem.

Life Skills: Realizing Your Dreams

What is a dream your student holds? A career dream perhaps, like being an astronaut or ballerina, for example. Manya's dream is to become an educated scientist. She understands that to achieve her dream, she must start small, where she is now. Since attending the university in Paris isn't going to happen yet, Manya works hard to learn as much as she can on her own.

Realizing your dreams can be a long process, but you can always begin reaching your dreams in small ways. For example, if a child wants to be a zoologist, she can do many things even when she is young to work toward that goal. Taking good care of her pets, talking with the veterinarian when she takes them in for checks, visiting and studying the animals in an area zoo, reading books about famous zoologists, volunteering at a local animal shelter, etc.

Sometimes children get frustrated or think their dreams will never arrive. Talk with your student about things she can start doing today to make her dreams come to pass. Manya is an excellent example of determination and focus, even in the face of denying circumstances. If you work toward a dream by taking small steps, you'll arrive there sooner than you think!

Chapter 5—The Turning Point

Teacher Summary

Finally, Manya has finished her work as a governess! She continues to work, however, in order to save more money and help her father and little sister, Hela. Manya studies chemistry and works on experiments at the Floating University. There, many Polish students learn science and mathematics in secret—away from the watchful Russian government.

Soon, in 1891, Manya decides to go to Paris and attend the Sorbonne. She has enough money, and her sister has invited Manya to live with her. Manya finds it difficult to leave her father, but he knows going to Paris is the best thing for his beloved daughter.

What we will cover in this chapter:

Social Studies: Geography - Baltic Sea*
Science: Chemistry - Experiments
Language Arts: Locating Information Without the Internet
Language Arts: Writing and Discussion Question

Social Studies: Geography - Baltic Sea*

For awhile, Manya works for a family who is vacationing on the Baltic Sea. Have your student find and look at the Baltic Sea on a world map. Point out to your student that the Baltic Sea is a large body of water that separates the north shore of Europe from the countries that make up the Scandinavian Peninsula (Norway, Sweden and Finland).

The Baltic Sea (as well as its eastern neighbors—North Sea, Norwegian Sea) is an arm of a major body of water. Can your student find it and name it? The Atlantic Ocean. The Baltic Sea is fed by the Atlantic Ocean, and covers more than

160,000 square miles (414,000 square kilometers). It is nearly 1,000 miles long and almost 400 miles wide.

Important aspects of the Baltic Sea and its impact on Poland and nearby countries (Russia, Estonia, Latvia, Lithuania, etc.) are the harbors that lie on its banks. Cities such as Copenhagen, Denmark; Gdansk, Poland; and Kiel, Germany have huge, prosperous harbors that allow boats and trading vessels to sail through the Baltic Sea and conduct commerce. Another important source of connection and travel is the small strip of water at the southernmost tip of Sweden. It is called the Gota Canal.

Science: Chemistry - Experiments

Manya is a smart woman. She knows she must work hard even though she isn't attending the university in Paris yet, learning all she can about chemistry, physics and math. But Manya loves science! Particularly doing experiments where she can see chemical reactions and changes. Your student can be inspired and educated by conducting some simple chemistry experiments herself.

Here are a few experiments your student can explore and try just like Manya.

Pulling Colors Out

This experiment helps your student observe the separation of colors in ink. Remind your student of what she learned about Isaac Newton's studies on the color spectrum (*Neil Armstrong* unit earlier in this volume).

You will need:

> green water-soluble pen
> black water-soluble pen
> coffee filter

> plate or saucer
> paper clip

Fold the coffee filter in fourths, so you have a four-layered, pie-shaped piece of paper. Flip the layers open a bit so the filter can stand up in the saucer (secure with a paper clip, if necessary). Now draw a nice bold stripe of black ink about 1" from the bottom of the filter on one side. Next, draw a bold stripe of green ink near (but not touching) the black stripe. The green ink should also stop about 1" from the bottom of the filter. Have your student fill the saucer with some water. Now wait one hour and see what happens.

As the water is drawn through the paper, it begins to separate the ink colors. Black ink reveals blues, yellows and purples. Green ink reveals blue and yellows. Ask your student why he thinks certain colors bleed/seep higher on the filter than others. Those colors have lighter chemicals in them. The heavier the chemical, the less it climbs.

Surface Tension Exploded

This experiment will show your student how the surface of a liquid reacts when it touches the air. It has a special property called "surface tension." It is kind of like a skin for the liquid. To illustrate for your student how this "skin" works, you will need:

> a clean plate
> ground pepper
> bar of soap or dish soap

Fill the plate with water. Sprinkle pepper across the surface, as evenly as possible. Notice how the pepper floats on top of the water. Each grain is being held up by the surface tension. Now, have your student gently touch the water's surface with the bar of soap, or add a drop of dish soap. At once, the pepper grains float away from the soap and cling to the edges of the plate. Why?

Soap changes the surface tension of water. As it breaks the surface tension in the center of the plate, the pepper is pulled to the edges by the "skin" that has broken apart and moved toward the sides.

Super Dilution

This experiment will show your student how dilution affects a solution using color.

You will need:

> one-gallon glass jar
> one-cup measure
> red food coloring

Have your student pour 1/2 cup of water into the jar. Now, he can place one drop of red food coloring. Now, start adding more water, one cup at a time.

Encourage your student to watch the color of the water carefully and record each cup of water he adds. Continue adding water until the color disappears (usually around eight cups of water).

Why does the color disappear? Your student can see red in the water at first, because the molecules of red dye are close enough together. As the water is added, the color molecules are spread far apart among the clean water molecules. Eventually, they are so far apart you cannot see the red anymore. However, the red molecules are still present—only invisible to the human eye.

Just like Manya, your student can "develop a taste for experimental research" by conducting simple experiments at home.

Language Arts: Locating Information Without the Internet

Manya no longer has a teacher to help her learn what she needs to know, so she must work hard to research and teach herself. Learning how to locate information is an important skill that helps your student to self-educate, research reports and papers, and explore topics that interest her. This lesson will help you share with your student the sources that are available to her.

In the 21st century, most people will find a great deal of the information they are looking for online. Your student probably already knows how to do an internet search for information or images. Use this lesson to teach or review online skills, but also share with your student that there are other sources of information she can use when doing research. A few of these are:

- books
- periodicals
- newspapers (including newspaper archives from years past)
- special reference books (i.e., encyclopedia, almanac, quotation books, etc.)

Some of the sources are available to your student at home, but most she will find and explore at her local library. If your library has a reference room or reference section, explore the books there with your student. Open a few and see what kinds of information they hold.

Challenge your student to come up with a subject she would like to learn more about, and then do research on that topic *without* using the internet. She can use available reference books at home first, and then go to the library for further study. Encourage your student to take simple notes as she does her research, taking care to also record where she read the fact.

Does your local library use the Dewey Decimal System? If so, review that with your student and remind her of the 10 main categories of books by call number:

000.........................Generalities
100.........................Philosophy
200.........................Religion
300.........................Social Science
400.........................Language
500.........................Pure Science
600.........................Technology
700.........................The Arts
800.........................Literature and Rhetoric
900.........................General Geography/History

Learning about different informational resources (besides the internet), knowing her way around the library, and asking librarians for assistance are all useful experiences and skills for your student to develop. Getting her excited and active in the research process will increase the quality of her schoolwork now and will set her up for success in college, work and life.

Language Arts: Writing and Discussion Question

Every child is sad when he or she must leave a parent for an extended period of time. Why do you think Manya found it particularly difficult to leave her father?

Chapter 6—A French Education

Teacher Summary

When Manya arrives in France to attend the Sorbonne, she begins by changing her name to its French version—Marie. At first, Marie doesn't understand nearly anything her fellow students/professors are saying. She doesn't speak French, and they don't speak Polish! She learns French quickly, however, and is soon fully absorbed in her studies.

Unfortunately, she becomes *too* absorbed and forgets how important taking care of her health is to her studies. She forgets to eat and doesn't sleep very much. Soon she is weak and sick, but her sister and brother-in-law take her home for a few days and help her rest and eat.

In 1893 Marie reaches her first goal, getting her Masters in Physics. She continues her studies, wanting to receive her second Masters in Mathematics, and is fortunate to receive a large scholarship from Poland—600 rubles! This allows Marie to study full time, and she seizes this opportunity with gusto.

Our author tells us that years later, Marie repaid the foundation the entire sum of 600 rubles. She wanted another Polish student to have the opportunity she did. Once again Marie exhibits her noble spirit.

What we will cover in this chapter:

Science: Nutrition and the Brain*
Language Arts: Learning Foreign Languages
Language Arts: Writing and Discussion Question
Language Arts: Vocabulary
Life Skills: Thinking of Others

Science: Nutrition and the Brain*

Manya, because she doesn't have much money and is so focused on her academics, forgets the importance of health and nutrition. Our brains don't function well without proper food and rest. Research has proven that children who receive balanced breakfasts in the morning do better in classes across the board. They aren't distracted by growling tummies, and their brains and bodies have energy to work with. Point out to your student how foolishly Manya behaves in this chapter and then share with her reasons nutrition and your brain are connected.

In chapter 7 of *Neil Armstrong*, earlier in this volume, your student may have studied digestion and how our stomach and intestines break down foods we eat. When your organs break the foods down, your body obtains certain chemical substances it needs for good health. These substances are often referred to as "nutrients." Talk about the three functions of nutrients in the body:

1. They help the body repair, build and maintain tissues.
2. They help the body regulate digestion, brain activity, sensory skills, and more.
3. They provide us with energy. Energy is required for *all* functions in the body.

To live well and in order to learn in school, our bodies need the right nutrients. Breakfast, in particular, is an important meal. While we've been asleep all night, our bodies have been resting and repairing. After those several hours, however, the body is ready for a good dose of nutrients to break down and use throughout the day. People who skip breakfast tend to be more sluggish, less creative and more ill prepared to face the challenges that come to them.

Encourage your student to view Manya's behavior in this chapter as a lesson in what *not* to do, in terms of nutrition and proper rest.

Language Arts: Learning Foreign Languages

Manya faces a big obstacle when she arrives in France. She doesn't speak French! She quickly sets to learning this new language and soon accomplishes the feat. In fact, our author tells us Marie learns French so well her friends can barely detect her Polish accent.

Learning a foreign language is a great deal of work, but it can be very rewarding and a lot of fun. Perhaps your student has already explored learning a new language.

There are many important reasons for learning a foreign language, but here are a few for your student to consider:

1. When you speak another language, it increases your ability to communicate. You can speak with so many more people in the world.
2. Learning another language opens your eyes to another culture.
3. Understanding a foreign language can help you understand your own language better.

Mastering any language requires you to do four separate things: speak, understand, read and write.

The language Manya must learn, French, is a part of a group of languages called Romance languages. These languages all developed from Latin and are similar— French, Italian, Romanian and Spanish. If you learn one of these languages fluently, learning another of the Romance languages is much easier.

If your student is interested in learning some foreign phrases (or in learning a foreign language), foster this interest by obtaining books, listening to foreign words and languages online, or trying one of many free foreign language learning websites. Learning a foreign language will enrich and deepen your student's life and her perception of the world around her!

Language Arts: Writing and Discussion Questions

Marie is frugal with her money, but she is also generous. Where do you think she learned these values?

Language Arts: Vocabulary
(This word is found in chapter 6)

gaiety   The state or quality of being joyous.

Life Skills: Thinking of Others

Although Marie doesn't exhibit the best choices in the area of nutrition and personal care, she does exhibit excellent choices in how she treats others. In this particular chapter we see another example of Marie's unselfish behavior—her decision to think of others and their needs.

Talk to your student about Marie's choice to repay the scholarship funds she received from Poland. Certainly the foundation didn't demand or even expect to be repaid. A scholarships is, by definition, gift money. Marie, however, knows what a gift the money was and longs to share the same fortunate gift with another Polish student.

Imagine how surprised the foundation must have been to receive the 600 rubles back from Marie years later, and be told to use it to help fund another student's education. Imagine how blessed that student felt who was able to attend a university because of Marie's generosity—perhaps even the Sorbonne!

Thinking of others and their needs helps us become stronger people with deep characters.

Chapter 7—Changes

Teacher Summary

Marie begins doing scientific research for pay. She studies magnets and works in a space located at the School of Physics and Chemistry. There she meets her future husband, Pierre Curie.

Pierre is fascinated by Marie and enjoys her company, knowledge of science and her dedication. Marie has strong feelings for Pierre, but wants to return to Poland as soon as she can in order to teach. That summer she receives her second Masters Degree (mathematics) and prepares to go home. Pierre eventually convinces her that she can help Poland through her scientific research from Paris, and the two marry.

What we will cover in this chapter:

Science: Magnets
Science: Crystals*
Language Arts: Writing and Discussion Questions
Language Arts: Vocabulary
Life Skills: Egotism - Learning to Value
Other Opinions

Science: Magnets

Marie works diligently on her scientific experiments. She is studying steel and its magnetic properties. Your student can work on experiments using magnets just like Marie.

Magnets are pieces of metal, ore or stone that have the power to attract or repel (push away) certain other materials. Magnets occur naturally in the earth. Magnets are made into a variety of shapes like bar, horseshoe, button, etc. Some magnets have a weaker strength and size than others. Refrigerator magnets, for example, are fairly small and generally only hold a sheet or two of paper. Other magnets are huge and so strong they can be used to lift scrap iron and entire cars!

Marie's experiments dealt with steel and magnets. There are other materials magnets attract besides steel, such as iron, nickel and cobalt. If your student has a magnet, she can test for different metals. Holding it near a frying pan, for example, can tell your

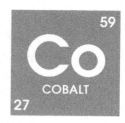

student what material the pan is made from. If the magnet sticks, you know the pan is made from some type of iron, steel, nickel or cobalt. If it doesn't, the pan must be made from some other metal, such as copper or aluminum.

Your student can test many things with a magnet. Most magnets will stick to the hood of a car (made of steel). It shouldn't stick to a soda pop can (aluminum). It should stick to a tuna can (steel), etc.

Your student can make her own permanent magnet fairly easily. Remind your student that each magnet and each magnetic material (things which are attracted to magnets) can be thought of as being made of many tiny magnets. The difference between a magnet and magnetic material, is that in a magnet all the tiny magnets are facing in the same direction. In magnetic material, the tiny magnets are facing different directions.

To make a permanent magnet, your student will need to take a magnetic material and line all the tiny magnets in the same direction. She will need:

1 steel knitting needle (or a long steel nail)
paper clips
a strong bar magnet

First, your student can test her needle (or nail) to see if it is magnetic. Does it pick up a paper clip? Now, put the needle on a table and stroke it 30 times with the magnet. Stroke with the same end of the magnet each time, and stroke in the same direction. Now test the paper clip again. Does it pick it up? How many paper clips will dangle from the needle? Stroke the needle 30 more times with the magnet. Test it again. Continue this exercise until your student has stroked the needle 120 times. How many paper clips will it hold?

As your student rubs the magnet across the needle, she is pulling and lining up all the tiny magnets in the needle and forcing them to go in the same direction!

Your student can also conduct experiments to see if magnets work through various substances. For example, set a paper clip on a table. Now slowly move a magnet closer to the paper clip. When the magnet comes close enough, the paper clip should jump off the table and attach itself. Magnets work through air!

Put the paper clip in a bowl of water. Have your student hold the magnet in the water and move it closer to the paper clip. Soon, the paper clip will attach itself. Magnets work through water!

Continue this experiment. Your student can test a magnet's power through fabric, paper, glass and more. Encourage your student to set her own hypotheses and record her results. If your student continues these experiments she might discover that the ends of a magnet are stronger than the sides of a magnet. She can see a magnet's magnetic field quite clearly by doing the following experiment.

Rub a file against an iron nail. Catch the iron filings on a sheet of paper. Lay a bar magnet on the table and then lay the paper sheet covered in filings over the magnet. Tap the sheet gently. The filings should arrange themselves in a pattern. The pattern shows the "lines of force" around the magnet. The lines of force will demonstrate to your student that the strongest pull is at the end of the magnet. The ends of a magnet are called the poles. One end is the north pole, and one end is the south pole.

If your student is interested in doing more experiments, just like Marie, find some books on magnets and magnet experiments, or look online for articles or videos.

Science: Crystals*

While Marie tested magnets, her husband Pierre worked on studying the structure of **crystals**. Crystals are a fascinating piece of nature. Explain to your student that a crystal is a solid form of material (substance). Unlike other solid forms, however, a crystal's molecules are arranged in an orderly pattern that is repeated again and again throughout the entire crystal. It is almost like little buildings. Crystals come in seven different types (or structures), the most simple of which is the cube. Table salt is made up of cube-shaped crystals.

Pour some table salt onto a dark background (fabric or plate) and have your student look at it through a magnifying glass or microscope. What does she see? Dozens of small cube crystals. Now do the same observation experiment with sugar. Are the crystals different? (Yes, and you can easily tell the difference between salt and sugar crystals with a magnifying glass or microscope.)

Many things are made up of crystal structures. Snowflakes, for example, are crystals that form from a gaseous substance—water vapor. Each of the snowflake crystals is six-sided and no two are alike! Crystals are found in other areas of nature as well. Geodes, for example, appear to be ugly brown rocks. Inside, however, you see many beautiful black, purple, green and clear crystals. Crystals are also the form most gems are found in, such as diamonds, amethysts, tourmaline, emeralds, and more. With your student, look online or in library books at the wide variety and beauty of the many different types of crystals.

Your student can make her own crystals at home using simple ingredients! Here are two experiments to try today:

Crystal Rope

2 Tbs. rock salt (the type used for making ice cream)
1 cup hot water
spoon for stirring
piece of string or yarn
pencil

Add the rock salt to the cup of hot tap water. Stir until dissolved. Tie the string around the pencil and place the pencil across the top of the cup, so the string is dangling into the salt water (3"-4"). Place the cup in a sunny, warm place.

Check the experiment often, but don't expect results in one day. Over the course of 2-5 days your student will begin to see the salt crystals attaching and building on the yarn.

Floating "Iceberg" Crystals

1 cup water
2 cups sugar
1/2 tsp. unflavored gelatin
a small pan
a pint jar
a spoon for stirring
an old towel

Pour the water into the pan. Stir in gelatin and heat on the stove until nearly boiling. When the gelatin has completely dissolved, remove the pan from the stove and allow it to cool for about five minutes. Then stir in the sugar, 1/4 cup at a time. Continue stirring the sugar until no more will dissolve. Let cool a few minutes more.

Rinse the jar with hot water, and pour the supersaturated solution (the gelatin/sugar/water mixture) into the jar. Wrap the towel around the jar to help slow down the cooling process. Place the towel-wrapped jar in a place out of the way, and do not disturb it for three days. Finally, remove the towel. What do you see? The sugar crystals will appear as though they are "floating" through the solution. Actually, they are suspended in the gelatin. If you can, continue to let the crystals grow for several weeks. As you wait, you will see the crystals form larger and larger specimens.

Language Arts: Writing and Discussion Questions

1. Marie decides to stay in Paris and marry Pierre. Do you think Marie is really abandoning her dream to help Poland? Do you think she'll find a different way? Write about it.

2. Pierre Curie believed that working for political change was not as important as working to make new scientific discoveries. He said to Marie that science could only benefit mankind. Do you agree or disagree with Pierre Curie? Why?

3. Why did Marie Curie hesitate before agreeing to marry Pierre Curie? What finally convinced her?

Language Arts: Vocabulary

crystal   A regularly shaped solid substance with angles and flat surfaces into which many substances solidify.

magnet   A piece of iron, steel or stone which attracts iron, steel, nickel or cobalt.

Life Skills: Egotism - Learning to Value Other Opinions

Pierre and Marie want different things at first, don't they? Pierre believes helping the world means working in science. Marie believes helping the world means teaching children. Ask your student who she thinks is right?

Often when people are passionate about what they do, they begin to believe that only their way is right. We call people who act as though they are the "best" egotistical. Egoists are not open to new ideas. But learning to see value in others' opinions enriches your life and helps you understand the world around you.

Both Marie and Pierre have pure motives. Both their ideas are right. Teaching is an excellent way to give back to the world and help others. Making important discoveries in science is also helpful. In the end, Marie decides to share Pierre's dream, but it doesn't make her original plan wrong.

Talk with your student about a time when perhaps she thought her way was the best. Did she listen to someone else's idea? Did she compromise or learn from someone else? What did she learn?

Chapter 8—A Surprising Discovery

Teacher Summary

Marie and Pierre work diligently together on their scientific research projects. Marie is also working toward her doctorate degree—trying to become the first woman in Europe to obtain one. In the fall of 1897 the Curies' first daughter is born (Irene).

In order to complete her doctorate, Marie must come up with a thesis. She and Pierre begin studying various research by other scientists, in order to come up with an idea for her paper. They finally settle on research conducted by the French scientist Henri Becquerel. He had recently discovered rays given off by uranium salts. Marie decides to try to find where the rays come from and what is causing them. Soon her research leads her to an amazing discovery—she thinks she has uncovered an unknown element!

What we will cover in this chapter:

Social Studies: History - Henri Becquerel
Science: Uranium*
Language Arts: Writing Your Own Science Thesis
Language Arts: Writing and Discussion Questions

Life Skills: Grandparents
Life Skills: Persistence
Life Skills: Cooperation

Social Studies: History - Henri Becquerel

Marie decides to base her doctoral thesis on the foundation research conducted by Henri Becquerel. Your student is probably unfamiliar with this scientist.

Henri Becquerel [ahn REE behk uh REHL] was born in Paris, France (1852-1908). His father and grandfather were both physicists, so he grew up around the field. He was highly successful, and by the age of 40 was teaching physics at the Museum of Natural History in France. In just three short years, he moved and began teaching in the same position at the esteemed Ecole Polytechnique.

His highest achievement, however, was shared with Marie and Pierre Curie. In 1903 the three scientists shared the Nobel Prize for physics—Henri, for his discovery of natural rays in uranium, and the Curies for their work to isolate the chemical element, radium.

Becquerel was elected president of the French Academy of Sciences in 1908 and died the same year.

If your student is interested in learning more about Henri Becquerel and his findings, locate a biography at your local library or look online.

Science: Uranium*

Henri Becquerel discovered rays given off by an element called uranium. Uranium is a silvery-white, radioactive metal. When we say something is "radioactive," we mean that substance spontaneously and singly radiates energy. When people are able to contain and channel that energy, it can be used for many things.

Uranium, for example, is used to generate the electric energy at many nuclear power plants. It is used to produce the vast explosions in some nuclear weapons. Explain to your student that uranium is a very heavy element. In fact, only the element plutonium is heavier. Uranium is heavy and powerful! A small piece of uranium (the size of a grapefruit) contains more energy than a trainload of coal—weighing three million times as much!

Where is uranium found? Uranium is mainly found in rock. It was discovered in 1789 by the German chemist Martin H. Klaproth. Just like Marie, Klaproth was working with the blackish-brown mineral, pitchblende, when he found uranium. Can your student guess what uranium was named for? (The planet Uranus.) This planet had been discovered only eight years prior.

Marie and Klaproth were definitely working with the right substance. Pitchblende contains more uranium ore than any other substance. Pitchblende (and therefore uranium) is found in several areas of the world, including Canada, the Democratic Republic of the Congo, and the silver mines of the Ore mountains in Europe. In the United States, large uranium ore deposits are mined in Arizona, Utah, Colorado and New Mexico.

If your student has studied the periodic table of elements, look together at the atomic weight of uranium. With an atomic weight of 238.029, uranium is the heaviest element that occurs in large quantity. Have your student compare that number with another element—nitrogen, for instance. Nitrogen's atomic weight is only 14.0067. Find the weight of plutonium, the heaviest element in terms of relative atomic mass. Can your student find the lightest? (The element helium—atomic weight 4.00260.)

Remind your student that an element is any substance that contains only one kind of atom. All chemical substances are combinations (or compounds) of elements. For example, water is a combination of hydrogen and oxygen.

Uranium is a powerful and amazing element. Perhaps your student can write a small report or oral presentation on this element for a sibling, parent or friend. She may wish to study another element—helium, for example—and do a comparison.

Language Arts: Writing Your Own Science Thesis

Marie had to write a research paper, or a thesis. She had to select a subject for her thesis. As the author tells us, it was a big decision to make. The paper had to be her own original work (or findings), but it could be based on the preliminary findings of others.

Your student can be stretched mentally and have a great time by writing her own thesis—just like Marie. She found something she felt was important and interested her. Set your student on the same search.

To begin, she needs to carefully consider the many subjects she can explore. Help her narrow her search by asking the following types of questions:

What is your favorite aspect of science (e.g., animals, weather, technology, chemistry, microscope work, botany [plants], etc.)?

Who have you studied in that area (e.g., John Muir, Thomas Edison, Wright Brothers, etc.)?

What is something you've always wondered about?

Is there an experiment you've wanted to conduct that we haven't been able to tackle yet?

Obviously, your student is not going to delve into experiments using radioactive materials or deep ocean exploration, but she can research and experiment on a variety of levels in a variety of subjects. Just like Marie, she can select a topic she thinks is important and interesting.

She may wish to begin by doing background research. What have other scientists discovered about his topic? What were their experiments? Who were they? When did they live?

Your student's thesis can contain two kinds of research. One is primary research (first person). This will include her own ideas, and the results of her own experiments. The second kind of research she may wish to include is secondary—ideas from the works of others. Remind your student of a researcher's responsibility, however, to document and give attribution for the work of others.

Here are some tips for your student, to help her get the most out of her thesis project:

1. Once you decide on your thesis topic, concentrate on that topic. It's okay to take awhile to decide; but once you've made your choice, don't waver.

2. Never rush a research paper. Make sure you work slowly and steadily.

3. Do your own first-hand research or experiments. Include these as a main source in your paper.

4. If you don't understand the information you're collecting, ask for help. If you can't explain your topic or information, how will you write about it?

5. Talk with your teacher and others as you develop your paper. Sometimes the best ideas for exploration come from others.

This project can be as simple or lengthy as your student is able to make it. A project like this sparks interest, creativity and excellence in your student because it gives her some control over her own education. She will get excited as she compiles her own findings and compares them with the work of others. Try hard not to influence your student's topic selection. This project should come from her own interests and pondering.

Language Arts: Writing and Discussion Questions

1. Marie and Pierre's workspace is in awful conditions—damp, cold and poorly ventilated. Why do you think they agreed to work there?

2. What is an experiment?

Life Skills: Grandparents

Little Irene Curie is cared for much of the time by her grandfather, Dr. Curie. He is a loving man who enjoys spending time with his son's family since his wife died.

Grandparents are special, wonderful people in our lives. They are different than parents, but just as important. Ask your student what she thinks are some differences between grandparents and parents.

Grandparents remember many things from long ago. They are older than you and even older than your mom or dad! Talking about times they experienced when they were children is a wonderful way to bond with grandparents and learn more about history.

The best way to learn more about grandparents and great-grandparents and their lives is to ask them! If your student is comfortable doing it, a wonderful activity is to set up some "grandparent interviews." Using a notebook or audio or video recording, your student can ask her grandparents about when they were young. She will learn so much about history, politics, social and cultural changes, pop culture from long ago, how people lived and what they enjoyed doing as children, and her written or taped interviews can be kept to show even her own children!

Being a grandchild and spending time with grandparents teaches a child many things like sharing, history, love and the importance of family. One of the most important things a child can learn from her grandparents, however, is about getting old. If children are around grandparents (or elderly friends or neighbors) they learn that people age. They learn to fear older people less, and understand the natural changes all of us will go through. It can help your student think through what kind of person she wants to be when she gets older.

Grandparents are a rich source of comfort, love and learning. If your student isn't close to, or doesn't have any grandparents, find an older person who needs some company and develop a relationship. The most sensitive, prepared and mature children are those who have had the wonderful experience of being close to an older person.

Life Skills: Persistence

Talk with your student about how dedicated Marie is to her research. We read, "At the end of several weeks of experimentation, Marie discovered something very interesting." Several weeks! As you continue to read in our book, you will see Marie's persistence in her research. She spends weeks, months, even years finding all she can!

Persistence is an important character trait in both science and life. Sometimes situations seem so difficult or even boring, we want to give up quickly. Persistence is the opposite of that—it means continuing the job even when we don't feel like it.

Ask your student if she remembers the difficulties the Wright brothers first faced as they tried to design a flying machine. She may recall the how hard Neil Armstrong worked to pay for and obtain his first pilot's license. Or even how diligent and persistent the

Boxcar children were as they worked in Dr. Brown's cherry orchard (FIAR Vol. 5).

Persistence is easier when we are doing something we want to succeed at so much we don't want to give up. It is more difficult, however, when we are doing things we don't really enjoy. In both instances, however, persistence always pays off. Even if you only have a sense of accomplishment, you will always feel better having finished what you set out to do.

Life Skills: Cooperation

Marie's thesis is based on the findings of another scientist, Henri Becquerel. We see her comparing her findings with the work done by her husband and his brother. Remind your student that in order to succeed, all scientists must cooperate with others. Their work must be compared, based on and added to the work of others. Without this kind of cooperation, discoveries would be much more rare and slow in coming. No one scientist really works alone. She is always aided by the work done by other men and women.

In your student's life, learning about this kind of cooperation is important. Understanding that we all depend on each other helps children develop healthy social consciences and a sensitivity to their place in a whole. When we cooperate with others in our lives, we naturally avoid egotism and self-centeredness.

This lesson might be a good jumping-off point for a simple essay project. You can assign the essay after you've discussed this lesson, or even before. Give your student the word "cooperation" and ask her to write a short essay (one paragraph to two pages) on what this word means to her. Or, your student might rather write a short story that depicts cooperation of some sort as a creative writing exercise.

Chapter 9—More Discoveries

Teacher Summary

Marie works hard to find the new element she believes exists in pitchblende. Pierre is so fascinated by her work, he soon joins her. Soon, they discover what they believe are two new elements! One, Marie successfully isolates and names polonium for her beloved Poland. The other remains a mystery and the work continues. Soon, after many more months of hard work, Pierre and Marie isolate what they believe to be the second new element. They name it radium. Now they must set out to isolate more of this element and study it. Pierre and Marie do take a much-needed break, however, and the vacation does them good.

What we will cover in this chapter:

Social Studies: History and Geography - The Spanish-American War
Science: The Importance of Asking Questions
Language Arts: Using Transitional Words and Phrases*
Language Arts: Writing and Discussion Question

Social Studies: History and Geography - The Spanish-American War

Marie and her husband Pierre began their long, exhaustive work on pitchblende in 1898. Another important event was taking place that year: the Spanish-American War.

Although the United States had been involved with previous wars, the Spanish-American War established the U.S. as a major world power. It was a short, but intense conflict between the United States and Spain.

The Spanish-American War took place between April and August of 1898. The issue was the liberation of Cuba. Find Cuba on a map and show your student how close it is to the coast of Florida.

At the time, Spain controlled Guam, Puerto Rico, the Philippines and Cuba. For several decades, Americans had been upset by what they felt was the cruel treatment Spain inflicted on these small countries. Spanish rule had created economic depression, oppression and brewing revolt.

Many Americans felt it was their duty to help free Cuba from the control of Spain. Remind your student that this war followed the Civil War closely. There was a certain segment of the U.S. population who felt slavery was a crime. There were others who did not. Two big newspaper moguls, William Randolph Hearst and Joseph Pulitzer, printed many, many headlines and articles in their papers about the horrible conditions in Cuba. They wanted Americans to free the country. Some believed that their articles exaggerated the situation in order to stir up empathy.

In January of 1898, President McKinley sent the battleship *Maine* into Havana's harbors. He wanted the battleship and its crew to help protect the innocent Cubans and Americans from rioters and cruel people. Unfortunately, just one month later (February 15, 1898) an explosion destroyed the ship and killed nearly 300 people on board.

Americans believed the Spanish were responsible, and immediately demanded retaliation. The popular slogan during this war became, "Remember the *Maine*." In just two months, April of 1898, America declared war on Spain.

The war only lasted five months (April to August of 1898). Spain ceded their hold on Cuba and surrendered to American forces. It was an important war for several reasons. To begin, it was the first war since the Civil War where (formerly) Yankee and Confederate troops fought together for a common purpose. Second, it helped free Cuba (as well as Guam, Puerto Rico and the Philippines) from cruel Spanish rule. And finally, it led to the building of the Panama Canal. The battles and war lines showed people how important a canal through the Isthmus of Panama could be. Show your student the Panama Canal on a map, leading boats to the Caribbean Sea from the Pacific Ocean. Find a simple book on the building of the Panama Canal. It is a fascinating story.

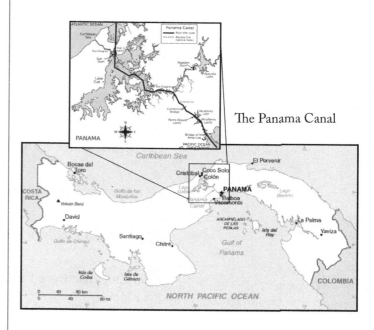

The Panama Canal

If your student is interested in doing an art project or activity to correspond with this lesson, one idea would be to make her own slogan board. She can decorate the background (perhaps with a drawn or cut-out map of Cuba and the other islands) and then stencil or letter the slogan "Remember the *Maine*!" You may wish to discuss with your student other famous war slogans—for example, the famous Uncle Sam posters used during World War I blaring, "I want YOU for U.S. Army!"

Science: The Importance of Asking Questions

In this chapter, we read, "Scientists have a habit of questioning everything. They don't believe what they see the first time."

As your student works through different science explorations and experiments, remind her of the importance of questions. Often called an "hypothesis," scientists formulate possible ideas and scenarios for their experiments by questioning their results. "This might happen if I do this..." But it is only through questions—through wanderings—that scientists come up with their new ideas.

Children are born with a wonderful natural curiosity. Anyone who has raised a three-year-old knows the question, "Why?" It is important to encourage these questions, and continue posing more yourself. As your student begins to see her questions answered, she will be excited and will come up with more.

Language Arts: Using Transitional Words and Phrases*

This chapter offers your student an opportunity to learn and review the use of transitional phrases. To begin, draw your student's attention to the paragraphs that begin (italics are added):

"*At that time*, scientists thought they already knew..."

"*By* June of 1898, Marie believed her element..."

"*Soon* they discovered this first radioactive..."

Our author, Ann E. Steinke, is using what is known as transitional phrases. In these sentences, her transitions are used to denote a change in time. Most writers naturally use transitional phrases in their writing. Every writer, however, can be helped by a review of more transitional choices. Here are four main categories of transitions:

1. To show time
2. To compare/contrast two things
3. To conclude an idea or thought
4. To add more information

Show your student some examples of each:

1. To show time: soon, after, finally, meanwhile, during, as soon as.
2. To compare/contrast two things: also, similarly, like, on the contrary, conversely.
3. To conclude an idea or thought: as a result, finally, in conclusion, in summary, in brief.
4. To add more information: for example, for instance, furthermore, additionally, along with.

By reviewing transitional phrases, your student is gaining two enrichment lessons—better vocabulary and smoother written compositions. To help your student remember these new words, encourage her to use two, three or even four in her next composition. You may also wish to look over some recent written work and point out to your student where she successfully used transitional phrases (she may not even realize she was doing it!), and where she could have had a smoother transition.

Language Arts: Writing and Discussion Question

Marie's sister, Bronya and her husband have opened a sanitarium for tuberculosis patients back in Poland. Why do you think Bronya wanted to do this?

Chapter 10—Four Hard Years

Teacher Summary

Marie and Pierre announce their discovery of radium, but the scientific community wants more proof. In order to allow other scientists to observe and study their new find, the Curies must isolate and produce "pure" radium.

Over the next four years, Pierre and Marie work diligently separating radium from pitchblende. They work in a terrible facility—an old shed with poor ventilation, a broken roof, and a weak stove for warmth. At one point a university in Sweden offers the scientists and their family a new workspace in Geneva. The Curies consider the offer, but don't want to risk a single wasted moment of work time. They continue, boiling and reducing nearly eight tons of pitchblende to produce one tenth of a gram of pure radium. Marie is exultant, but exhausted. Unfortunately, during this time her father passes away and Marie misses him greatly.

What we will cover in this chapter:

Social Studies: Geography - Bavaria
Science: Periodic Table of Elements*
Life Skills: Meaningful Work

Social Studies: Geography - Bavaria

The Curies discover that pitchblende is being mined in Bavaria and the uranium is being removed. Your student has explored many of the regions of Poland. Take some time and explore a portion of Germany with this lesson.

Bavaria [buh VAIR ee uh] is an area and state in southern Germany. Two of the most important cities in Bavaria are Munich and Nuremberg. Munich is the capital of Bavaria and is a city of industry and publishing. Nuremberg is known for the famous toys and baked goods produced there—especially their delicious gingerbread!

Bavaria is primarily a tourist area. People from all over the world visit this region every year to enjoy the amazing mountain ranges (Alps) and the numerous lakes.

Just as Poland was divided, conquered, and brought together again over the course of history, Bavaria has also had a similar history. As different rulers controlled the land (Germanic tribes, Napoleon and even the Allies during WWII), Bavaria changed in name. At times it was a kingdom, or a republic or a state. After the unification of Germany in 1990, Bavaria became a state again, situated in southeastern Germany.

After you complete this short geography lesson, you may wish to make or buy some gingerbread and enjoy it with your student!

Science: Periodic Table of Elements*

The Curies are successful in isolating a small amount of pure radium. This is important because in order to list it officially on the periodic table of elements, the scientists must be able to determine the element's atomic weight.

Your student may have already begun a study of the periodic table of elements with *Thomas Edison* in FIAR Vol. 6, or with *Betsy Ross* in FIAR Vol. 5. Use this opportunity to build on that knowledge and complete a periodic table in the activity sheet for this chapter.

With your student, find a colorful copy of the periodic table to use for reference. What does your student notice? Can she find Polonium? Radium? Uranium?

Draw your student's attention to a specific square—Polonium, for example. Each square has a lot of information in it, including the element's symbol (Po for Polonium), the atomic weight (210 for Polonium), the atomic number (84 for Polonium) and the name of the element.

What else does your student notice about the periodic table of elements? The elements are listed in rows. These rows are called **periods**. Elements that are somewhat similar in properties are grouped together in vertical columns. These columns are called **groups**.

The table of elements also uses different colors to indicate the **classes** of elements. For example, blue might be used to designate a class of elements such as the noble gases.

For a related activity and two suggested go-along books for the periodic table, see the activity sheet for Chapter 8.

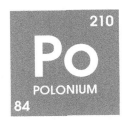

144

Life Skills: Meaningful Work

Beneath the illustration of the old shed, we read a quote from Marie. She said, "It was in this miserable old shed, that the best and happiest years of our life were spent, entirely consecrated to work."

Why do you think Marie was so happy in those horrible conditions? All she did was work—and work hard! Explain to your student that in life it is important to find "meaningful work" to do. Doing a chore or having a job which holds no meaning for you or anyone else can be frustrating. Many jobs, however, become meaningful when we think about who they will benefit. Humans need meaningful work to do because it helps us form noble characters and happy hearts.

Even menial jobs can be made meaningful. Does your student complain about having to do her chores? Setting the table, for example, or washing the dog. Encourage your student to think about how her job helps her family. If the table wasn't set, everyone would have a hard time eating, wouldn't they? If the dog was never washed, the poor animal would be uncomfortable, matted and dirty.

Marie and Pierre were happy because they knew their discoveries would help mankind. They believed in what they were doing.

Encourage your student to look around her and find meaningful work to do. If, beyond her schooling and home chores, she doesn't find something to inspire her, maybe she can get involved in a volunteer program (helping at a soup kitchen, visiting the elderly at a nursing home, volunteering at a local animal shelter, offering an older neighbor help in her garden, etc.). Meaningful work doesn't have to be a paid profession. It is mainly a way to give of yourself to others. Marie found it in her life—find it in yours!

Language Arts: Writing and Discussion Question

When the Curies discovered how to separate radium from pitchblende they could have patented their discovery and made a great deal of money. Why didn't they? Would you? Explain.

Chapters 11-12—Awards and Sorrows, Tragedy

Teacher Summary

Marie and Pierre continue to work on their great scientific work. Many people are anxious to learn about their research, and the Curies try their best to answer all their questions. They refuse to charge for their knowledge as well. They believe it would not be in the interest of "pure" science if they sold their work, instead of sharing it.

Soon, they discover another important property of radium. It can burn skin tissue. Immediately people begin thinking of using radium to destroy skin cells—like cancer, tumors and growths. The process began to be known as Curietherapy, but we now call it radiation therapy. Marie also achieves her last academic goal—her doctorate.

Many awards are given to the Curies, including the coveted Nobel Prize in Physics (1903). They share the award with Henri Becquerel, the French scientist upon whose discoveries Marie based her work. Even though all the attention and awards are nice, the Curies long to get back to their quiet laboratory and continue to work.

Soon, in 1904, Marie gives birth to her second and last child—a daughter named Eve. Although Marie is very tired and sick, she loves her new baby and the family is doing well. Pierre and Marie are able to get a new laboratory to work in, and although they are both weak and ill from the exposure to radium, they continue to work every day.

On April 19, 1906, an unexpected tragedy occurs. Pierre is accidentally drug down by a horse carriage and crushed beneath the wheels. With her husband dead, Marie gathers her daughters to her and grieves.

Soon, she is back to work. The Sorbonne, where Pierre taught, must hire a new physics teacher. They can only think of one person—Marie. Although she is the first woman to ever teach at the university, Marie accepts the challenge and sets her mind on continuing the work she and Pierre set out to do.

Along with teaching, Marie develops a method of measuring radium. The scientific world is amazed and grateful. Marie is granted a second Nobel Prize in Physics in 1911!

What we will cover in these chapters:

Science: The Dangers of Radioactive Materials
Language Arts: Writing and Discussion Question
Language Arts: Vocabulary
Fine Arts: Drawing - Using Our Illustrator's Line Technique
Fine Arts: A Famous Sculpture - *The Thinker*
Life Skills: Generosity - Comparing Carver and Curie
Activity Sheet: Who Was Alfred Nobel?*

Science: The Dangers of Radioactive Materials

Throughout the last several chapters of our book, we have read descriptions of how weak and sick Marie and Pierre have become. Eventually the sickness is attributed to the very substance Marie has dedicated her life to—radium. Her sickness is caused by radiation poisoning.

This lesson will introduce your student to a basic understanding of radioactive materials and the danger they pose to humans.

Radiation sickness (poisoning) is the term given for a variety of symptoms associated with a person's exposure to radioactive materials. Marie's type of exposure is rare. At that time, no one knew the dangers of radioactive elements. Today, many precautions are taken when working with radioactive materials.

Radiation sickness takes many forms. Remind your student of how tired Marie and Pierre always seem to be. Even with their level of hard work, no healthy person would be that exhausted. Fatigue is a main symptom of early radiation sickness. Other symptoms include hair loss, vomiting and loss of appetite.

If a person is exposed to large amounts of uncontrolled radiation, the rays can destroy blood cells, organ tissue, the immune system and can eventually result in death. Marie, unfortunately, had no idea of the dangers. Marie, her daughter Irene and Irene's husband, Fred, all died from radiation poisoning. Pierre would have assuredly died from the sickness as well, if his life hadn't been abruptly ended in the accident.

Remind your student, however, that radiation—with the proper controls—can be greatly beneficial to cancer patients, people who need x-rays, and more. Indeed, it can be lifesaving! Marie's discoveries have helped millions and millions of people stay healthy. Radiation is something that can be both beneficial and dangerous.

Fine Arts: Drawing - Using Our Illustrator's Line Technique

Perhaps your student has noticed the interesting illustration techniques used in our book. The illustrator is a man named Roger Xavier. His technique uses pen and ink, and includes many groups of lines going in the same direction. The groups of lines give the figures shape and movement.

One of the most interesting drawings in our book occurs where Marie is giving her oral responses to questions posed by a group of professors. She is completing the final step toward her doctorate.

What does your student notice about the drawing? How does Xavier achieve his background? He carefully draws sweeping lines, going slightly from top right to bottom left. These lines make the room seem expansive and give the impression of many people, don't they?

Xavier draws the professors in the audience as only small heads and a little shoulder definition. The further back in the picture you look, the smaller the people's heads appear, giving you the impression that the room is large.

Let your student try this technique for herself. Remind her that the lines don't need to be perfectly spaced, but that the direction is more important. Encourage her to draw a group of people, similar to Xavier's illustration.

If she enjoys this technique, she may wish to flip through the book and observe other illustrations by Roger Xavier. Let her try copying different pictures. Many artists learn from initial copying of others.

Fine Arts: A Famous Sculpture - *The Thinker*

Marie and Pierre enjoy their life in Paris and their friends. One of their friends is the famous French sculptor, Auguste Rodin [oh GOOSTE roh DAN]. The work of Auguste Rodin is very famous, and your student will enjoy learning a bit about the artist and looking at his work.

Auguste Rodin was born in France and lived from 1840-1917. He is considered by many to be the greatest sculptor of the 1800s. Rodin was fascinated with the human body. The intricacies of skin folds, delicate features, and powerful bone structure of the human body was the subject of many pieces. Some of Rodin's work focused on just one piece of the body—a hand, a foot or a face.

One of the most famous sculptures in the world, and a piece by the great Rodin, is called *The Thinker*. You can view this statue at left and also see it from different angles online. What does your student think? Does she like the piece? What does she think the gentleman is contemplating?

The Thinker was originally begun as a piece to be included in a large, sculpted door on the Museum of Decorative Art in Paris. It was commissioned by the museum in 1880. The door was never completed, but Rodin used his idea for a man deep in thought, and expanded it to create this bronze work of heroic size that we now call *The Thinker*.

If your student explores and studies more pieces by Rodin, she will notice the immense emotional intensity displayed in his work. He was a master at expressing feelings through movement and shape.

If your student is interested, this lesson might serve as a jumping off point for doing her own sculpture. She may even wish to try to copy Rodin's style by molding and sculpting her own version of *The Thinker*.

Life Skills: Generosity - Comparing Carver and Curie

Marie and Pierre are committed for now, to "share their work, not sell it." They don't want to make money with their discoveries. They only want to help people and other scientists doing research.

If your student worked through FIAR Vol. 7, she studied the life of George Washington Carver. This lesson presents an excellent comparison discussion topic. Carver, like the Curies, also never wanted to profit monetarily from his discoveries. Here are some things George Washington Carver said when people asked him why he didn't charge for his information or sell it:

The Thinker

148

"I want everything I do to be available to the public for the general good of all."

"If I know the answer you can have it for the price of a postage stamp. The Lord charges nothing for knowledge, and I will charge you the same."

"It is not the style of clothes one wears, neither the kind of automobiles one drives, nor the amount of money one has in the bank, that counts. These mean nothing. It is simply service that measures success."

Read these quotes with your student. Ask her to compare things she has learned about Marie with what Carver is saying. They are quite similar, aren't they? Marie's main interest is in helping people through science. She doesn't sell her discoveries. She does not live in luxury. She isn't concerned with fancy dresses, but instead prefers her dark clothes that are serviceable and don't show dirt, etc.

Are there any other similarities or differences your student can think of? This type of discussion—**compare or contrast**—is excellent for your student's mind. They force her to think using logic, synthesizing ideas and pulling information from earlier study topics.

Language Arts: Writing and Discussion Question

Marie goes through a serious period of grief after her husband, Pierre, is killed. She does not think she will ever be happy again. Will she? Why?

Language Arts: Vocabulary

radiation poisoning   Illness induced by exposure to radiation, including vomiting, hair loss and fatigue.

Chapters 13-15—Dreams and War, A Special Gift, The Final Years

Teacher Summary

Shortly after Marie receives her second Nobel Prize in Physics, the French Academy of Sciences chooses to nominate her for membership. Once again, if Marie is accepted as a member she would be the first woman to ever do so. Unfortunately, a terrible rumor is spread about her. A Paris gossip magazine prints an article saying that Marie is responsible for breaking up the marriage of a fellow scientist. The rumors are unfounded and lies, but they result in Marie's nomination being revoked. Marie is heartbroken. The membership would have been nice, but the damage to her reputation is what upsets her most.

Marie continues to work, and continues to be ill. Her kidneys fail twice in less than a year and she is forced to take time off. Her long exposure to radiation is taking its full toll. However, in 1913, Marie Curie realizes a lifelong dream—helping her country of Poland. She goes to Warsaw and helps dedicate a scientific laboratory specializing in the study of radium. Marie is thrilled to give the dedication speech in her native tongue—Polish.

World War I breaks out the following year, and Marie is separated from her children. She is in Paris, and they are vacationing in Brittany. Even with her children away from her and a terrible war looming before her, Marie does not despair. Instead, she thinks of a way to help with the war effort. Using her knowledge of radium and the current research on x-ray machines, she sets up x-ray transport units. Known as "Little Curies," over 200 cars transport x-ray equipment to front line hospitals to help care for the wounded. Marie personally trains over 150 women to operate the equipment! With Marie's idea and the hospital personnel, over one million wounded are helped!

As the war comes to a close, Poland is freed through the Treaty of Versailles. Marie is thrilled. She wants to continue her work with radium, and she does. Using the help of Americans and friends, she raises money and is able to purchase more pure radium. During this time, Marie meets President Harding and then President Hoover. They both help present her with the radium.

Marie's daughter, Irene, continues the work her mother had started. She and her husband, Fred Joliot, discover artificial radioactivity and consequently are awarded the Nobel Prize in Physics. Three Nobel prizes for one family—a feat that has never been duplicated!

Marie dies at dawn on July 4, 1934. She was 66, and she is believed to have had leukemia, caused by 30 years of exposure to radium. She was buried next to Pierre in Sceaux, France. On her grave is written: "We must believe that we are gifted for something, and that this thing, at whatever cost, must be attained."

What we will cover in these chapters:

Social Studies: History - Marie Curie's Daughter, Irene
Social Studies: History - Albert Einstein
Social Studies: History - The Treaty of Versailles
Science: Kidneys - Their Form and Function
Language Arts: Writing and Discussion Question
Language Arts: Vocabulary*
Life Skills: Rumors - Dangerous Talk
Life Skills: Being Gifted For Something

Social Studies: History - Marie Curie's Daughter, Irene

Although many people know the name Marie Curie and are aware of her tremendous contributions to science, not many know about her daughter Irene's amazing discovery and success. Thankfully, in our book Irene's work is also discussed.

Irene and her husband, Fred Joliot [Jho LEE OH], continued the work of Marie Curie even after her death. Before her mother died, however, Irene made a significant and lasting discovery—every bit as important as her mother's discovery of radium.

As Irene and Fred work in their laboratory, they notice something unusual. If they expose a piece of aluminum (another metallic element) to high doses of radiation, the aluminum remains radioactive! They discover how to make artificial radioactivity!

Explain to your student how important this finding was. At the time, pure radium was so expensive even Marie had a hard time buying it! If scientists could make other metal elements radioactive, they could begin to offer radiation therapy and x-rays to millions of people for much less money. More scientists could study radiation as well, without having to have pure radium. Radioactive materials could be produced, studied and used whenever scientists needed them.

If your student is interested, here are a few other facts about Irene. She had a baby girl, Helene, on September 17, 1927. Just like her mother, Irene worked in the laboratory until she went into labor and was back at work soon after. Just like Irene, Helene followed in her mother's footsteps and became a theoretical physicist.

Irene passed away on March 17, 1956. Fred died on August 14, 1958. Both lives were claimed by exposure to radiation.

Social Studies: History - Albert Einstein

One of Marie's best friends was the famous scientist, Albert Einstein. Can you imagine the conversations they had? You would probably need to be a scientist to understand anything they were saying!

Albert Einstein is considered one of the greatest scientists of all time. He was born on March 14, 1879 (Marie was born in 1867) in Germany. He was fascinated with science, even as a young boy. He attended the Swiss Polytechnic Institute in Bern, and became a Swiss citizen in 1905.

Although Albert Einstein's discoveries and contributions were many, he is best known for a theory he developed called the theory of relativity. The science community maintains, and accurately so, that the average person has a difficult time understanding the theory. It is a complex makeup of mathematical formulas and ideas. In brief, the theory of relativity deals with concepts such as time, space, mass and motion. It also treats mass and energy as the same thing—interchangeable factors. This idea revolutionized the scientific thought, and led the way to releasing energy from the atom (i.e., atomic bomb).

Einstein was married twice. He had three children from his first marriage, and two stepdaughters from his second. He lived the last 20 years of his life in Princeton, New Jersey, and died in 1955.

Social Studies: History - The Treaty of Versailles

After the end of World War I, Marie gets exciting news—Poland is finally free! Remind your student that for many years, Poland had been divided and ruled by other countries. The area where Marie grew up was ruled by the Russians (chapter 2 lessons), but other areas were controlled by the Germans and the Austrians.

The freedom Poland experienced after WWI was directly related to an important legal document, the Treaty of Versailles [ver SIGH]. Explain to your student that a **treaty** is a formal agreement between two or more independent governments. A treaty, in other words, is like a contract. Treaties are often used to end wars.

The Treaty of Versailles officially ended the fighting with Germany in WWI. Many people worked on the Treaty of Versailles including President Woodrow Wilson, Prime Minister David Lloyd George of Great Britain, Premier Georges Clemenceau of France and Premier Vittorio Orlando of Italy. These men became known as "the Big Four."

Included in the Treaty of Versailles were several important points. It stated that Germany was responsible for World War I, and it called for reparations. Reparations are actions to "repair" or to make right. Germany was required to completely demilitarize, revise its boundaries (this freed Poland and certain provinces of France), and give the Allies coal, livestock, ships, timber and tremendous cash payments. The Treaty of Versailles ended the war, and it also completely stripped Germany. Germany rebelled against the Treaty of Versailles and was humiliated, but it was forced to accept. It took effect in early 1920.

Remind your student of the lesson on Adolf Hitler covered in chapter 1 of *The Saturdays* (FIAR Vol. 6). Many people feel that the humiliation and anger so many Germans felt after the Treaty of Versailles was fuel for Hitler's fire. He spoke about raising up a new Germany—full of pride and strength. The Germans were so beaten down they clung to his words. Communism was spreading via Russia and the Germans were worried about their future. To many, Hitler's plans seemed like an answer.

For an activity to embellish this lesson, you might wish to have your student draw up a "treaty" of her own. She can use a recent family disagreement or current news event as the basis. What things does she feel need to be changed? How can each side work together to fix the problem? What does she think is wrong with the situation? All of these questions can help her form her treaty. When she has completed the main ideas, she can create a very formal looking document and entitle it "*The Treaty of*_____ ."

Science: Kidneys - Their Form and Function

Marie suffered kidney failure due to her radiation poisoning. **Kidneys** are vital organs in the human body and work together with the **ureters** and the bladder to filter blood, remove waste products and formulate urine.

Has your student ever eaten kidney beans? (If not, by all means go and buy some today!) Those large dark red beans got their name because they look like small kidneys. In reality, kidneys are about the size of a man's fist and are a dark purplish color. Together, they weigh around one pound. Look at those kidney beans again. Does your student notice how one side seems to curve inward a bit? Your kidneys are shaped the same way. The curved side points inward toward your ureters, while the rounded side points toward the sides of your body.

Look at a diagram of human anatomy and point out the kidneys. Kidneys are the body's "washing machine." They continually filter, clean and pump out clean blood. As our cells work, they sometimes produce harmful waste products in addition to the good things. The kidneys catch all the harmful toxins and pull them out of the blood. Even though your kidneys are small, they work really hard! Twenty-five percent of all the blood in your body passes through your kidneys every single minute (approximately one quart).

In four minutes, all the blood in your body has been filtered, cleaned and pumped back out into the blood stream!

The kidneys filter your blood using millions of tiny filters called **nephrons**. Each nephron is approximately 1/2 inch long, but it is so thin only a microscope can detect it. Along with the nephrons, the kidneys filter the bad things out of our blood just like an oil filter in a car. There are different membranes, with different size "holes". Most of the things in our blood stream, like glucose, amino acids, vitamins, blood cells and proteins, are reabsorbed by the body. The filter is too small to take them. Therefore, most of what the kidneys catch is water, salt, ammonia and urea. They will also remove certain dyes and drugs from the blood. This is why if you eat a lot of beets, your urine appears a little pink!

All of the jobs the kidneys perform help keep the body's fluids in balance. In doing so, the body's conditions are kept just right. Having all the body conditions in balance is called homeostasis.

One of the important functions of the kidneys is to remove excess salt in our bloodstream. Salt is important to the body, but too much can be harmful. Salt is attracted to proteins and too much can damage our cells. To illustrate this for your student, sprinkle a heavy layer of salt on a piece of raw meat. Check it in two hours. What happens? The salt begins to draw out the fluid and shrivel the meat's structure. Now soak the piece of raw meat in a bowl of plain water overnight. The next morning, check it. What happens? The water fills the cells of the meat to overflowing and they burst. The meat is mushy.

Keeping just the right amount of salt in our systems helps our cells retain just the perfect amount of water!

Your student might wonder why people are born with two kidneys. Two kidneys work to keep the body healthy. If one needs to be removed for any reason, the other kidney will increase in size and do the same amount of work. However, if both kidneys are lost, then a person must have a kidney transplant.

Kidneys are small but important organs!

Language Arts: Writing and Discussion Question

Why was Marie unwilling to face the fact that the radium was making her sick? Why did the American journalist, Mrs. William Meloney, help Marie Curie? How did she do it?

Language Arts: Vocabulary

treaty   An agreement between two or more nations, agreed upon and signed.

kidney   One of two organs found in the body which separates waste and water from the blood.

nephron   A filter unit found in the kidney.

ureter   A duct which carries urine from the kidneys to the bladder.

Life Skills: Rumors—Dangerous Talk

Marie had her nomination to the French Academy of Sciences revoked because of an ugly, untrue rumor. Discuss rumors with your student. Are rumors ever true? What should we do when we hear a rumor?

Sometimes rumors are based on a small grain of truth, but many times are complete falsehoods. When someone tells us a rumor our obligation should be to ignore the statement. If you must know, go to the person directly and ask him. If you listen to the rumor and then repeat it, you are gossiping.

Rumors and gossip are dangerous to a person's character. They can quickly get out of hand. No one checks to see if the story is true, and facts can quickly be deleted and added. Encourage your student to ignore rumors and stay away from gossip. You never know the real story unless you talk to the person who was there!

Having people talk about you is painful. Don't do the same hurtful thing to others!

Life Skills: Being Gifted For Something

At the end of our book, we read a statement by Marie Curie, "We must believe that we are gifted for something...". What does your student think of this statement? Ask her what she thinks she is gifted to do. Or maybe she is still searching for that "calling." That is fine! Lots of people don't find what they think is their special gifting until much later in life. But, every person on Earth has one. A gifting means that we are good at something, we love it and it often gives something back to others. It might be playing the piano or gardening. These things can make others feel good and inspire them. Maybe it's working with animals and giving them comfort, or teaching people.

If your student doesn't think she is gifted for something, encourage her to be looking for ways she is gifted and then to explore those things more fully. At the end of her life, your student will want to know she made a difference. She only needs to find her special gifting and then use it to the best of her ability. Just like Marie!

Teacher's Notes

Use this page to jot down relevant info you've found for this
Five in a Row chapter book, including favorite lessons, go-along
resources, field trips, and family memories.

MARIE CURIE AND THE DISCOVERY OF RADIUM

Dates studied: _____

Student: _____

Favorite Lesson Topics:

Social Studies:
_____
_____

Science:
_____
_____

Language Arts:
_____
_____

Fine Arts:
_____
_____

Life Skills:
_____
_____

Relevant Library Resources:
Books, DVDs, Audio Books
_____
_____
_____
_____
_____

Websites or Video Links:
_____
_____
_____
_____
_____
_____

156

Related Field Trip Opportunities:
_____
_____
_____

Favorite Quote or Memory During Study:
_____
_____
_____

Name:

Date:

History: **Timeline of Marie Curie's Childhood and Early Adult Years: Late 1800s**

The lesson **History: Exploring our Timeline - The Late 1800s** instructs you to research people and events that took place during the late 1800s. Use the timeline below to record information that you find during your research. Mark any people or events that you research; include printed images if desired and use hash marks along the timeline to represent specific dates and mark accordingly.

1900

1867

Name:

Date:

Fine Arts: **The French Riviera—Famous Painters: Henri Matisse**

In the lesson **Geography: The French Riviera**, you learned that this location's favorable climate was thought to be helpful medically, in the late 1800s and early 1900s, for people in poor health.

The French Riviera, known in French as the Côte d'Azur, also enchanted painters and artists with its views of the turquoise Mediterranean sea and the gray-blue Alps. During the late 1800s and 1900s, many famous painters flocked to the French coast, including Henri Matisse, Claude Monet, Pablo Picasso, Paul Signac and Marc Chagall.

Henri Matisse particularly loved the French Riviera. He wintered there beginning in the early 1900s and by the 1920s he resided there year-round. Like many artists, Matisse had several artistic styles. One style is called "cut-outs" and is easy and fun to replicate at home with scissors and colored construction paper. Use the templates below as a guide, and also create some similar shapes of your own to cut out in various colors. Glue them to a paper to make an interesting design or a recognizable object or scene.

Use these go-along books for inspiration:

The Iridescence of Birds: A Book About Henri Matisse
by Patricia MacLachlan (about Henri's childhood)
Henri Matisse: Drawing with Scissors by Jane O'Connor
Henri's Scissors by Jeanette Winter
Colorful Dreamer by Marjorie Blain Parker

158

Name:

Date:

Geography: **Alps & Carpathian Mountains—Photo Scavenger Hunt**

After completing the **Geography: The Alps and Carpathian Mountains** lesson, you can use this page to go on a photographic scavenger hunt of the biggest and most famous peaks in the Alps as well as a couple of photographs of the smaller Carpathian Mountains that Mayna loved.

Search online for the following: Mont Blanc, Matterhorn, Monte Rosa, Grossglockner and photos of the Carpathian Mountians. Print and paste images into the spaces below and label each photograph.

Name:

Date:

Language Arts: **Vocabulary Words**

After finishing chapter four use the crossword puzzle below to review the vocabulary words covered in **chapters 1-4**.

160

Across

2. (ch. 2) using no liquid (the opposite of a mercury barometer)

4. (ch. 4) second largest source of sugar, second only to cane

7. (ch. 3) a festive party and sleigh ride celebrated in Poland

8. (ch. 1) a green mineral

Down

1. (ch. 1) the equipment used in the study of physics

3. (ch. 4) main unit of Polish currency

5. (ch. 3) a large body of water surrounded by land

6. (ch. 1) the science and study of matter and energy

flip for vocab words: aneroid | zloty | malachite | physics | sugar beet | physics apparatus | kulig | lake

Marie Curie and the Discovery of Radium - Chapter 5

Name:

Date:

Geography: **Baltic Sea**

The lesson **Geography: Baltic Sea** provides information about important aspects of the Baltic Sea, as well as geographical information. An interesting part of the Baltic's Seas geography is how many countries surround it. Search "Baltic Sea map" online and view it and the bordering countries. Write out the list of surrounding countries. Then search each country's flag and color in and label the blank flags below with each counry that touches the Baltic Sea. The flag blanks below are all the same 3:2 ratio (which is a common flag size of many countries). For an interesting rabbit trail, dig deeper and research countries' flag ratios. There is only one country (not one of the ones in this activity sheet) that has a non-quadrilateral flag; can you find out which one it is?

Name:

Date:

Science: **Nutrition and the Brain**

The lesson **Science: Nutrition and the Brain** explains how and why forgetting to eat and rest caused Manya to struggle with her studies and become sick. To discover what doctors and scientists say are the healthiest foods for our brains, let's do some research. Search online for "best foods for brain health." As always, be sure to find credible sources to review—the Mayo Clinic has become world renowned for their medical care and approach to treating difficult conditions and is a good source of information regarding health. The American Heart Association is another well known, respected source of health guidence. Other hospitals and medical journals are also good resources for reserach.

Best foods for the brain:

Lentils

Olive Oil

Spinach

Almonds

162

Can you find a recipe online that contains several of the foods listed? Write the name of the recipe and website below:

Which foods are your favorites from the list?

What are some foods you haven't had that you could try?

Name:

Date:

Science: **Crystals**

After completing the **Science: Crystals** lesson, use this sheet to draw substances
that are crystals (or not) around your house. In each circle below, draw what you see
through a magnifying glass (or through a microscope). Two items are already listed for
you (sugar and salt) and two are up to you (you might try pepper, borax, brown sugar,
epsom salt, rock salt, or another household or kitchen substance). Place the substance
on a sheet of black or white contrasting paper to help you see the shapes better, and
then draw what you see! Is the substance a crystal ... or not?

sugar   salt

Name:

Date:

Science: **Comparing Two Elements**

Use the activity sheet below to compare the two elements that you chose in the **Science: Uranium** lesson. Search online or look for the books *Elements: A Visual Exploration of Every Known Atom in the Universe* by Theodore Gray or *The Periodic Table: Elements with Style!* by Simon Basher and Adrian Dingle. **Note:** for more information on the periodic table and a related activity sheet, see Chapter 10. Keep your go-along book(s) for that lesson!

164

TWO ELEMENTS IN THE PERIODIC TABLE		
Name:		
Date of Discovery:		
Atomic Number:		
Atomic Symbol:		
Atomic Weight:		
Phase:		
Color:		
Classification:		
Group in Periodic Table:		
Group Name:		
Period in Periodic Table:		
Block in Periodic Table:		
Melting Point:		
Boiling Point:		

Marie Curie and the Discovery of Radium - Chapter 9

Name:

Date:

Language Arts: **Transitional Phrases**

The lesson **Language Arts: Using Transitional Phrases** introduced you to four main categories of transitions with examples and encouraged the use of two or more in your next writing assignment. Below you'll find practice prompts that will help you develop your skills at writing transitional phrases before you incorporate them into your own writing.

Four Categories:

1. To show time
2. To compare/contrast two things
3. To conclude an idea or thought
4. To add more information

Examples:

1. Soon, after, finally, meanwhile, during as soon as
2. Also, similarly, like, on the contrary, conversely
3. As a result, finally, in conclusion, in summary, in brief
4. For example, for instance, furthermore, additionally, along with

Write a transitional sentence that takes a reader between breakfast and dinner of the same day.

_____

_____

_____

Write a transitional sentence in which Marie Curie is introduced to the reader, while adding more information about what she is known for, or her accomplishments, in the scientific field.

_____

_____

_____

Write a transitional sentence that compares Marie Curie to another famous scientist or another person you've read about.

_____

_____

_____

Write a transitional sentence in which you are finishing up an essay about a topic you are very interested in.

_____

_____

_____

Name:

Date:

Science: Periodic Table of Elements

Using a colorful periodic table of elements as a reference, fill in the chart below with all the elements you remember from your FIAR studies (with *Marie Curie, Thomas Edison, Betsy Ross*, etc.) or from your general knowledge. You can also fill in the rest of the chart (as detailed as you'd like) with the other elements, and color code it using highlighters or colored pencils to match your reference chart.

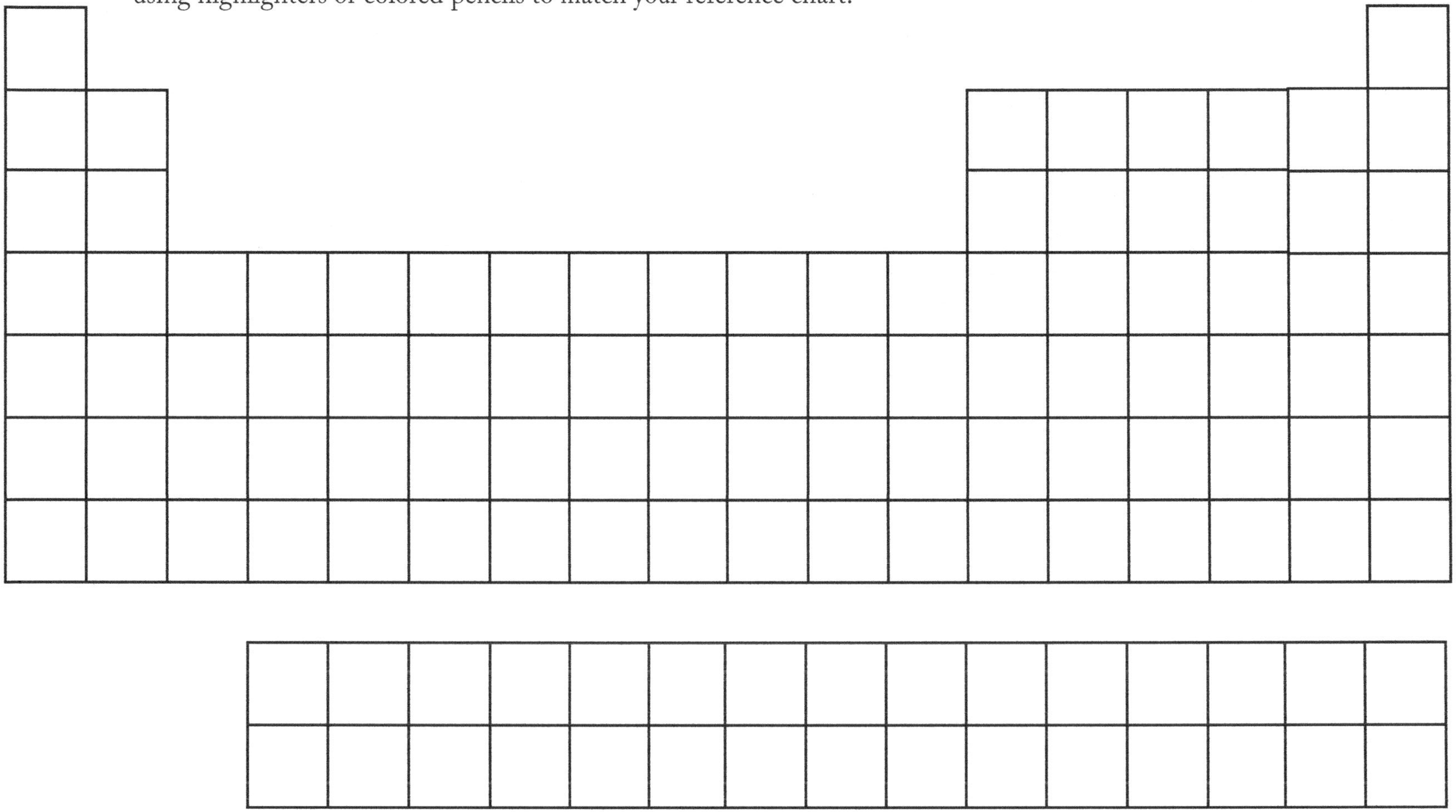

166

Marie Curie and the Discovery of Radium - Chapters 11 & 12

Name:

Date:

History: **Biography - Who Am I?**

Alfred Nobel (1833-1896) was a Swedish man who made contributions to science through chemistry, inventions and engineering, but is best known for leaving his fortune to establish the Nobel Prize.

To learn more about this man and his legacy, you can serach online or use books from the library.

Go-along books that you could use to research are:
Alfred Nobel: The Man Behind the Peace Prize
    by Kathy-Jo Wargin
The Nobel Prize: The Story of Alfred Nobel and the Most
    Famous Prize in the World by Michael Worek
Alfred Nobel: Inventive Thinker by Tristan Boyer Binns

Print and paste an image of Alfred Nobel into the frame.
Write information gathered through your research into the spaces below.

Name: _____

Lived: _____

Known for: _____

_____

_____

_____

_____

Connections to story: _____

_____

_____

_____

_____

_____

Marie Curie and the Discovery of Radium - Chapters 13-15

Name:

Date:

Language Arts: **Vocabulary Words**

Use the crossword puzzle below to review the vocabulary words covered in **chapters 6-15**. It's been a few chapters since you covered some of these words. Review the vocabulary words if needed before completing the crossword below.

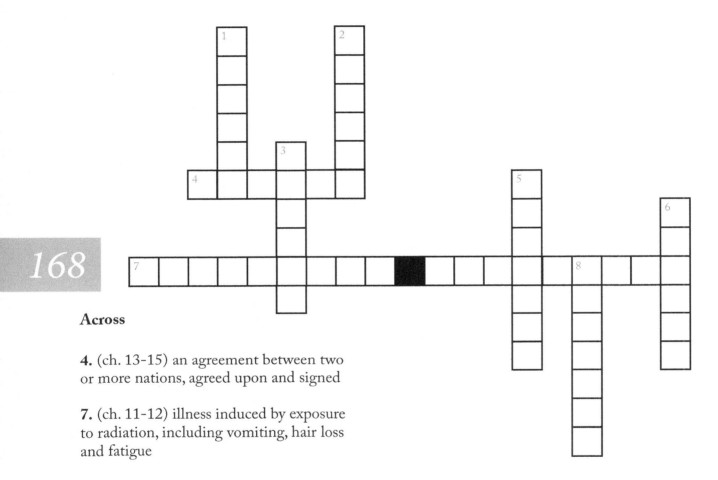

Across

4. (ch. 13-15) an agreement between two or more nations, agreed upon and signed

7. (ch. 11-12) illness induced by exposure to radiation, including vomiting, hair loss and fatigue

Down

1. (ch. 13-15) a duct which carries urine from the kidneys to the bladder

2. (ch. 13-15) one of two organs found in the body which separates waste and water from the blood

3. (ch. 6) the state or quality of being joyous

5. (ch. 7) a regularly shaped solid substance with angles and flat surfaces into which many substances solidify

6. (ch. 7) a piece of iron, steel or stone which attracts iron, steel, nickel or cobalt

8. (ch. 13-15) a filter unit found in the kidney

flip for vocab words: radiation poisoning | nephron | crystal | magnet | gaiety | treaty | kidney | ureter

Introduction and Tips for Hitty: Her First Hundred Years

In this final unit of Volume 8, your student will read a much longer chapter book than previously used with Five in a Row. *Hitty: Her First Hundred Years* is a Newbery award-winning novel by Rachel Field, written from the point of view of a handmade doll from the 1800s. Her many adventures include a harrowing ocean voyage on a whaling ship, a dramatic island escape, encounters with many cultures and people of other nations, ownership by children who love her, meetings with famous people, and a satisfying, full-circle ending to an exciting and far-reaching story.

This unit is necessarily **longer and more complex** than previous Five in a Row chapter book units. The **same academic subject areas** are covered, but there are sometimes many more lesson options per chapter. There are also **two large, ongoing projects** included with this unit (a research paper and a service project). And, unique to the FIAR curriculum, all of the lessons are **written directly to the student.**

One of the hallmarks of Five in a Row, at all levels, is its flexibility, and this *Hitty* unit is no exception. You know your student best. You can give them the chance to "own" their studies with *Hitty*. If independent work proves frustrating or too challenging for them, be prepared to guide them as needed, while still allowing them as much independence as possible.

Below are two different options for rowing *Hitty*; you may choose one of these methods or something in between to provide your particular student with the most benefit.

1. Your student can do this unit independently. Here is a real-life example of a weekly schedule (which can be modified as needed) for a student who is a very motivated, independent learner:

• Monday: read chapter, do copywork of your choice (this could be a few verses from the FIAR Bible Supplement or a favorite/interesting passage from the chapter). Vocabulary could also be added here, or done instead of copywork.

• Tuesday: read over all lessons. Choose one or more lessons and one writing prompt. Both are due on Friday.

• Tuesday through Friday are spent independently doing the lesson(s) and writing prompt. Use any extra time to be working on the research paper.

• Teacher involvement consists of helping when asked and a daily check-in of progress. Be sure to do a "walk-through" of the whole curriculum and your expectations together with your student before beginning. As with all FIAR chapter books, a "Teacher Summary" is provided at the beginning of every chapter to provide a quick reference for the parent's benefit, if neeeded.

• Research paper due at end of unit (semester); this paper will likely require more hands-on teacher involvement than the rest of the unit. Service project is ongoing.

2. Or, your student can do this unit in much the same way as previous FIAR chapter book units. This would involve more teacher planning and participation, which could include any or all of these from the teacher: choosing lessons, choosing activities, reading the chapter aloud, reading the lessons aloud, assisting with research, assisting with activities and writing, etc. Your student may want to assemble a notebook of assignments and activities. You also may find yourself assisting your student quite a bit at the beginning of the *Hitty* study, and allowing them to work more independently as the weeks go on.

More tips for success with *Hitty*:

• Decide how you'd like your student to use this unit using the ideas above, all depending on the needs of your particular student. As always, there is no "right or wrong" way to do Five in a Row.

• Your student may be an entirely independent learner, or may need daily assistance or participation from you, the teacher. Either is fine.

• *Hitty* may take as little as 6-8 weeks to row, or it may take an entire semester. Either is fine.

• No matter how you choose to row *Hitty*, it's a good idea for you (the teacher) to carefully preview the unit, become familiar with the various lessons and activity sheets, and make note of any recipes or activities your student may be interested in. This will likely affect how you decide to plan and use this unit with your student, whether they are an independent learner or not.

• Plan on being involved in your student's Research Paper and Service Project, no matter what level of independence your student has with the rest of the lessons. These two projects are complex and ongoing, and your student will likely need your direction, instruction, and assistance at several points along the way.

• You will need to continue to add math, plus the specific language arts areas of grammar, spelling, and handwriting (if necessary). As your student approaches the high school years, you may also already be adding other subjects depending on your student's interests and needs, such as foreign language, artist/composer study, musical instrument practice, computer or coding skills, other fine or practical arts, physical education, home ec or shop classes … the list could go on and on. What you add and to what extent will vary from family to family and from student to student.

No matter what options you choose, this *Hitty* unit, like every Five in a Row unit before it, offers "inspired learning through great books" and is designed to ignite a love of learning to last a lifetime.

A Note to the Student Before Beginning
Hitty: Her First Hundred Years

Welcome to a unique book in the Five in a Row curriculum, *Hitty: Her First Hundred Years*! This book is longer and more complex than others you've studied in Five in a Row. It's a fascinating story that crosses centuries and continents.

Part of the joy of using Five in a Row is being allowed to sometimes follow your own interests. You may find some lesson activities (such as a personal journal or a leaf collection, for instance) that continue for weeks as you pursue your studies—or perhaps even for months after your study is complete. Other activities may take only 30 minutes or so to complete. Remember that the goal is to continue to love learning, to know the joy of reading, and to gain knowledge in a relevant and memorable way. This study was designed to help you do each of these things, every day.

Remember, there's no prize for finishing first. Enjoy the learning journey. What you get out of any Five in a Row chapter book study is a direct reflection of what you put into it. You can use these lesson plans as a complete resource, checking them off your list as you complete them. Or you can use them as simply a "beginning point" from which to go on a wonderful learning journey. Move through subjects that are already familiar and then slow down to savor and enjoy topics of particular interest. The goal is to be learning every day, actively engaged in the process or expanding your knowledge, improving your character, and developing your gifts. The lessons in this unit are a great way to help you achieve all three of these goals.

Invest yourself in the process of learning. Spend time working on your research paper, mastering the steps to this important process. Pick a topic that genuinely interests you and your task will be much easier. Spend time developing a meaningful service project and work at serving others in a way that will be a blessing to both you and them. Some of these projects may far outlive your study of this book, becoming a part of your lifestyle for years to come. Most of all, enjoy the privilege of learning. Make the most of this opportunity and you will be rewarded in many ways!

Hitty: Her First Hundred Years

Title:	*Hitty: Her First Hundred Years*
Author:	Rachel Field
Copyright:	1929
Award:	Newbery Medal, 1930

172

Chapter One

"In Which I Begin My Memoirs"

Teacher Summary

In our first chapter, we meet the heroine of our story—Hitty. Hitty is a small doll, made of mountain-ash wood, who has experienced the most extraordinary travels in her first hundred years. Our story follows Hitty's life through her eyes.

We discover at the beginning of our story that Hitty has decided to record her memoirs. Currently, she resides in Miss Hunter's antique shop, but quickly we are taken back through time to Hitty's humble beginnings.

She was created for a small girl named Phoebe Preble. A local peddler carves Hitty out of mountain-ash wood and gives her the most beautiful face. Phoebe sews a simple dress for Hitty and the doll becomes part of the Preble family.

Hitty enjoys the Prebles and her memoirs are filled with specific details describing each member of the family, the home and their activities. Soon, Hitty experiences her first adventure. Phoebe Preble disobeys her mother and takes Hitty to church, tucked inside her muff. When the services end, Phoebe accidentally lets Hitty drop out of her muff and Hitty is stranded beneath a pew. She is there for several days and thinks all is lost, but finally Phoebe comes and claims her. As punishment for her disobedience, Phoebe must stitch a sampler and cannot play with Hitty until it is finished. Hitty doesn't mind because it is so nice to be home.

At the end of our chapter, we see Phoebe's father, Captain Preble, return home from sea. Phoebe quickly shows her father her new doll and the story of being lost at the church is retold with great dramatic skill.

What we will cover in this chapter:

Social Studies: History - The Time Frame of
  Our Story
Social Studies: History - Antiques
Social Studies: Geography - Ireland
Science: Bats
Science: Conch Shells
Language Arts: Point of View
Language Arts: Writing Your Own Memoirs
Language Arts: Onomatopoeia
Language Arts: Understanding Verse
Language Arts: Writing and Discussion Question
Language Arts: Vocabulary
Fine Arts: Quill Pens
Fine Arts: Drawing Animals More Realistically
Life Skills: Listening to Your Conscience
  Two Ongoing Projects:
Research Project: Beginning the Process*
Service Project: Choosing Your Service Project

Social Studies: History - The Time Frame of Our Story

As we begin our story with Hitty, the author chooses not to give us the specific year or decade the story takes place. Remember that the story begins with Hitty in Miss Hunter's antique shop. As Hitty begins to record her memoirs, the story jumps back to her creation 100 years before.

Since the author doesn't tell us directly what year it is, we must use context clues from the story to figure it out. What type of clues do you think we might be able to use?

Technology is often a good clue in stories. What types of inventions, cars, cooking utensils, etc., are they using in the story? When were those things invented? Fashion and food are also excellent clues used to deduce a time frame.

In our tale, we find two major clues early in the chapter. First, we read that Hitty enjoys using her quill pen instead of those "new-fangled" fountain pens. We also read that corsets and poke bonnets are very out of fashion. Both these clues can be used to help us figure out our time frame "mystery."

If we do our research, we can find that fountain pens were not perfected and sold until around 1900. If fountain pens were "new fangled" to Hitty, then we can assume our story begins sometime around 1900.

Also, we can infer from Hitty's comment about the corsets and poke bonnets that she herself remembers when these were in fashion. If we research poke bonnets, we discover that they were in fashion in the early 1800s. (As a side note, the word "poke" in the name of this bonnet refers to the fact that the hair could be poked up into the bonnet, thus concealing the entire hairstyle.)

Armed with both of these clues (technology and fashion) we can assume that our story begins around the turn of the 20th century. We can also deduce that when Hitty begins her memoirs, the time frame is around the beginning of the 19th century. So Hitty's story probably runs from around 1800 to around 1900.

We can discover the time frame of a story through context clues. Knowing a story's time frame makes enjoying and comprehending the story much easier!

Social Studies: History - Antiques

"The antique shop is very still now." Our story opens with Hitty in her present home—an antique shop. What is an antique? Something old? Something expensive? For an object to be considered an antique, people look at three different factors. They are: the age of the item, the artistic value of the item and the historic value of an item. As a rule of thumb, in the United States items over 100 years old are often considered antiques. Cars are considered antiques when they are 25-45 years old.

Look at the title of our story: *Hitty: Her First Hundred Years*. Hitty is a doll that is over 100 years old and, therefore, she is considered an antique!

An antique can be nearly any item that is from the past and has either artistic or historical value. For example, some antiques people seek out and collect include: quilts, flatware, cars, costumes, watches, tractors, toys, dolls, vases, needlework, knives, swords, tea cups, cars, etc. Antiques vary in monetary value depending upon the item, its age, the demand for that item and its quality.

Commercial objects and pop culture items that are collected (including baseball cards, stamps, limited edition figurines, bean bag dolls, etc.) are fun and worth money, but are not considered antiques. Instead, those items are called "collectibles."

If you are interested in antiques, or perhaps in starting a collection of your own, take an afternoon to visit a local antique shop. Make a list of the things you see. What items do you like the most? Did you see any dolls? Are they wooden like Hitty? Perhaps the shop owner would even take a few moments to share his experiences with you and what he enjoys collecting personally.

Learning about antiques will help you gain an appreciation of art, historic perspective and knowledge of other people's interests.

Ireland

Social Studies: Geography - Ireland

In this chapter, we learn the Old Peddler brought the mountain-ash wood used to carve Hitty across the sea from Ireland.

Ireland is often called "The Emerald Isle" because of its vibrant green hills. The grass covering these hills is particularly lush and colorful because of the moist climate. Look at a map or globe and find Ireland.

Ireland juts out into the Atlantic Ocean on the southeastern edge of the United Kingdom. For many years, the United Kingdom ruled Ireland, In 1921, however, the country was split in two. The lower half became known as the Independent Republic of Ireland. The upper portion is called "Northern Ireland" and is still ruled by the British. Tension is present between these two portions of Ireland. Many Irish people who reside in the Republic think that British rule is wrong and that Ireland should be free.

Find the city of Dublin. Dublin is the capital of Ireland and also the largest city. Nearly one-third of Ireland's population lives in Dublin.

Find a picture of Ireland's flag. Notice the three colors: green, white and orange. What do you think those colors represent? Green is the color of the original Irish clans. The white represents peace. Orange is the color of the province of Ulster. Ulster makes up the major portions of Northern Ireland. Why do you think designers chose white (peace) to be color between the green and orange? It signifies a hope for peace between "Orange" (Northern Ireland) and "Green" (The Independent Republic of Ireland). Remember, flags always tell stories!

Ireland has two official languages: Irish and English. Regardless of which language they speak, the Irish have a strong sense of community and family. They enjoy music and sports as entertainment. Have you ever heard of a musical "jig" or "reel?" These two terms are famous folksongs and dances started in Ireland. Seek out some Irish folk music and listen to these intricate and happy songs.

Sports are quite popular in Ireland. Gaelic football is a favorite sport. It is similar to a cross between American soccer and American football. The Irish also love hurling. Hurling is a fast, intense game involving throwing and kicking a ball, as well as moving the ball along the ground with a long bat called a "hurley." Ireland is also famous for more familiar games including soccer and golf, and fishing.

If you have enjoyed a glimpse into Ireland, you may wish to explore this fascinating country even further. A few topics which may interest you include agriculture, Irish folk music, Ireland's castles, the IRA (Irish Republican Army), and the strife between Catholic and Protestant groups.

Science: Bats

"Then there were the bats." Poor Hitty! Trapped in the church with bats flying about! Did you know that bats are the second most numerous type of mammal? (Rodents, such as mice and squirrels, are the most numerous of all mammals.) There are almost 1,000 different species of bats. Bats live on every continent in the world except Antarctica and on many of the islands.

Bats are the only mammals that can fly. Many people are frightened of bats but their fear is unfounded. Bats are harmless to humans and also help us a great deal! They eat many insects, including mosquitoes. Scientists estimate that one bat can catch over 500 mosquitoes in one hour! That is nearly one mosquito every eight seconds! Also, their manure (called "guano") helps farmers who use it in commercial fertilizers.

When you think of a bat, you probably picture a tiny fragile creature. This is an accurate picture of certain bats, including the brown bat which resides in the United States. The brown bat is about the size of your hand and has a wingspan of eight to 12 inches. The flying fox bat, however, has a body the size of a seagull and a wingspan of nearly five feet!

If you would like to know more about bats, you may wish to locate a copy of *Stellaluna* by Janell Cannon. This sweet and simple story centers on a small baby fruit bat who is adopted by birds. The story follows the baby bat until she finds her mother at the end. The book includes many factual notes about bats within the story, as well as two pages of scientific facts. The illustrator, Jewel Cannon, uses colored pencils and acrylic paints for the illustrations, making them appear to glow.

Science: Conch Shells

Rachel Field gives us a wonderful description of Miss Hunter's antique shop, doesn't she? Through Hitty's eyes, we are given a glimpse into the shop's treasures, including an old conch shell.

Have you heard of a conch? What does it look like? A conch (kahnk) is any large sea snail which lives in a heavy, spiraled shell. The most common conch is the pink conch (or queen conch). The shells are approximately one foot in length, and they are highly prized by collectors. The pink conch can be found mainly in the West Indies. Many people also value the snail as a source of food.

Conch shells are also the shells commonly used to "hear the ocean." Have you ever done this? By holding the shell over your ear, you can hear what sounds like the rushing of ocean waves. In reality, the echo of blood rushing through your ear canals causes this sound. But you can always imagine it is the lapping of waves where Miss Hunter may have found that conch shell.

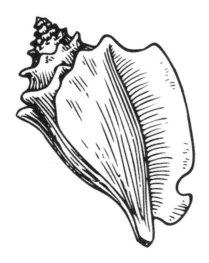

Language Arts: Point of View

Who is the main character in our story so far? Who is describing the story for us? The answer to these questions is, of course, Hitty. When we read this book, we are hearing the story from Hitty's point of view.

As you practice your creative writing techniques, one decision you must always make is the point of view. Will you use first person (words like I and me, just as Hitty does in our story) or will you use third person (using words like he and she)?

You could look at books you may have studied in previous Five in a Row lessons as examples. The author of *Sarah, Plain and Tall*, for instance, uses first person. (Anna, the main character, speaks in first person.) In *Homer Price*, however, Robert McCloskey employs third person.

The character you choose for the point of view is an important decision. Think about our story, *Hitty: Her First Hundred Years*. How would the story be different if it were told from Mr. Preble's point of view? Mrs. Preble's? The Old Peddler's? Notice the point of view of the next story you read.

Language Arts: Writing Your Own Memoirs

When a person writes a book about his own life, we call this an "autobiography." Specific accounts within that work are called "memoirs."

Our book is a fictional tale. Hitty is not a real doll and, of course, dolls cannot think and speak like Hitty does. Our book is, however, a fictional autobiography. Hitty writes about her life using a quill pen in Miss Hunter's antique shop. She writes her memoirs so we will be able to see what has happened in her life.

Anyone can write his or her own memoirs—even you! Many students (and adults) keep journals or diaries. Memoirs are similar with one exception. A person generally assumes no one will ever read his diary, but memoirs are written specifically for others' enjoyment.

Are you interested in trying your hand at writing a memoir? Would you prefer to try a factual memoir or fictional memoir? Would you rather use yourself as the main character or another person?

Write about whatever you think would be interesting to someone else. If you enjoy this assignment, you might want to consider keeping a small paper or digital notebook titled "My Memoirs." Who knows? Perhaps people will read these written sketches of your life someday—just as we are reading Hitty's.

Language Arts: Onomatopoeia

Onomatopoeia is a word whose sound suggests the sound it refers to. In this chapter, we read: "...the whistle of the whip as the Old Peddler cracked it, and the gay tinkle-tankle of our sleigh bells."

The words "tinkle-tankle" are an example of onomatopoeia. Can you think of other examples?

"Hoot," said the owl.
The rain went splish-splash on the windowpane.
The glass of cola fizzed merrily.

Try to employ onomatopoeia in your own stories.

Language Arts: Understanding Verse

Phoebe Preble is stitching faithfully on her sampler. Phoebe disobeyed her mother and the consequence was working that sampler. You probably read over the poem on the sampler quickly. Did you understand what it means?

Young people often read poetry verse so quickly they don't take the time to understand what the poem is saying. You often need to take special care to understand ideas when you read poetry. This special care is required because poetry reduces thoughts to just a few words and uses various literary devices such as personification. Using Phoebe's sampler as an example, take time to understand this verse more thoroughly:

Conscience distasteful truths may tell,
But mark her sacred lesson well.
Whoever lives with her at strife
Loses his better friend for life.

In the second line, to whom or what does the word "her" refer? In the fourth line, to whom is "his" referring? Who is the "better friend?"

In this poem, personification is being used. Instead of talking about a person's conscience as an idea, this poem describes conscience as a woman. The words "her" refer to the conscience. The words "whoever" and "his" refer to the person who has the conscience.

Just because we read the words or even memorize a poem doesn't always mean we've taken the time and given the necessary thought to understand it fully. This is true in all writing but sometimes even more so with poetry.

The book tells us that Phoebe knew this verse "by heart." Do you think Phoebe really knew what the poem meant?

Language Arts: Writing and Discussion Question

How do you think Miss Hunter acquired Hitty for her antique shop? Write about it. Hint: You will discover how she did at the end of our book, but don't peek! Instead, when you reach the end of the book, compare your idea with Hitty's memoir.

Language Arts: Vocabulary

Note: The vocabulary words in this unit are taken from our book. If you come across a word you don't know in the chapter you're reading, check the vocabulary list to see if it's defined there. You'll also find an activity sheet following Chapter 2 that applies to all vocabulary words in this unit.

confidante   A person we trust with our secrets.

infirmity   An illness or weakness.

memoir   A short biographical or autobiographical account.

muff   A covering (usually fur) which has openings at both ends for a woman's (or little girl's) hands; used to keep the hands warm.

prowlishly   Behaving like a prowler; sneaking around.

reprove   To find fault with; to show disapproval.

tippet   A scarf.

wadgetty   To be impatient; inability to sit still.

Fine Arts: Quill Pens

Hitty seems to enjoy writing her memoirs almost as much as we enjoy reading them, doesn't she? And she certainly enjoys using her old quill pen instead of those "new-fangled" fountain pens.

Have you ever seen or used a quill pen? Quill pens were first developed in 500 B.C. and were used nearly exclusively until the mid- to late-1800s. People used the wing feathers of birds such as geese, ducks and swans. They dried the feather, cut and shaped the end of the quill and then used it to dip in ink and write.

We read about Hitty sitting by a "spattered square of green blotting paper" and a "pewter inkstand." When you use a quill pen, the ink is "loaded" onto the quill by dipping the end into a small container of ink. After the ink has been loaded, it is important to blot the very tip of the quill gently onto paper in order to remove excess ink and prepare the tip for writing.

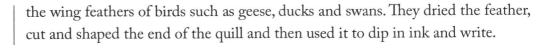

Would you like to try your hand at using a quill pen? They are fairly easy to make. Locate a large duck or goose wing feather. These can sometimes be obtained from farms or petting zoos. They can also be purchased at many art supply, science or nature stores. You will also need to purchase some ink at an art or office supply store. Blotting paper can be whatever paper you choose (newsprint works well).

You will need to slice the tip of the quill at an angle in order to create a pen. The tip of the quill pen is called the **nib**. Search online for "how to make a quill pen" for more detailed instructions.

You may enjoy trying to write like Hitty with your newly-made quill pen—you may even want to use it to write your own memoirs!

Fine Arts: Drawing Animals More Realistically

Our illustrator for *Hitty* is Dorothy P. Lathrop. Find the picture that shows Hitty and an adorable, furry chipmunk. Look at the chipmunk's fur. Notice how Lathrop uses her pen to draw the fur. Each line on the hindquarters, head, back and tail goes in a specific direction. This technique gives a realistic look to the creature. This is the way a chipmunk's fur really grows. There is another example of this technique in chapter 13 with field mice as the subject.

Try this technique: Using white paper and a rolling ink pen, trace the chipmunk in this chapter (or draw it freehand if you'd like). Now, using the same pen, try to copy Lathrop's technique by drawing the animal's fur with directional strokes. When you finish with the fur, look at the chipmunk's eye in the book. Notice how the illustrator drew the eye with a specific shape. Notice how she uses white highlights to accent the eyes and make them appear brighter. Now try drawing the eyes on your chipmunk.

Learning to draw animals in a more realistic manner is easier when you observe and mimic the technique of great artists!

Life Skills: Listening to your Conscience

Phoebe Preble struggles to decide whether or not to obey her mother (and the rules of their faith) and not play with Hitty. Unfortunately, Phoebe falls victim to temptation and disobeys.

This chapter offers an excellent opportunity to revisit the subject of conscience. It can be difficult sometimes to do the right thing. It is also important. Phoebe would have been so much happier if she had just obeyed. Hitty would have been safe in the drawer that evening—all ready to play with!

Hearing that "little voice" we call our conscience is what makes us human. Hitty, a doll, has no conscience. An animal doesn't have a conscience either. Knowing the difference between right and wrong and having the ability to choose elevates us above other living creatures. And choosing what is right can make us noble! You must listen and obey your conscience when you are faced with a decision like Phoebe's.

Two Ongoing Projects:

Research Project: Beginning the Process*

In this Five in an Row unit, you have the opportunity to write a research paper. It may be your very first project of this kind and it will be challenging, but it can be enjoyable! In the activity sheet for this chapter, you will find an outline taking you through each of the important steps in the writing process. You can use this as a quick reminder page as you write, but you will also find reminder lessons throughout this study. These lessons will serve to encourage you and remind you of what stage you should be at as you write. (You could also choose to do the research paper at the end of this unit, after completing the other lessons.) Here are five research paper topics to choose from for this study. If you have an idea for a topic of your own, feel free to discuss it with your parent/teacher and use it instead.

The History of Whaling Ships
The Caribbean
Charles Dickens
Antique Dolls of the 1800s
Coral Reefs

As you read the story, you will see where these topics come into play in Hitty's tale. You can begin the writing process by fulfilling the first step: prewriting.

Prewriting is doing your background research. If, for example, you chose the topic of coral reefs for your research paper, you will want to find out as much as you can about your topic. Look for library books, internet sites, and videos about coral reefs. Begin formulating questions you will want to answer in your paper: Where are coral reefs located in the world? What kinds of coral reefs are there? How do the reefs differ? What animals live there? What do people get from coral reefs? How are coral reefs being destroyed or maintained? Remember that your information can be from both primary and secondary sources. **Primary sources** are direct quotes gathered by interviewing people. **Secondary sources** come from written or audiovisual material. The majority of your sources will be secondary, but primary resources give your paper a fresh and immediate feel that readers appreciate. Interviewing someone directly also gives you a much better feel for your topic.

This process of research and gathering will help you form the main point of your paper. This main point is called your **thesis**. A thesis is the central statement of your paper. As you perform your early research, make sure to do two things: **make notes** of everything you've found that might prove helpful or interesting in your writing, and **make a bibliography** of all the books you've found for information, as well as any articles or videos. In this way, you can quickly refer back to them as you are writing instead of wondering, "Where was that article I found?" This bibliography will also prove important to your writing if you decide to quote from any other book or article. You can give attribution to the author of the text instead of plagiarizing. **Plagiarizing** means to write using someone else's words without saying who originally wrote the text.

You will see a few more reminders throughout this unit that will help you keep focused on your writing project. By the end of this project, you should have a paper you can feel really proud of to show to others. Enjoy the process!

Service Project: Choosing Your Service Project

Every day countless opportunities arise where we can help out and serve others. As a part of this unit, you will have several service projects to choose from. If it is something you want to work on alone, feel free. If your family would like to undertake the project together, all the better! Helping others makes us feel good because we know we're doing something to make a difference.

Here are three ideas to consider for your service project:

1. Making/collecting new or gently used dolls and teddy bears for area children's hospitals/police stations. Contact a nearby children's hospital and see if they accept donations of dolls and teddy bears to give their patients. Children who are in the hospital are scared and sick. Think how much a friendly face like Hitty's could brighten their day! Police stations may also accept these toys to give to children who have been involved in a violent or emergency situation. Giving a small toy to a child whose parents are missing will help comfort him in a crisis situation. You can either make the dolls and teddy bears, or collect them. You will probably find many, many individuals and families who are interested in either donating dolls or money to buy dolls that will be given to charities. You may even be able to contact a company you know of that makes dolls or teddy bears and get them to contribute their products.

2. Helping nursing home residents write letters to friends and families. Can you imagine wanting to share something with your mother or brother and being unable to hold a pencil steady to write them a letter? How tragic and frustrating! By going to an area nursing home and volunteering your writing services, you can help some lovely people say hello to their friends and family by writing the letters for them. Just like Hitty's memoirs, you will probably learn a great deal about each person as you write his/her letters. You will learn about his life and his history. It will be as fascinating to you as it will be a service to them.

3. Achieving your CPR and/or Red Cross certification so you will be ready to help those in need. You never know when someone in distress may require your help. Having these skills at your fingertips will be a wonderful asset.

Any of these ideas would make an excellent choice for a semester service project. You may also think of other options, such as serving in an animal shelter, volunteering at a community garden, working with an organization that is already serving in some way, etc. This project could take you through this unit, but if you find it something you truly love and you're making a good contribution, you may wish to continue your work for some time. Go and serve with joy!

Chapter Two

"In Which I Go Up in the World and Am Glad to Come Down Again"

Teacher Summary

In our second chapter, we find Phoebe Preble and the Prebles' houseboy, Andy, picking raspberries. The day is fine and Hitty is along for the trip. Suddenly, some Indian wives come into the thicket and frighten the two children away. Hitty is unfortunately abandoned in the confusion.

Hitty is convinced Phoebe will return to look for her, but before that can happen a large crow swoops down and picks her up in its large beak. The Mother Crow carries Hitty to her nest where she deposits her alongside her three babies.

Hitty remains in the nest for several days until she is finally able to drag herself up to the edge of the nest. When she looks over the side, she realizes the Mother Crow's nest is located near the top of the ancestral pine tree on the Preble's property. Hitty is close enough to Phoebe's house she could throw a pebble at it!

Overjoyed, she decides her only chance to be found is to hurdle her body over the edge of the nest and hope she is discovered down below. Unfortunately, she doesn't fall clear to the ground but, instead, falls onto another branch and is stuck. Thankfully, Andy soon discovers Hitty in the branches and after much work on the part of the entire family, Hitty is returned to Phoebe. Her clothes are ripped, but she is safe.

What we will cover in this chapter:

Social Studies: Native Americans
Science: Prairie Flowers
Language Arts: Foreshadowing
Language Arts: Writing and Discussion Questions
Language Arts: Vocabulary*
Fine Arts: Cooking - Raspberries
Life Skills: Courage
Life Skills: Racism and Words

Social Studies: Native Americans

Hitty, Phoebe and Andy are all surprised by the small group of Native American wives at the raspberry patch. These women are a part of the Passamaquoddy (PASS uh muh KWAH dee) tribe. The Passamaquoddies are an Indian nation that resides in and around the state of Maine. Their name, Passamaquoddy, literally means "plenty-pollock-place," or "people who fish for pollock." The Passamaquoddy tribe still resides in Maine and has a voice in the state legislature.

There are many ways you can explore the vast topic of Native Americans. For example, you may wish to learn about other Native American tribes/nations and where they live. A fun activity to use for this lesson would include a small United States map and tracing paper the same size. You can lay the tracing paper over the map and mark out the territories and regions different tribes once inhabited.

You might also be interested in researching which Native American tribes still exist and where, the daily lives of Native Americans in pre-Revolutionary War America (or pre-Mayflower America), particular tribes that lived or live near your own area of the country, etc.

Science: Prairie Flowers

Chapter 2 begins with a beautiful description of prairie flowers blooming in Maine. List the flowers mentioned in this chapter and look them up online. Each is unique and beautiful!

If you completed the *Sarah, Plain and Tall* unit study from FIAR Vol. 6, you remember working on a prairie notebook—recording different nature references covered in that book. You may want to refer to those lessons and review the information you gathered then.

For now, research one or more of the flowers listed. See what facts you discover. For example, if you were to choose the buttercup, you might report the following:

Buttercup

• The buttercup is also known as the crowfoot. The scientific name is ranunculus aeris. Buttercups get their name from their bright yellow color.
• Each buttercup is made up of five shiny petals.
• Buttercups can grow up to four feet tall. Farmers consider buttercups annoying weeds. Cattle and other animals won't eat buttercups because of their bitter taste.
• An old folk game suggests if you hold a buttercup under someone's chin and his chin looks yellow, he likes butter.

You may also wish to draw or paint an example of the flower you explored.

Language Arts: Foreshadowing

Hitty writes, "I felt suddenly bereft and very small indeed. But this was nothing to what I was about to feel."

When you read that sentence, what do you think? It probably makes you think something even more dra-matic is about to happen. Our author, Rachel Field, does an excellent job at tucking in exciting tidbits throughout our story. This way of suggesting what is to come later in a story by giving hints and clues is a literary device known as foreshadowing.

Here's another example of foreshadowing, from chapter 1: "How strange it seems to remember those words now! How little we thought then of all that was so soon to befall us!"

Foreshadowing is an excellent tool to employ when you write fiction. It gives the reader a clue of what is to come, which keeps him reading. It also gives the reader a sense of the unknown that can be very exciting!

Compose a short story or fictional essay. Try your hand at foreshadowing. Then, continue looking for Rachel Field's use of foreshadowing throughout our story.

Language Arts: Writing and Discussion Questions

1. Think about Hitty's comment, "...feeling things behind one is always so much more terrifying than when they actually appear." When have you had this experience? What was something you were frightened about but when it actually happened was not as bad as you had feared? Write about it. (See the Life Skills: Courage lesson below for more thoughts on this topic.)

2. After Hitty is saved, Captain Preble says, "More'n one way to harpoon your whale...and more'n one use for a doughnut fork!" What do you think he means? Write about a time when you discovered this to be true.

Language Arts: Vocabulary*

bereft   Deprived; without.

cove   A small bay; mouth of a creek.

disconsolately   Being without hope.

dory   A small rowboat used by fishermen.

foraging   Hunting or searching for food.

ignominiously   With shame and disgrace.

gig   A light, open, two-wheeled carriage pulled by one horse.

gullet   The esophagus.

tantalizing   Enticing; tempting.

turnpike   A road that has, or used to have, a gate where toll was collected.

Fine Arts: Cooking - Raspberries

Phoebe and Andy are certainly tenacious in their search for raspberries, aren't they? Raspberries are a delicious treat. Pick some fresh raspberries if you are able, or get a pint from your local grocery store or market. You can enjoy the same delicacy Phoebe surely did while picking that day!

Also, why not take this opportunity to try your hand at making muffins or preserves? Any fruit muffin recipe (such as blueberry) can be easily adapted to incorporate raspberries—simply substitute the fruit you want to use. Below you will find a recipe for raspberry preserves—probably quite similar to what Mrs. Preble made. This recipe is fast and easy. It uses the freezer instead of traditional canning techniques, making it great for the student chef. You will be so pleased to surprise family and friends with your new creation!

Raspberry Preserves

4 cups raspberries
4 cups sugar
1/4 tsp. finely shredded lemon peel
1/2 (6 oz.) pkg. liquid fruit pectin (1 foil pouch)
2 Tbs. lemon juice

Crush the raspberries; measure 2 cups berries. In a bowl, combine berries, sugar and lemon peel. Let stand 10 minutes.

Combine pectin and lemon juice. Add to the berry mixture; stir for 3 minutes.

Ladle at once into jars or freezer containers, leaving a 1/2-inch headspace. Seal; label. Let stand at room temperature about 2 hours or until jam is set. Store up to three weeks in the refrigerator or one year in the freezer. This recipe makes four half-pints.

Life Skills: Courage

In two different sections of this chapter, we see the subject of courage addressed. First, we see Hitty abandoned in the raspberry patch and we read, "... feeling things behind one is always so much more terrifying than when they actually appear."

Think about that sentence. Do you think this is true? Are things we imagine often more terrifying than reality? What can we learn from Hitty's comment? It is important to remember it takes courage to face things directly. When we do, however, the situation or person is often not nearly as frightening or upsetting as we imagined.

Later in the chapter, we hear Hitty quoting a favorite motto of Captain Preble's: "Nothing venture, nothing have." Have you heard the modern version of this motto—"Nothing ventured, nothing gained?" Think about this motto. What is it really saying? Risking takes courage, but with risks we often discover great things.

Think of a time in your life when you took a risk and it paid off. Were you frightened? What happened in the end?

Life Skills: Racism and Words

Chapter 2 provides you with an excellent opportunity to discuss racism with your parents/teacher. Racism can be found in language as well as in historic context in books.

In this chapter, we see Phoebe and Andy frightened by five Native American (called "Indians" at the time) wives coming through the thicket. Both children repeatedly use the racial epithet "injun." Today, we find this word offensive. Just like other racial slurs, this word would be inappropriate and destructive for any child or adult to use. Have you ever heard someone use words like this? What was the situation? How did it make you feel?

Prejudice is at the root of racial slurs and feelings. Consider the word "prejudice." A prejudice is a "*pre-judged* opinion." When you prejudge something it means you have formed an opinion without knowing about it. People often form prejudices from environmental influences, i.e., their parents, their friends and where they live. There are different kinds of prejudice. Physical prejudice is prejudging someone based on his or her appearance. Mental prejudice is prejudging someone based on their perceived intelligence, how well they think, etc. Sexual prejudice is prejudging someone based on his or her gender. Age prejudice is prejudging someone based on his or her age. Racial prejudice is prejudging people based on their ethnicity (like the Passamoquaddy women in our story).

It is important also to learn about **discrimination**. Prejudice leads to discrimination. Discrimination can cause people to be left out of groups, activities, living situations, jobs and more. When you discriminate against someone, you deny him his rights and you can deprive yourself of having a relationship with that person—a relationship that could be wonderful and enriching. Discrimination is not only against the law, but it is wrong.

This chapter also raises the issue of historical context in stories. If it is wrong to use the word "injun" or "squaw," you may wonder why our author uses such language. Today, we better understand the hurtful and destructive result of racial slurs. In our story, the year is sometime during the early 19th century—more than 200 years ago.. These terms and others were commonplace. If you have ever heard of or read the book *The Adventures of Tom Sawyer* by Mark Twain, you may remember that the character "Injun Joe" plays a large part in the plot of that book. When was that book written? 1876. Historical context is applicable in that example, as well. Historical context doesn't make racial slurs and prejudice right, but it does serve as an explanation.

Strive to avoid prejudice and discrimination in your own heart. It is also important for you to stand up for people who are victims of discrimination. If we learn to appreciate our differences, we can begin enjoying each other.

Chapter Three

"In Which I Travel—by Land and Sea"

Teacher Summary

The long stay with the crows ruins Hitty's dress, so Mrs. Preble kindly makes her new garments. Phoebe is thrilled to have her doll back at home, and Hitty is equally thrilled to be home. The Preble family gets back to a normal routine and Captain Preble prepares for a new whaling voyage.

His ship, the *Diana-Kate*, is being outfitted in Boston for her next voyage. Captain Preble decides he needs to go to Boston in order to oversee the work. He invites his wife, daughter and Andy along for the ride. While in Boston, Captain Preble realizes he needs more sailors. He also has trouble finding a cook for the ship. He asks Mrs. Preble if she would be willing to come. She agrees and soon Hitty and Phoebe are preparing for their first step onto a whaling ship.

What we will cover in this chapter:

Social Studies: History - Whaling
Social Studies: History - Ships
Social Studies: Geography - Northeast
  United States
Science: Motion Sickness*
Language Arts: Greek Mythology - Diana
Language Arts: Sea Jargon
Language Arts: Writing and Discussion Question
Language Arts: Vocabulary
Fine Arts: Cooking - Homemade Gingerbread
Fine Arts: Illustrating Text

Social Studies: History - Whaling

The Prebles' voyage on the *Diana-Kate* will be a whaling adventure. You are probably unfamiliar with whaling, so take this opportunity to learn more about these historic hunting expeditions.

Native Americans were the first people in the United States to take part in whaling. Instead of going out in ships, they hunted whales from the shore—mostly baleen whales, including the bowhead, humpback and right whales. These whales lived close to shore and were fairly small (around 50 feet long). By the 1600s, American colonists were also trying their hands at whaling near shore. They, too, hunted the baleen whales. The work was long and hard and the baleen whales produced very little oil.

It wasn't until 1712 that a whaling ship brought back a new species of whale never hunted before—the sperm whale. It was much larger than the baleens, had more teeth and produced a great deal of oil. The sperm whale's head held a large amount of oil called "spermaceti." The discovery of the sperm whale began what became a huge whaling industry. Suddenly, whaling became profitable. The oil from the sperm whale was put to many uses, including lubricants, lamp fuel, candles and even a base for expensive perfumes. Sperm whales were much larger than the baleen whales and were worth much more money for the sailors who hunted them. The whaling voyages changed. People no longer hunted from shore (sperm whales live far out in the ocean), but, instead, began to set up long sea voyages (like Captain Preble's) lasting from months to years in length!

The life of a whaler was difficult and dangerous. The following quote is from *Clippers and Whaling Ships* by Tim McNeese:

"Whaling ships were not known for their comfort. Crews were not paid well. Even as late as 1860 a regular seaman on a whaling ship was paid only about 20 cents a day. An unskilled worker on land could receive nearly a dollar a day. Many whaling ships carried crew who were taken from the lower classes...Rendering the blubber made deck life difficult for sailors, and not only because of the smell. The oil coated the deck, making walking hard. Oil fires sometimes occurred, setting oil-soaked decks ablaze. Then there were the rats and roaches. Whale oil and blood attracted them. Cats were brought onboard to kill the rats. Nothing could be done to combat the cockroaches. The freezing temperatures of the waters around Cape Horn killed some of them. But in the Pacific they bred wildly. And they grew—some of them were 1 1/2 inches long! Their most annoying habit was to crawl into sleeping sailors' beards in search of food particles."

Several things contributed to the slow decline of whaling in the United States. The first came in 1849. Perhaps you have studied the California Gold Rush. This dramatic event in the middle of the 19th century lured many of the captains and sailors from their whaling work to the gold-laden hills of California. This proved to be a downfall for the whaling industry. Then, just a short time later, during the Civil War, ships from the South sank many whaling ships. This again hurt the whaling industry tremendously. Finally, in 1859, petroleum was discovered in Pennsylvania. This new fuel, called kerosene, began being used almost exclusively instead of whale oil. By 1920, there were only two commercial whaling ship outfits still working in the United States.

The whaling industry sealed its own fate, as well. Because so many whales were being caught as the harpooning and other technology modernized, many species of whales bordered on extinction. The sperm, right and humpback whales were particularly hard hit. The United States government began to realize the problems and in 1971 passed a law making all commercial whaling illegal. The government also banned any importation of whale oil products. The only exception to this law applies to native people who depend on whales for their food and supplies, and who hunt within certain parameters. These people would include the Inuit Indians (also called Eskimos) who live in Alaska. You might want to research to find which other countries today still allow whaling—there are very few.

An obvious connection with our story and this lesson is the book *Moby-Dick*. The author, Herman Melville, spent many years sailing around the world and experienced exciting moments on different whaling ships. This book is considered one of the best books ever written but it is quite long. If you're interested in reading it, there are many good, abridged versions available.

If you want to expand this lesson further, look for books on whaling at your library, or research articles or videos online. As you study whaling, you will be amazed at this fascinating piece of history.

Social Studies: History - Ships

We see magnificent descriptions of the *Diana-Kate* in this and subsequent chapters. If you are interested in learning more about ships, look online or at your library for books on ships or the history of ships, paying special attention to books that have cross-section illustrations so you can see inside each level of the vessels. Topics to study also might include floating, displacement, hulls,

190

rowboats, sailing a boat, submarines and more. You can also research different kinds of ships, including clipper, whaling, and packet ships. You might want to sketch, draw, or copy and paste different kinds of ships or cross-sections onto posterboard and include information about each.

Social Studies: Geography - Northeast United States

Although our story is certainly fiction (dolls can't really speak or write!), it is definitely grounded in realism. Hitty's travels take her to real cities and ports. This would be an excellent opportunity to review the northeastern region of the United States. In this chapter, we see the following cities discussed:

Portland, Maine
Boston, Massachusetts
Portsmouth, Maine
Salem, Massachusetts

Print out a blank regional map of the northeastern U.S. Label the states accordingly and then write in the different cities we read about. Do a simple report on one or more of them and include on your map a few symbols to depict things you have learned. For example, a small picture of a cup of tea might be appropriate to put near Boston (i.e., the Boston Tea Party). Another example would be to place a small gavel near Salem (i.e., the Salem Witchcraft Trials).

Science: Motion Sickness*

Phoebe and Hitty are both excited to be a part of this new adventure on the *Diana-Kate*! Unfortunately, Phoebe's first few days on the ship are marred by motion sickness:

"...After we had been jolting and rumbling along for about an hour she complained of not feeling well... none [of the home remedies] made her feel any better. She grew very pale and was glad to lie still with closed eyes as we rolled along at a fine pace.

"'I am afraid,' her mother told the other ladies with a doleful head shake, 'that she must have inherited a weak stomach. It runs in our family.'"

Phoebe is suffering from motion sickness. You may have heard it called carsickness or seasickness. You may have even experienced this uncomfortable feeling. Do you know what causes it?

Motion sickness is when motion causes a person to have nausea and dizziness. Often the ill person becomes pale (just like Phoebe) and may perspire. If the motion continues, the person may vomit. Generally, if the motion stops, the symptoms go away after a few hours. If you are on a ship, like Phoebe, and the motion persists, the body will generally adjust after several days and the symptoms slowly disappear.

To understand why motion sickness happens, it is important to understand what gives us our sense of balance. The organs that control our sense of balance are located in our inner ear. These organs are called our **vestibular system**. The vestibular system is made up of tiny organs and semi-circular canals. This system of organs, along with our eyes and other nerve endings, reports to our brains what is happening around our body. The brain then responds by positioning our body to match up with the movement. We get sick when the movement or motion exceeds the limits that our inner ear and other organs can accurately report to our brains. The brain doesn't understand and our body begins to feel "off balance." This is what creates the dizziness and nausea.

It makes sense, then, that in order to prevent motion sickness (or lessen the symptoms) it is important to keep the head as motionless as possible. This is why Phoebe felt better lying down. If you are in a car or plane and cannot lie down, the best option is to keep your head pointing straight ahead and rest it against the back of your seat.

If you are interested in exploring this topic further, you may want to look into the vestibular system, the brain's role in balance and even how drugs such as Dramamine™ help prevent motion sickness. (Clue: These drugs depress the central nervous system in the human body so the conflicting motion information between eyes, ears and brain are not noticeable.)

Language Arts: Greek Mythology - Diana

Why did Mrs. Preble refuse to step foot on Mr. Preble's ship? She didn't like the name of the ship—the *Diana*. She seems to think the name is "un-Christian."

The ship's name, *Diana*, is the Roman name for the Greek mythological goddess, Artemis. Diana is often depicted wearing hunting clothes and carrying a bow and quiver. She was the daughter of Jupiter (Greek name: Zeus) and the twin sister of the god Apollo.

If you are interested in reading some of the myths surrounding Diana, an excellent resource is *D'Aulaires' Book of Greek Myths* by Ingri and Edgar d'Aulaire. This book has been recommended in previous Five in a Row volumes, as well. It's a classic, illustrated title that is a perfect introduction to the topic of Greek mythology, for all ages.

Throughout your future studies, whether in high school or college, you're likely to come across allusions (literary references) to names of Greek and Roman gods and goddesses in many contexts. Becoming familiar with some of their names will make your future learning more enjoyable and easier to understand.

Language Arts: Sea Jargon

Rachel Field has a remarkable ability to create a complete and accurate setting for her characters. We really believe Hitty and her friends are aboard the *Diana-Kate*. We like the sailors and Captain Preble—the way the men speak and the activities they do each day. One thing that helps us feel this reality is the jargon Rachel Field uses in our story. **Jargon** is a word that means the language of a specific group, profession or activity. In *Hitty*, we see excellent examples of what we will call "sea jargon"— words that are specific to seafarers, ships, sailing, whaling, etc.

It is strongly encouraged that you put together a "Sea Journal" for your study of *Hitty*. You can include terms and jargon, observations, pictures, clippings, drawings, poems, artwork, etc.

The following terms are in two categories. One is ship jargon, and the other is sea jargon. For the first category, it might be helpful and fun to find, draw or trace a ship (preferably a whaling ship) and label all the terms we'll be learning on the drawing.

Ship Jargon

cabin: a private room on a ship

cabin boy: a boy or man whose work is serving the officers and passengers of a ship

cargo: the load of goods carried by the ship

crew: the men required to work a ship

"fitting out": equipping the ship with all the things required for a voyage

hull: the main body and frame of a ship

mast: a long, upright pole of wood or metal in the middle of a ship used to support the sails and rigging

masthead lantern: a lantern hung from the top of the mast

stern: the rear part of a ship

"weigh anchor": to pull up the anchor in order to set sail

chart: a map used by sailors to show the rocks, shallow places and coasts of the sea. A ship's course is marked on a chart.

gale: a strong wind

harbor: an area of deep water, protected from wind, providing a place of shelter for ships

port: a place where ships and boats can load and unload cargo

wharves: platforms built on or near the shore where ships can pull up and load and unload their cargo

Throughout the next several chapters, you will see lessons entitled "Sea Jargon." These are more terms that you should include in your journal.

Language Arts: Writing and Discussion Question

Captain Preble loves his ship, the *Diana-Kate*. What would your dream ship be like? What would its name be? Where would you sail? Write about it.

Language Arts: Vocabulary

doleful   Sad or dreary.

Fine Arts: Cooking - Homemade Gingerbread

The Prebles enjoy a delectable treat of cider and gingerbread at Cousin Robinson's on Congress Street. The gingerbread of that time (the early 19th century) was different than what we think of today. Instead of crispy gingerbread cookies, gingerbread was a warm, soft cake. Here is a recipe which is probably quite similar to what the Prebles enjoyed. Perhaps you would like to fix this along with a mug of cider to enjoy while you work through a few of these lessons!

Cousin Robinson's Gingerbread

Preheat the oven to 350°.

In a pan, melt 1/2 cup butter over medium heat; allow to cool. Add 1/2 cup sugar and 1 egg; beat well. Set aside.

Mix the following dry ingredients together:
2 1/2 cups flour
1 1/2 tsp. baking soda
1 tsp. each cinnamon and ginger
1/2 tsp. salt

Mix the following wet ingredients together:
1/2 cup dark molasses
1/2 cup honey
1 cup hot water
1 Tbs. orange rind (optional)

Add the dry and wet ingredients alternately to the butter mixture until just blended. Bake in a greased 9"x9" pan for about 1 hour. Serve warm, plain or with a bit of whipped cream. Delicious!

Fine Arts: Illustrating Text

Our author does a wonderful job of describing the magnificent stagecoach the Prebles take. Look back at that description:

"There are no such stagecoaches nowadays, or such fine, prancing horses to draw them. This one was painted red and yellow, and the four horses were matched in pairs, two grays and two chestnuts. The spokes of the wheels were painted black and when they turned very fast it made one quite dizzy, especially if one hung out of the window and looked down."

194

Consider an illustrator's goal. An illustrator wants to enrich the text, but stay true to what the author has written. For example, if there were a picture of the stagecoach described in that paragraph which had four black horses, the reader would be confused. The author specifically says, "two grays and two chestnuts." On the other hand, the author doesn't give any details as to how tall, broad, well groomed, clad, etc., the horses are. These things are left to the illustrator's imagination! Our author specifically states the colors of the stagecoach—red and yellow. The illustrator has that parameter, but can then decide exactly how he thinks that stagecoach might look.

Try illustrating this portion of text. If you don't know what a stagecoach looks like, find a picture to use as reference. Remember to remain true to the text, but to enrich the picture with your own creative choices.

Chapter 4

"In Which We Go to Sea"

Teacher Summary

Hitty, Phoebe and Mrs. Preble soon grow accustomed to sailing on the *Diana-Kate*. They learn all the sailors' names and a few of them even become close friends. Hitty and Phoebe particularly like Bill Buckle and Jeremy Folger.

After many days of smooth and beautiful sailing, the weather turns rough. The *Diana-Kate* rises and plunges in the crashing waves. Soon the sailors and Captain Preble are working around the clock trying to keep the ship safe.

Finally the storm quiets down, and although the crew lost the main topmast of the ship, they are safe. The voyage will continue!

What we will cover in this chapter:

Social Studies: Geography - Cape Hatteras
Social Studies: History - Horsehair
Science: Ocean Waves
Science: The Science of Sailing
Language Arts: Characters - Dynamic, Static and Stereotypical*
Language Arts: Sea Jargon
Language Arts: Writing and Discussion Question
Language Arts: Vocabulary
Research Project: Creating Your Writing Plan*
Service Project: Initiating and Beginning Your Project

Social Studies: Geography - Cape Hatteras

The first days of the whaling voyage on the *Diana-Kate* go smoothly. Phoebe and Hitty enjoy the new sights and adventures the trip affords them. Andy warns them the smooth days may come to an end when they get near Cape Hatteras.

Look at the coastline of North Carolina on a United States map. Cape Hatteras (HAT uhr uhs) is located at the southeastern tip of the Hatteras Islands.

Andy was right when he warned the girls of the possible danger of Cape Hatteras. Cape Hatteras is known as the "Graveyard of the Atlantic" due to the strong winds, waves and shallow areas (called **shoals**).

Social Studies: History - Horsehair

Phoebe and Hitty spend their first few nights aboard the *Diana-Kate* on a horsehair sofa located in the aftercabin. Horsehair was used as an upholstery covering throughout the 19th century. Just as the book describes, horsehair furniture is very slippery. It can be difficult to stay seated on furniture covered in horsehair, but it can also be fun!

Perhaps you remember another famous literary reference to horsehair furniture. Laura Ingalls Wilder wrote a famous and delightful series of books—the *Little House* series. In the third volume, *Farmer Boy*, Laura Ingalls Wilder describes the childhood of her husband, Almanzo Wilder. In that book, set in the late 19th century (approximately the same time frame as our story), she writes about Almanzo's experience with a horsehair chair. Here is the reference:

"They tiptoed in, without making a sound. The light was dim because the blinds were down, but the parlor was beautiful. The wallpaper was white and gold and the carpet was of Mother's best weaving, almost too fine to step on. The center-table was marble-topped, and it held the tall parlor lamp, all white-and-gold china and pink painted roses. Beside it lay the photograph album with covers of red velvet and mother-of-pearl.

"All around the walls stood solemn horsehair chairs, and George Washington's picture looked sternly from its frame between the windows.

"Alice hitched up her hoops behind, and sat on the sofa. The slippery haircloth slid her right off onto the floor. She didn't dare laugh out loud, for fear Eliza Jane would hear. She sat on the sofa again, and slid off again. Then Almanzo slid off a chair.

"When company came and they had to sit in the parlor, they kept themselves on the slippery chairs by pushing their toes against the floor. But now they could let go and slide. They slid off the sofa and the chairs till Alice was giggling so hard they didn't dare slide any more."

If you have read the *Little House* series, you probably remember this scene! If not, this series is highly recommended. It also makes a wonderful family read-aloud.

Science: Ocean Waves

The *Diana-Kate* lifts and dips on the waves constantly. Waves often break over the edges of the deck and wash everything in salt water.

You may have learned about salt water, beaches and the different oceans of the world by this point in your education, but have you ever looked at ocean waves specifically? What makes waves? How big can they get? Why are some regions better for surfers than others?

Waves are amazing. If you live near the ocean (or have visited) you have heard that rhythmic, constant swell and crash on the beach. It is a soothing and beautiful sound. During storms, it can also be loud and terrifying. Ocean waves are truly one of nature's miracles.

Three different things cause waves (or currents) in the ocean. The first is wind. The second is temperature. The third is salinity (or level of salt).

Wind-driven waves are caused by the wind blowing across the surface of the water. The wind moves the water and sets it in motion. If you stand on a beach, you can watch the water rolling toward you. This is because wind-driven waves almost always flow parallel to the earth's surface. (During hurricanes and other storms the water's surface can be blown in a direction other than parallel to the earth.) Wind has a powerful effect on ocean water. These wind-driven currents generally affect nearly 500 feet of ocean depth!

The second and third causes of ocean waves are temperature and salinity. The scientific term for this is "thermohaline circulation." Just as wind-driven waves flow horizontally, thermohaline circulation causes the ocean water to flow in vertical currents. Do you know which rises—heat or cold? Heat. Hot water rises just as hot air rises. In areas where ocean water is colder (polar regions) and heavier (more salt or saline) the water tends to sink toward the bottom. This water is then dispersed and rises back toward the surface.

If you wish to learn more about waves, you may want to continue your exploration by studying tides. As with everything in nature, things are always connected. The tides affect waves and vice versa.

Look at the library or online for information about waves, and perhaps even some hands-on experiments you can do at home to explore the science of waves.

Science: The Science of Sailing

The *Diana-Kate* is a beautiful ship! She has enormous masts and sails. Have you ever been on a sailboat or sailing ship? One *without* motors, paddle wheels, etc.?

Sailing can be so much fun! It also takes a lot of time, instruction, practice and knowledge. Let's look at a few sailing basics.

Sailing requires a cool head, good choices and a knowledge of the natural elements. The most important factor in sailing is *wind*. Wind is your "motor," if you will, and learning to know the wind is imperative to sailing effectively and safely.

You may enjoy learning some of the main **courses** of a boat in relation to the wind. When you say you're "following a course," this refers to the boat in relation to the direction of the wind. A boat can never sail directly into the wind. Instead, as the sailor, you want to steer the boat into the wind in different directions depending upon where you want to go. Here are a few course terms to learn:

Heading up means keeping the boat heading steadily toward the wind.

Bearing off means turning the boat away from the wind.

Coming about or **tacking** means turning the front of the boat across the wind.

Gybing (JY bing) means turning the back of the boat across the wind.

Every maneuver a ship or sailboat makes must fall into one of these four groups. You can find many short videos online that will show you exactly what these terms mean, using animations and real-life examples.

As we discussed previously, wind has everything to do with sailing. On a sailboat, the sails (large pieces of canvas) are pulled up toward the top of the masts. As the wind blows, it fills the sails and the pressure of the wind moves the sail and thus the boat. This is why wind is so vital. If you're in the middle of a lake and the wind suddenly dies down, you are stuck! Good sailors know the wind and the weather better than anyone. In order to predict your course and make good choices, you have to understand what the weather is doing.

If you are interested in learning how to sail (or more about sailing) contact your local community college or outdoor equipment store. Many cities have local sailing clubs and lessons specifically geared for youth. Even if the lessons begin in a large pool or pond, it can be great fun and can set you up for a lifelong love of sailing.

Language Arts: Characters - Dynamic, Static and Stereotypical*

When we write a fictional story, the people in a story are called "characters." We find three different types of characters in fictional stories— dynamic, static and stereotypical.

Dynamic characters have various emotional levels, they grow or change, and they adapt to different situations. Hitty is an example of a dynamic character. Dynamic characters tend to be more "fleshed out" in a story. We know a lot about them—likes, dislikes, fears, hopes, etc.

Static characters are very consistent. They are clear, concise and do not change much. Captain Preble is an excellent example of a static character. Throughout our story, he always reacts and relates in a predictable, controlled way.

Finally, stereotypical characters are seen again and again in other stories. For example, the spinsterly school-marm, the handsome and dashing hero, the kind milkman who always smiles, the evil and cold-hearted villain, etc. It is not bad to include stereotypical characters in a story, if we remember two things: 1) Stereotypes are not interesting as main characters, and 2) stereotypes should be kept to a minimum in our stories. The sailors in *Hitty* are great examples of stereotypes. Bill Buckle, Elijah and the others exhibit stereotypical characterizations. They are strong, brawny, swash-buckling, joke-telling, etc.

Every good story will include one or more of these three types of characters. If every character in a book were dynamic, the story would be too wordy, overly detailed and confusing. Likewise, if every character in a book was static, the story would be boring, with little detail and a predictable plot.

Good writers can employ all three of these character types in their stories. Try using these techniques in a story of your own today!

Language Arts: Sea Jargon

In this chapter we discover more new sea terms to learn and explore. Remember to include them in the Sea Journal you began in the last chapter. You can add any of the ship terms to your labeled drawing or diagram. Your journal can include anything that you wish, i.e., printed images, drawings, sketches, colorful type, etc.

Ship Jargon:

aftercabin: area in the ship where the captain could entertain

amidships: halfway between the bow and stern of a ship

berth: a bunk or bed on a ship

bowsprit: a pole projecting forward from the bow (rhymes with cow) of a ship—ropes attached to the bowsprit help to stead the sails and rigging

crow's nest: a small, enclosed platform near the top of the mast, used as a lookout by sailors

figurehead: a statue or carving placed for ornament on the bow of a ship

foc's'le: (FOX uhl) this is the contraction of "forecastle"—a forecastle is the upper deck in front of the foremast

ratlines: small ropes which cross the mast of a ship helping to support the mast

rigging: all the ropes, chains and equipment used to support the masts and sails of the ship

topsail: a sail attached to the topmast

try-works: located amidships, brick areas that surround the try-pots used to boil down the whale blubber

try-pots: large kettles set in brick aboard the ship's deck, used for boiling down the blubber and rendering the oil

yardarm: either end of a long pole used to support a square sail

"batten down the hatches": a phrase meaning to nail small strips of wood (battens) across the openings in a ship's deck in readiness for a storm (the openings are called hatches)

"heave to": to lift or hoist rigging, sails, etc.

mate: sailors who answer to the captain, i.e., first mate, second mate

Language Arts: Writing and Discussion Question

Phoebe whispers to Hitty, "I didn't think going to sea would be like this, did you?" Phoebe perhaps had unrealistic expectations for the voyage. When was a time you have had unrealistic expectations of something and you were surprised by what really happened? Write about it.

Language Arts: Vocabulary

combers   Breaker waves.

enlivening   Making lively or cheerful.

scud   To run or move swiftly.

Research Project: Creating Your Writing Plan*

Now that you have selected a topic for your paper and you have gathered enough research to begin, you may begin creating your writing plan. A writing plan is a bit like a map. It tells you where you are going with your paper and reminds you of what you have left to write. A writing plan involve two things. The first is an outline. There are several ways you can do an outline for a research paper; one example is provided as a bonus activity sheet for Chapter 4 at the end of this unit.

Second, a writing plan involves gathering any additional information you will need for your paper. For example, if you see that your third point on the outline is "Types of Coral: Stony and Soft," and you don't have any information on soft coral, you can quickly gather it and be better prepared to write.

Create a writing plan and outline for your introduction, body and conclusion of your paper. Work carefully as you formulate your writing plan. If you create a clear and concise outline, you will be able to follow it and always know what goal you are working towards throughout your research paper project.

Service Project: Initiating and Beginning Your Project

Depending upon which service project you chose, it is now time for you to begin the process. Make any necessary contacts and begin writing down a list of goals. Ask your parent/teacher for help if you need assistance in finding phone numbers or making contact in other ways.

If, for example, you decided to obtain your CPR certification, you will need to find the number for your local Red Cross office. Contact them and ask when and where they are offering certification courses in your area. You might also want to ask if there are any good references or books on the topic you can be reading to prepare for your first class, or check out library books on this topic ahead of time.

Chapter Five

"In Which We Strike Our First and Last Whale"

Teacher Summary

The voyage aboard the *Diana-Kate* continues smoothly after the storm. Quickly, the first whale is sighted and the capture begins. Phoebe and Hitty witness firsthand the elation and victory, as well as the stench and filth associated with a whale's capture.

The situation on the ship becomes dangerous when fire breaks out on the decks. The flames spread quickly, and the whale oil soaking the wood planks makes the fire worse.

Soon, the crew realizes that the ship cannot be saved. Most of the crew reject Captain Preble's authority and leave on their own. The Prebles, Hitty, Andy and three of the sailors make plans to abandon the ship, as well. For Hitty, the situation grows even worse.

Phoebe puts Hitty in a basket and sets her on a keg of provisions. As the fire gets more intense, Bill Buckle works to get everything loaded. Hitty's basket is missed and soon she hears her family pulling away from the ship. She has been abandoned on board the fiery vessel! At the last possible moment, the ship breaks in two and Hitty is thrown from the basket into the ocean waves.

What we will cover in this chapter:

Social Studies: Career Path - Marine Biologist*
Science: Whales
Language Arts: Sea Jargon
Language Arts: Writing and Discussion Question
Language Arts: Vocabulary
Life Skills: Loyalty

Social Studies: Career Path - Marine Biologist*

In the next lesson for this chapter, you will learn more about whales. If these majestic mammals of the sea interest you, perhaps you would like to explore a career involving them. Have you ever heard of a **marine biologist**?

Many marine biologists are specialists in the study of whales, dolphins and porpoises. They work with nonprofit organizations, universities and government agencies to gather information used to learn more about whales.

To be a good marine biologist, you need to be compassionate, hard working, detail-oriented, have good math and science skills and work well with others. You also need to be patient! Many of the experiments and studies that marine biologists do can last years. Gathering data and compiling information may seem tedious, but it is important if we want to learn all we can about whales and other sea creatures.

If you would like to know more about being a marine biologist, you can look online or at the library about this career, or contact your local university about its biology programs. Remember that the best marine biology programs (indeed, some of the only!) are located in coastal cities.

Science: Whales

Captain Preble and his crew are anxious to capture the enormous whales they sight. With so much description of a whale hunt, you may wonder what whales are really like. If you have never studied whales, this would be an excellent opportunity to explore these fascinating members of the animal kingdom. If you

Blue whale and calf

have spent time looking at whales before, use this lesson as a review.

Whales are mammals. (The blue whale is the largest mammal on our planet.) Do you remember how a mammal is defined? Mammals are warm-blooded, have hair or fur, and nurse their babies. Humans are mammals, too! You may think because whales spend so much time under water, that they are like fish—breathing under the water. This is not true. They breathe air just like we do, but they are able to stay under the water for much longer periods of time.

The scientific name for the entire group of whales is **cetaceans** (si TAY shuns). Within the different families of whales are dozens of different species. Some people think dolphins and porpoises are different from whales, but they are not. Dolphins and porpoises are just smaller whales with distinctive shapes. Actually, each of the different families of whales has its own special shape and traits.

Because there are so many different kinds of whales, you can find them in every ocean in the world. Some live in polar regions and others live in warm seas. Some whales even live in freshwater lakes and rivers!

A whale breathes through an opening on the top of its head. This opening is called a "blowhole." Just like our nostrils, blowholes allow the whale to exhale and inhale. Although whales normally hold their breath for only a minute or so, many are able to stay underwater for nearly 45 minutes if they need to look for food or escape from enemies.

You can research a specific type of whale on your own. Perhaps you would like to learn more about the kind of whale Captain Preble and his crew were hunting—the sperm whale. You may want to explore the char-

Orca, or killer whale

acteristics and history of the beautiful orca, or killer whale—distinctly marked with black and white.

Here is a list of some questions to help you get started with your research. Armed with these facts, you can easily put together an excellent written or oral science report.

What does an orca look like?
Where do orcas live?
How long do orcas live?
Do orcas migrate?
Does an orca sleep?
How does an orca breathe?
What is a blowhole?
Who are the orca's enemies?

From this list, you can quickly see how much you will be learning about *all* whales from the exploration of just one species.

If you are a budding artist, you may enjoy looking at a book about drawing whales and other sea creatures. There is an excellent book entitled *Draw 50 Sharks, Whales, and Other Sea Creatures*. Written by Lee J. Ames and Warren Budd, this book showcases step-by-step drawing instructions for many types of whales, dolphins, porpoises and more.

Language Arts: Sea Jargon

You will find new words and ideas to add to your Sea Journal in this chapter:

"in fast": stuck tightly

harpoon: a barbed spear with a rope tied to it used
for hunting large sea creatures

gamming: a visit between two ships' crews

Language Arts: Writing and Discussion Question

This chapter touches on loyalty to our friends and family. Can you think of a time when you stuck by a friend during a difficult time? Perhaps you have a friend who has been especially loyal to you. Write about your experiences. (See the following Life Skills lesson on Loyalty for more information on this topic.)

Language Arts: Vocabulary

concocted   Devised; made up.

wallowing   Rolling about; floundering.

Life Skills: Loyalty

In this chapter, most of Captain Preble's crew reject his authority and leave on their own. When a ship's crew ignores the Captain's orders and makes their own plans, it is called "mutiny."

Three of Captain Preble's sailors do not commit mutiny. Bill Buckle, Jeremy Folger and Reuben are loyal to the Preble family and their captain.

This is an excellent opportunity to think about loyalty. Loyalty is being faithful and true to someone. Loyalty to a friend is easy when everything is fun and light. Loyalty is proven, however, when circumstances get difficult. If you are a loyal friend, you don't say mean or disparaging things about another person. You also stick up for that person if you hear someone else saying hurtful things to or about him.

Only three of Captain Preble's crew believed it was more important to do what was right and be loyal to their friend and Captain than to look after their own interests.

Loyalty is an important character trait. Being loyal isn't always easy, but if we are intent on building strong characters and pursuing noble actions we must strive for loyalty to our friends and family.

Chapter Six

"In Which I Join the Fishes and Rejoin the Prebles"

Teacher Summary

After Hitty is washed overboard, she spends some time floating along the coral reef. Miraculously, she is not far from the island shore where the Prebles landed near the wreck. Eventually, they spot her and bring her home to Phoebe once again.

The Prebles work hard on the island, gathering food and fuel and trying to decide what to do next. Soon, they are not alone on the island. Island natives arrive on shore and the two ill-matched groups meet. The Prebles are frightened of the natives. They can't communicate with them and are not sure what will happen.

The next turn of events surprises everyone! The natives like Hitty. They seem to think she is some sort of idol. They carry her away, much to Phoebe's horror, and Hitty is once again in a perilous situation.

What we will cover in this chapter:

Social Studies: History - Carib Indians
Social Studies: Geography - Caribbean Islands

Science: Coral Reefs*
Science: Distillation
Language Arts: Literary Recommendation
Language Arts: Writing and Discussion Question
Language Arts: Vocabulary
Fine Arts: Watercolor

Social Studies: History - Carib Indians

The island natives arrive where the Prebles are stranded. Although we are not told what ethnic group these people belong to specifically, we might assume they are a part of the Carib Indian (Kalinago) tribe. The *Diana-Kate* was sailing down the Atlantic coastline, toward the Caribbean Islands. It would make sense the ship might have gone down near those islands.

The Carib Indians (KAR ib) were a group of violent, marauding South American tribes who resided mainly in the Amazon River Valley. The Carib Indians were greatly feared because of their tradition of eating their war captives (cannibalism). During a battle with the Arawak Indians, the Carib Indians captured a group of islands and moved their homes there. The islands are now known as the Windward Islands. Find the Windward Islands on a map or globe. They are located right off the northern coast of Venezuela.

In our story, the natives who approach the Prebles arrive on the island via small boats and canoes. The Carib Indians are known for their expert canoeing abilities. They also are prize fish hunters, using harpoons and poison arrows.

Columbus visited the Caribbean islands during his four voyages. After Columbus, the Spanish sailed the high seas toward the Caribbean. This proved deadly for the Carib Indians. Outnumbered and without comparable ammunition, thousands of Carib Indians were captured and killed during the Spanish invasion.

Today, the Caribbean islands are highly populated with Carib Indians. They also reside in the Guianas and in the Amazon Valley. However, very little remains of the Carib Indians' original lifestyle and traditions. Most of the Carib Indians today are highly saturated in the European and American influences of the last 500 years.

You will learn more about the Carib Indians and their religious practices in the following chapter.

Social Studies: Geography - Caribbean Islands

In this chapter, we are looking at the Caribbean islands. It is important to understand the geography of these islands. You should be able to identify them on a world map.

Find where the Caribbean islands are located. These islands lie in a line stretching from the United States to the northern coast of Venezuela. They form a natural buffer between the Atlantic Ocean and the Caribbean Sea.

The Caribbean is filled with people from all over the world. Some were immigrants trying to flee oppression. For example, many Jews fled the Spanish Inquisition and went to the islands. Other people were looking for freedom from rulers they disagreed with. Many British loyalists rushed to the Caribbean after the United States won independence from England. Still others were brought to the islands under duress. Many European colonists in the islands stole people from west African coasts and brought them back (by the thousands) to serve as slaves on their plantations.

Because of this diverse population, the Caribbean today is a rich tapestry of different backgrounds, colors, beliefs and more.

Today, the Caribbean is a large agricultural area. Many world exports come from this region. Bananas, tobacco, coconuts, sugar, rum, spices, citrus fruits and cotton are just a few of the important exports we find in the Caribbean.

Tourism is also a large part of the Caribbean's economy. The tropical (and in some seasons temperate) climates, beautiful beaches, hospitable people and delicious food are large draws for travelers worldwide.

Take some time to look at pictures of the region. The beauty of the islands is simply breathtaking!

Also, you may enjoy creating a traditional Caribbean meal. Rice and beans is a great example of simple Caribbean fare. Serve it with iced pineapple or guava juice, and perhaps bananas with cinnamon sugar for dessert. It might also be fun to play some Jamaican music in the background—maybe even dance!

Rice and Beans

2 cups rice
1 cup dried red beans
1 coconut
1 slice of bacon (chopped)
salt and pepper

Soak the beans overnight.

To prepare the coconut: Place coconut in preheated 300°F oven for 20 minutes; let cool. Pound coconut with a hammer until it breaks into pieces. Using a flat-head screwdriver placed between the white flesh and the brown shell, pry off portions of the coconut meat. Grate these pieces and squeeze to extract the juice or "milk."

Add the coconut milk to 3 cups of water and boil the beans in it for 2 hours. Add the bacon and continue cooking until beans are tender. Add rice, salt and pepper and cook slowly until all the water is absorbed. Serves 6.

Science: Coral Reefs*

Read the following paragraph from our story:

"I think I must have become too water-soaked from days of buffetings to know what went on about me or by what devious and salty ways I came to the Island. But come I did in time, along with other bits of wreckage. At any rate, I knew nothing till I found myself in the quiet waters of a rock pool. This was a deep hole worn in the coral and all manner of bright seaweeds clung to the sides, trailing long, wavering fingers or tresses like green and scarlet hair in the clear water. Small, shelly creatures were moving about on busy missions of their own, and a huge spiked starfish was twining about my ankle."

Our author, Rachel Field, has done an excellent job describing a beautiful tide pool and coral reef. What makes a coral reef? Where are they found? What types of animals live there?

A coral reef is like a country all its own. Millions of "citizens," or animals, reside in their own nooks and crannies, and everyone depends on everyone else for survival.

Coral is a limestone formation created by billions of small animals. Each individual animal is called a **polyp**. Hundreds of thousands of these polyps living together in the same skeleton are called a **colony**. These corals have skeletons that are limestone. As the animals die, they leave behind their skeletons and these form the rock-like coral. It takes hundreds of years to create the enormous coral reefs we see today. For those small animals to survive, they require warm, clean salty water. They also need sunlight; therefore the water cannot be too deep. These conditions are vital for a healthy coral reef.

The largest coral reef in the world is the Great Barrier Reef off the coast of eastern Australia. The Great Barrier Reef is over 1,200 miles long!

If you have never explored coral reefs and the wildlife that reside in them, you will be amazed! Perhaps no other area of nature contains so much teeming life in one place—and life which is extremely varied!

Sea horses, emperor angel fish, sea cucumbers, clownfish and sea slugs are just a few of the fascinating and beautiful creatures you find in a coral reef. As you begin to study these animals, you may want to set up small reports on each, including fast facts you gather as well as drawings or images.

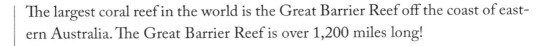

For example, you may choose to research an incredible animal called a sea cucumber. Sea cucumbers are bizarre and wonderful. They are shaped like fat sausages and are between four and ten inches long. In some very warm tropical regions, they can grow up to three feet! Sea cucumbers belong to the scientific family **echinoderms**. Echinoderms also include sea urchins and starfish. Sea cucumbers have an unusual way of distracting predators. If being pursued by an attacker, the sea cucumber will split its body open and push out some of its internal organs. The organs, floating through the water, distract the attacker and the sea cucumber remains safe. Later, the sea cucumber's body can regenerate new organs. Another way the sea cucumber protects itself is by changing shape and color in order to camouflage itself. Sea cucumbers are also caught, dried and sold as food in Asia and California. The dried sea cucumber is called trepang.

Coral reefs are lovely to look at and interesting to study. Remember that coral reefs are threatened every day by pollution and ships. Scuba divers can also damage coral reefs by accident or by illegally gathering coral and animals.

If you want to explore coral reefs in more depth, you can get books at the library that explain more about each creature and plant. If you live near a science museum or aquarium, a trip to see a tide pool or coral reef would be marvelous.

Science: Distillation

The Prebles' situation seems desperate. They are stranded on this tropical island with little food sources and even less fresh water. A human being cannot survive if he drinks any significant amount of salt water. The high concentrations of salt destroy body cells and organs.

How were the Prebles able to collect a small amount of fresh water? By collecting rainwater in barrels. Do you know any other way they might have been able to obtain fresh water?

This lesson centers on the scientific principle called distillation. Distillation has been used to gather fresh water for nearly 2,000 years and is still used today.

Distillation is based on the observable, natural water cycle. Every day, all over the earth's surface, water from the oceans and seas is evaporated by the sun (millions upon millions of gallons). The water vapor becomes clouds. As the clouds grow heavier and heavier, they release their moisture and the water falls to the earth—as *fresh* water! This is how Bill Buckle and the others gathered their water—from rain.

Thousands of years ago, people observed this natural water cycle and began to understand an important principle. When water is heated, the salt is left behind as the vapor rises. If that vapor can be collected and then cooled and condensed, it is no longer salty!

Anyone can distill water using the sun. Fill a container with salt water (5:1 water to salt ratio) and cover the container with a sloped plastic dome (an inverted 2-liter pop bottle works well). Place the container in the sun. As the water evaporates and beads up on the sides of the dome, it can be collected. The result is fresh water.

Solar distillation is labor intensive; it takes a lot of time for very little payoff. Still, it works!

Today, modern distillation plants use a process called multistage flash distillation. It uses the same principles of solar distillation, but instead of waiting for the sun to turn the water into vapor, seawater is preheated and put through chambers that force the water into steam. The steam is then cooled and collected.

This method of distillation is vital today for ship crews and at the United States naval base at Guantanamo Bay, Cuba. The base in Cuba produces over 3.4 million gallons of pure water each day using this method.

Why do you think the Prebles didn't try solar distillation on their own? (Perhaps they didn't have enough containers to hold the seawater; they didn't have anything in which to collect the vapors, etc.)

Language Arts: Literary Recommendation

As you enjoy the adventures of Hitty and the Prebles on the island, you may want to incorporate another book which follows a similar theme. A classic, *The Swiss Family Robinson*, is an exciting and adventurous book to read alone or as a read-aloud with siblings.

Written by Johann David Wyss, the story centers on one family, the Robinsons, and their adventures after being shipwrecked near New Guinea. The family must work together to survive.

The author, Johann David Wyss (1743-1818), was a Swiss pastor and scholar. The book originated as a series of stories created for his sons. The original illustrations were done by one of those sons, Johann Emmanuel. His son Johann Rudolf published the book after Johann David Wyss' death.

Language Arts: Writing and Discussion Question

Hitty describes the situation on the island, writing, "I knew that things were going to happen. It seemed like the moments before a thunderstorm." What does she mean by that second sentence? Describe what you think it feels like just before it begins to storm.

Language Arts: Vocabulary

buffetings   Knocks, strokes, or hurts.

gesticulating   Making or using gestures to help communicate.

gimcracks   Trinkets, novelty items.

marlinspike   A pointed iron tool used by sailors to separate the strands of a rope by splicing.

providence   The hand or protective care of God (from the word *provide*).

Fine Arts: Watercolor

Look at the illustration of Hitty floating in the rock pool. This art lesson involves two elements. First, you will do a small amount of scientific research. Second, you will practice your water color technique.

This lesson will work better if you are able to enlarge the picture using a copy machine. After it is enlarged, trace the picture using tracing paper. Transfer the illustration onto watercolor paper using tracing and carbon paper.

Now, look at some color illustrations or photographs of sea creatures. You will look for pictures of the creatures from the illustration, i.e., starfish, snails, anemone, sea urchins, seaweed, etc. You should be making notes of the vibrant colors of these creatures in nature.

Using watercolors, try to recreate the beautiful colors of the sea creatures on your copy of the illustration.

Chapter Seven

"In Which I Learn the Ways of Gods, Natives, and Monkeys"

Teacher Summary

Hitty is taken by the natives and made their "god." The chief builds a small temple for Hitty out of leaves and branches. The monkeys in the treetops above are especially enthralled with Hitty and she likes their mischievous behavior. The natives bring her fruit and shells each day, and they "paint" her face with berry juice. Hitty likes the attention but misses the Prebles tremendously!

One night, without warning, Andy comes and saves her—snatching her from the temple and stealing away in the darkness. Unbeknownst to Hitty, the Prebles and the sailors have decided to try to escape the island. They have a boat ready, and the stranded family and sailors and one very happy doll are soon floating away from shore.

Captain Preble believes there is a ship nearby, but their tiny boat must catch up to it and signal it. This takes all night, and there are many times when the Prebles think the end is near. Miraculously, the ship sees them with their last signal and is soon pulling about to pick up the stranded family.

What we will cover in this chapter:

Social Studies: History - Carib Indians
  and Religion
Science: Bioluminescence*
Language Arts: Writing and Discussion Question
Language Arts: Vocabulary

Social Studies: History - Carib Indians and Religion

In the last chapter, you learned why the natives the Prebles encountered were probably a part of the tribe of Carib Indians (Kalinago). In this chapter, we see even more convincing evidence.

The natives treat Hitty like an idol. If you explore the history of Carib culture, you will learn they were very religious and worshipped small idols, often made of wood! Hitty would certainly fit that description. The Carib tribes called their idols "zemis" and the Chief's zemi was kept in a small temple—just like Hitty.

This lesson is offered simply to remind you to look in the text of stories for clues to help you understand it better. Even though Rachel Field chooses not to name the Caribbean tribe described in chapters 6 and 7, we can deduce who they are by her descriptions. Back in chapter 1, we used fashion and technology to help us figure out the probable timeline of our book. Noticing these sorts of details will increase your reading comprehension.

Science: Bioluminescence*

When Hitty recalls the ocean water during the Prebles' attempt to hail the ship, she writes: "The warm tropic water was alive with the most brilliant phosphorescence I have ever seen. Each time our oars dipped and rose again they made showers of shining miniature stars on either side."

Do you wonder what she means by "brilliant phosphorescence?" The scientific term for phosphorescence in living things is **bioluminescence** (by oh loo min NEH sense). This is an excellent scientific term and topic for you to study.

Bioluminescence is the ability of some living animals and plants to give off light. The light is created by chemical reactions in the living organism, and does not produce heat.

Most examples of bioluminescence appear in aquatic life, primarily in the ocean. Over 1,000 species of fish are bioluminescent. The lanternfish is one example of a fish that displays bioluminescent properties. Lanternfish live deep in the ocean. They have small, light producing, bead-like organs called **photophores** on their bodies. These photophores glow and are used by the lanternfish to communicate, distract predators and provide camouflage. Lanternfish most often live and travel together in schools of hundreds, even thousands!

There are many fascinating bioluminescent animals to explore. For example, the sea cucumber you learned about in chapter 6 (coral reef lesson) is bioluminescent. If you used FIAR Vol. 1, you may remember a book called *Night of the Moonjellies*. Jellyfish are bioluminescent, too!

Other living organisms in ocean water, such as algae, can be bioluminescent. Microscopic organisms and plant materials can glow and cause the water to look brilliant at night.

But bioluminescence is not just found in aquatic life. Some land organisms also display this property. Certain mushrooms and insects are bioluminescent. One such mushroom is the *Omphalotus Olearius* or the Jack O'Lantern mushroom. This mushroom is a fiery orange, but at night its spores glow a vibrant green color. This mushroom is also poisonous!

Insects that are bioluminescent include the click beetle, railroad worm and the common firefly. You are probably familiar with fireflies. Also called lightning bugs, fireflies are winged beetles whose abdomens include light organs. By means of chemical reactions, these organs glow with a greenish-yellow light. The lights are used to communicate, to find mates and more. On a summer evening, you can spot these small glowing creatures by the hundreds!

If we look again at the original passage of this lesson, Hitty is describing the waters surrounding their boat as "phosphorescent." Can you now offer some suggestions as to what was causing that glow?

Language Arts: Writing and Discussion Question

For a while, the Prebles do not believe the ship will rescue them. We can only imagine what they must have been thinking. If you were stranded as they were, with little chance of rescue, what would be going through your mind? What or who would you be thinking about? Why? Write about it.

212

Language Arts: Vocabulary

cutting Becoming, presenting (an old-fashioned use of the word).

phosphorescent Glowing without burning or heat.

porringer A serving dish deeper than a bowl or saucer, used to eat porridge or saucy items.

skirmish A quick, small fistfight.

stealth Secret or sly action.

talisman Anything which acts as a magic token or charm.

Chapter Eight

"In Which I Am Lost in India"

Teacher Summary

After the ship's crew sees the Prebles' frantic signals, they pull around and take the weary family (and sailors) aboard. This new ship is called the *Hesper* and Hitty writes they like it almost as much as their beloved *Diana-Kate*. The *Hesper* is a trading vessel between India and China.

The ship soon reaches its next port, Bombay, and everyone goes ashore to purchase new clothes and supplies. The Prebles, Bill Buckle, Reuben and Folger are particularly thankful for this turn of events. Their clothing is either badly torn or missing.

Soon, they are all well outfitted and Phoebe is tired from all the excitement. Bill Buckle offers to carry her back to the Hesper. Unfortunately, the little girl is so exhausted she falls asleep and accidentally drops Hitty into a gutter.

Hitty never sees the Prebles again. She is lost in India in a gutter! The next thing she remembers is an old man picking her up from the dirty street. The old man takes her home. He turns out to be a snake charmer. Hitty is not excited by the cobra, but doesn't have any options. She travels with the man and his snake for a long while, until one day a couple sees Hitty sitting by the cobra's basket. The couple, who is American, recognizes that Hitty is not an Indian doll. They offer the snake charmer money and he agrees to sell Hitty. The couple wants the doll for their daughter, Little Thankful. Hitty is thrilled! She is finally going to belong to a little girl again!

What we will cover in this chapter:

Social Studies: Geography - India
Social Studies: History - World Religions: Hinduism
Science: Cobras
Language Arts: Sensory Descriptions*
Language Arts: Sea Journal - Finishing Up
Language Arts: Writing and Discussion Question
Language Arts: Vocabulary
Research Project: Writing a First Draft
Service Project: How Is It Going?

Social Studies: Geography - India

The Prebles enjoy walking through the streets of Bombay, buying clothes and items they have needed for so many days. In this chapter we are introduced to India and its many interesting sites and people.

Find India on a detailed world map. What do you notice about the country? Bangladesh, Nepal, China and Pakistan surround the upper third of India. The lower two-thirds jut out into the Indian Ocean. Can you find Mumbai (formerly called Bombay)? It is located in the middle of India's western coast. Being located on the ocean makes Mumbai/Bombay a port city and explains why the *Hesper* arrived in that city.

If your map has topographical lines, you can look at the majestic and beautiful Himalayas (hi muh LAY uhs). The Himalayan Mountains are located between the southwestern portion of China and the northern rim of India. Among the highest mountains in the world, the Himalayas are often called "the top of the world." The tallest mountain in India is called Kanchenjunga and is nearly 30,000 feet tall!

India has three main seasons—cool, hot and rainy. In the cool months, the temperature can be as low as 40°F. In the summer the temperatures can rise far above 100°F. In India, when it rains it isn't just a sprinkle. Have you ever heard the term "monsoon?" This comes from India. The rains, called monsoons, occur from June to September. They are so heavy, devastating floods happen nearly every year!

India

Indian women wear beautiful wrapped robe-dresses, called saris. Many Hindu women wear small dots of powder on their foreheads. These dots were traditionally red and represented their religion, but today the dots can be many colors and are simply for beauty.

Indian food is delicious. The main spices (coriander, mustard, turmeric, garlic, onions and anise) are blended together to form what is called "curry." In America, we buy curry powder premixed, but in India the women mix their own curry fresh daily. Curry, yogurt, fruits, nuts, rice and flat breads are foods enjoyed daily in India. Have you ever tried a curried dish? Here is a quick and simple recipe featuring this unusual spice combination:

Curried Rice

2 cups hot water
1/2 cup uncooked rice
1/2 cup chopped tomatoes, drained
3/4 tsp. salt
1/4 cup sliced onion
2 Tbs. melted butter or margarine
3/4 tsp. curry powder

Pour hot water over rice. Place where the rice will stay hot but will not cook. Let it rest for 45 minutes.

Meanwhile, preheat your oven to 350°F. Add remaining ingredients to rice; mix. Bake in an 8"x8" baking dish for 1 1/2 hours or until liquid is absorbed and rice is tender, stirring occasionally. Serves 4.

Serve this curried rice with grilled vegetables or chicken kabobs for a delicious Indian meal!

India also boasts what many consider to be one of the most beautifully designed and structured buildings in the world—the Taj Mahal (TAHJ muh HALL). This stunning building is located in Agra, a city just southeast of New Dehli in northern India. The Taj Mahal looks like smooth carved snow. It is made of white marble and rests on a foundation/platform made of red sandstone. Each corner of the platform features tall, slender towers called minarets, or prayer towers. The Taj Mahal is an excellent example of Indian architecture. Find a picture of this beautiful and famous structure. You will love the peaceful, smooth lines of the design.

If you are interested in studying famous people of India, two excellent choices are Mother Teresa and Mahatma Gandhi.

Mother Teresa (1910-1997) was a beloved Roman Catholic nun who devoted her life to serving "the poorest of the poor" in Calcutta, India. Mother Teresa was born in Yugoslavia, but became an Indian citizen after she began her work. She was known to many as "the saint of the gutters." This reminds us of where Hitty was lost, doesn't it? Mother Teresa won the Nobel Peace Prize in 1979 for her amazing life work. The world mourned her death in 1997.

Mahatma Gandhi (1869-1948) (ma HAHT ma GAHN dee) was one of the most important social reformers of the early 20th century. He helped free India from British rule through nonviolent peace protests. Gandhi wanted India to be a free, united country and worked toward that goal until it was achieved in 1947. Gandhi did not believe in violence of any kind, including the killing of animals. He lived a simple life and encouraged people to be self-sufficient—growing their own food and hand spinning/weaving their own clothing.

Mahatma Gandhi lived to see the freedom of India, but was tragically shot and killed by a terrorist just six months later in 1948. At his funeral, India's Prime Minister Nehru said, "A light has gone out of our lives and there is darkness everywhere..." The famous scientist Albert Einstein said of Gandhi, "Generations to come will scarcely believe that such a one as this walked the earth in flesh and blood."

You can continue your exploration of India by looking at the capital (New Delhi), the city where Hitty was lost (Mumbai, formerly called Bombay), the monetary system (based on the rupee), or the food of the land (kabobs are from India).

Write a report or present an oral report on something you have learned in your study of India. You may want to include some artwork, perhaps your own drawing of the Taj Mahal. You might also want to include a recording of Mother Teresa or Mahatma Gandhi speaking.

Social Studies: History - World Religions: Hinduism

Note: In the text of our story, the spelling of Hindu is "Hindoo." This spelling can be found in the 1913 edition of Webster's Dictionary, and was an accepted variant for the time period of our story. The correct modern spelling is now "Hindu" and "Hinduism."

The old man who rescues Hitty from the gutter is a Hindu. Hinduism is one of the major world religions. The major principles and unique aspects of this religion are outlined here.

In brief, Hinduism is a polytheistic religion. Do you know what this means? This means Hinduism believes in many gods—not just one God. Hinduism is very complex and structured. Hindus believe in reincarnation and karma. Reincarnation is the belief that when people die, they return in different forms to the earth for another lifetime. The law of karma states that the actions and behaviors of a person affect their next life. For example, if a Hindu follows his religion strictly and is kind to others, he might be reincarnated in his next life in a better position socially—richer, more power, etc. Likewise, the law of karma holds if that same man rejects his religion and behaves in a dishonorable way, he might be reincarnated as a worm—literally! This cycle of reincarnation continues until a person reaches "spiritual perfection." At this point, called "moksha," the person's soul does not return.

Hinduism also holds to a stringent social class system—called a caste system. In this system, people live in certain areas and hold certain jobs depending upon their social standing. People aren't allowed to move "up" in social standing or marry outside their caste. Although the caste system of India has become less popular in modern times, it is still followed by many.

Science: Cobras

Hitty is not exactly thrilled with her new travel mate—the cobra. Cobras live in Africa, the Middle East and Asia. Cobras can live in almost any climate (except Arctic).

You probably already know that cobras are a part of the reptile family. Reptiles do not have skin like we do; instead, scales cover their bodies. Scales are not slimy but, rather, they are silky, dry and smooth—a little like the skin of an onion. Reptiles are also cold blooded. This means they require heat (sunlight, for example) to maintain their internal body temperatures and keep warm.

Because they are poisonous, cobras are feared all over the world. Cobras have poison (also known as venom) sacs at the back of their heads. The cobra uses its venom to obtain food and for protection. Some cobras can shoot venom at a victim—even at a distance of ten feet! This type of attack will only hurt a human if the venom reaches his eyes—at that point, blindness is almost inevitable. Other cobras inject the venom into a predator or prey by means of fangs. This requires the cobra to bite the victim. Cobra bites are quite dangerous. The most common cobra bite is that of the Indian cobra. Doctors and scientists have studied the venom of the Indian cobra extensively and have developed an injection called "antivenin." This medicinal injection can save a human, but it must be administered as quickly as possible.

As dangerous as cobras seem, they have their own natural enemies. Eagles and other birds eat many cobras. The most dangerous enemy to the cobra, however, is a small, furry animal called the mongoose. Mongooses are only around 12-15 inches in length, but they are so fast they can quickly seize and kill a cobra before the snake has even a moment to react. A wonderful children's story by the famed author Rudyard Kipling centers on the tale of a mongoose and a cobra. The story is called "Rikki-Tikki-Tavi," and adults and children alike love this exciting and heartwarming story.

Perhaps you are wondering about the cobra in our story. Is he really "charmed" by the Hindu man and the music? The answer is no. This interesting sideshow of snake charming has been popular in Asia and India for hundreds of years. It looks very magical, but, in reality, there is a simple explanation. The charmer plays an instrument called a pungi (in *Hitty* it is called a flageolet) and sways back and forth. The cobra, which cannot hear the music but can sense the sound, raises up and responds to the movement because it sees the person and the pungi as a possible predator. This is a natural reaction; the snake would do this if there was no music and the person swaying was not the charmer.

Cobras are fascinating creatures. Although many people are fearful of these snakes, in reality they usually do not strike humans unless they are scared or provoked. They also serve a good purpose by eating mice, rats, and other animals which could become great pests if their numbers were not controlled.

Language Arts: Sensory Descriptions*

Hitty describes her first meeting with the cobra:

"As it swayed, it would move its head with its layers of skin, fold on fold, slowly from side to side. I saw the glitter of bright, lidless eyes and the flicker of a darting tongue; I heard its scales making a faint scraping sound on the floor. Once, even, it came very close to me, so close that I felt part of its chilly body slide across my feet. At the touch I stiffened till it seemed I must surely crack in two..."

Identify which words in this description address Hitty's five senses. We see three of the five described in this short paragraph: sight, hearing and touch. Hitty sees the snake beginning to move. Hitty hears the scales on the floor. Hitty feels the snake on her feet.

Sensory description is an important and dramatic literary device. It can help "spice up" an otherwise boring paragraph. Here are two short paragraphs describing a snow cone, for example. Which do you think is more interesting?

1. Johnny held the snow cone in his hand. He ate it slowly. Johnny enjoyed the snow cone very much. He wanted another one.

2. Johnny held the dripping snow cone in his hand. As he ate, he watched the cherry red syrup fill the point of the cone. It was so delicious he wanted to eat it quickly, but instead he savored it, trying to let each individual icy cold crystal touch his tongue before it quickly melted away. It tasted sweet—like liquid candy. Finally, he reached into the bottom of the paper cone and picked up the last frosty piece of ice. As it slipped through his fingers and into his mouth, Johnny was already thinking how much he would love another snow cone.

Hitty: Her First Hundred Years

Can you see the difference? As the reader, we want to see sensory details in stories because it helps us feel like we are "there" in the story.

Language Arts: Sea Journal - Finishing Up

The first third of our story centered a great deal on ships and sailing. In this chapter we find a final few seafaring terms to add to your journal.

keel: the main timber or steel piece that runs underneath the ship; the entire ship is built on its keel

sailing needle: a long, sturdy needle with a large eye used for stitching heavy sailcloth

Depending upon the format you chose to use for your Sea Journal, you may want to put it together in a three-ring binder or bind it like a book. You can decorate the cover however you want. Perhaps your own drawing of the *Diana-Kate* or a picture of the men working on the try-pots could be included.

Language Arts: Writing and Discussion Question

What do you think William means when he says, "God moves in mysterious ways?" Write about it.

Language Arts: Vocabulary

bazaar   A street(s) filled with shops and booths.

bullock   An ox, steer.

fakir   A Muslim (or sometimes Hindu) holy man who lives by begging.

flageolet   A small wind instrument something like a flute.

foreboding   A prediction, warning.

gaped   Stared with the mouth open.

precarious   Dangerous or risky.

voluminous   Of great size or volume.

Research Project: Writing a First Draft

The time has finally come to begin writing. Can you believe it? All of your preliminary work (prewriting, creating the outline, gathering information, creating a bibliography, making notes) will now come into play.

Begin by writing your introduction. In the introduction you will want to quickly gather your reader's attention. You can do this by using an exciting or dramatic quote or statistic, an interesting question, or some other kind of attention-grabbing statement. Once you have his attention (this will probably take two or three sentences), you will want to focus on your thesis statement—the main topic of your paper. The thesis statement is most often placed as the last sentence of the introduction.

Once you have the first draft of your introduction, you can begin working on the body of your paper. The number of paragraphs in the body of your paper directly relates to the number of main points you want to make. If you have four main points, then your paper will have four body paragraphs. If you have three main points, then your paper will have three body paragraphs. Your paper should include a minimum of three main points.

When you have written the first draft of the body of your paper, you can begin writing your conclusion. A conclusion paragraph usually begins by restating your original thesis in an interesting way. Then conclude the paper for the reader by writing more generally about your topic, wrapping up your research, and sharing any final thoughts.

Your next reminder will appear in Chapters 12 and 13 of this unit.

Service Project: How Is It Going?

How is your service project going? At this point, you may have identified areas that are going smoothly and other areas that are more challenging than you expected. Keep up the good work. When you get discouraged, focus on the people you are helping to keep you motivated. Don't forget to ask an adult if you have any questions or have run into any problems. You might want to talk things over with your parent or with someone related to your service project, such as a supervisor, mentor or fellow volunteer.

Chapter Nine

"In Which I Have Another Child to Play with Me"

Teacher Summary

Hitty is now living with a missionary family in India. Her new owner, a girl named Little Thankful, isn't as devoted as Phoebe was, but Hitty is thrilled to be back in the arms of a child.

One day, Little Thankful grows sick with a fever. When she is well, her parents agree that India is no place for a small child. She has lived all of her life in India, but they decide to send her back to Philadelphia to live with her grandparents. Hitty, of course, is taken along. America! Hitty is ecstatic to be going home! The little girl and doll embark on a long voyage, but soon arrive in Philadelphia.

Little Thankful's grandparents are very wealthy. They buy Little Thankful new clothes. Soon, Little Thankful and Hitty are on their way to their first party. Unfortunately, the other little girls at the party are spiteful and mean. They make fun of Little Thankful's freckles and mock Hitty. Little Thankful, having been humiliated, decides she wants nothing more to do with Hitty. It only takes a moment, but Little Thankful stuffs Hitty deep into an old horsehair sofa. Hitty is frightened and horrified, but there she must stay until she is found.

What we will cover in this chapter:

Social Studies: History - Missionaries*
Social Studies: Geography - Philadelphia
Social Studies: History - Tailor-Made Clothing
Language Arts: Writing and Discussion Question
Language Arts: Vocabulary
Life Skills: "Beautiful Inside and Out"

Social Studies: History - Missionaries*

Little Thankful's parents are in India because they are missionaries. A missionary is someone who is sent by a specific religious group to teach others about his faith. Missionaries often do more, however, than just talk about their faith. Many missionaries are skilled and trained at helping people with education, farming, medical care and other practical areas.

Some missionaries work in their home country or city. Others work in foreign countries like Little Thankful's family. There are missionaries all over the world!

Hundreds of thousands of Christians work as missionaries in the world today. Christian missionaries are made up of ordained clergy as well as everyday people (like you and me) called "lay people." Christian missionaries serve on every continent and help spread their message by preaching sermons, translating the Bible, organizing group meetings and churches and helping new converts understand the Christian faith.

Just one example of a well-known missionary is David Livingstone (1813-1873), who worked for the London Missionary Society, converting African natives and working to end slavery. His work also included many explorations and discoveries in Africa. It was David Livingstone who named Victoria Falls for Queen Victoria.

Two excellent book series covering dozens of different missionaries are:

Christian Heroes: Then & Now (dozens of volumes), by Janet and Geoff Benge, published by Youth with a Mission (YWAM)

Hero Tales: A Family Treasury of True Stories from the Lives of Christian Heroes (four volumes) by Dave and Neta Jackson

Social Studies: Geography - Philadelphia

Hitty and Little Thankful arrive in Philadelphia, much to Hitty's excitement!

Philadelphia is a wonderful, historic and thriving city today. In FIAR Vol. 5, Philadelphia was covered in detail in the *Betsy Ross* unit study. If you completed those lessons, this would be an excellent time to review what you learned about that city.

Founded in 1682 by Quaker William Penn, Philadelphia became the capital of Pennsylvania in 1683. The name comes from the Greek word philadelphia, which means brotherly love. For this reason, Philadelphia is known as the "City of Brotherly Love."

Often called the "birthplace of the United States," it was in Philadelphia (at Independence Hall) that the Constitution and the Declaration of Independence were created and signed. It was also in Philadelphia that many famous Americans such as Benjamin Franklin and Thomas Jefferson lived and worked.

If you want to learn more about Philadelphia, you can do research to draw a simple map locating the most famous 18th century buildings still present in the city. You could also build a model of Independence Hall or do research and write a paper about the Declaration of Independence, the Constitution, Ben Franklin or Thomas Jefferson.

Social Studies: History - Tailor-Made Clothing

"In those days, ready-made dresses had not been invented. It would have seemed a real calamity not to have one's clothes fitted and stitched by a nimble-fingered dressmaker, who stayed at a house for weeks in order to fit out different members of the family."

Isn't that interesting? Can you imagine having someone come to your house and live there while your clothes are being measured, sewn and sized? How unusual!

Actually, the way we buy our clothing today is unusual. It is only in the last 150 years that ready-made clothing has been available. In Hitty's day, saying you were a size 10, or that you wear a medium, would have been utterly useless. They wouldn't have understood what you were talking about. Instead, seamstresses measured each person and made clothing that fit his or her specific measurements. It took a long time and cost money, but that was the only way to have it done. If you couldn't afford a dress or suit maker, then you sewed your clothing yourself.

This is just another example of how many things changed during the 20th century. Just think of how many more will change in the 21st century!

Language Arts: Writing and Disscussion Question

Have you ever been teased like Little Thankful and Hitty were? What happened? How did it make you feel?

Language Arts: Vocabulary

balustrade   The banister railing of a stairway.

calomel   A white, tasteless powder that darkens on exposure to light; used in medicine to fight bacteria.

catechism   A handbook of questions and answers for teaching the principles of a religion.

222

devious   Not in a straight path; deceiving.

dimity   A thin, corded or patterned cotton cloth.

fan rope   The rope used to move a manual fan.

merino   A light, thin cloth made from soft wool.

Life Skills: "Beautiful Inside and Out"

The other little girls at the party are mean and hurtful, aren't they? What horrible things to say to Hitty and Little Thankful!

In Hitty's first observations of the girls, she says, "They looked like a flock of tropical butterflies...with their bright bows, their starched ruffles, lacy pantalettes, and shining curls. I was enchanted by the sight..."

Then Hitty's observations take an interesting turn. She continues on by saying, "I had no idea that they were not as charming *in manner* as in appearance."

"Beautiful inside and out" is a saying that means someone is both attractive and kind. Their pleasant outward appearance is a reflection of their inner being. The girls at the party are demonstrating that their beauty and charm is only on the outside.

An older, similar saying is, "Beauty is as beauty does." It means that you will never be considered lovely unless you act lovely from the inside out. Those little girls wore beautiful dresses and sashes, but when they opened their mouths, ugliness came out—pettiness, teasing and hurtful comments.

Remember to check your heart and mouth as often as you might check your outfit!

Chapters Ten and Eleven

"In Which I Am Rescued and Hear Adelina Patti"

"In Which I Sit for My Daguerreotype and Meet a Poet"

Teacher Summary

Hitty is finally rescued from the horsehair sofa. Many years have gone by, and some young children discover Hitty during a game in the attic. The little girl who "adopts" Hitty is named Clarissa Pryce.

The Pryce family are Quakers, and Hitty is excited to belong to a family again (and to be out of that horrible sofa). Clarissa makes her new outfits—Quaker outfits—and it is with the Pryce family that Hitty learns how to write. Clarissa provides Hitty with a proper desk (doll sized) and a beautiful green feather quill pen.

Hitty is enjoying her new life with the Pryce family. One night, Clarissa disobeys her parents and attends a concert of the great singer, Adelina Patti. Her parents don't believe a musical concert is appropriate for a young Quaker girl. The evening is quite eventful and ends in tumult as Clarissa must tell her parents what she has done.

Some time later, Clarissa's grandfather decides he wants a daguerreotype of his youngest granddaughter. Clarissa is thrilled and enjoys her sitting very much. In a surprising turn of events, Hitty herself enjoys a sitting with the photographer and the Pryce family displays both Clarissa's and Hitty's daguerreotypes on the mantel.

Hitty also has the supreme pleasure of seeing and

meeting the famed Quaker poet, John Greenleaf Whittier. He even writes a small but delightful poem about the little doll and gives it to Clarissa.

The Pryce household becomes more sober toward the end our chapter, as the Civil War becomes a reality. The Pryce family, like many Quakers, does not believe in slavery, but they also hate violence. They spend their time working toward peace and helping with war relief.

What we will cover in these chapters:

Social Studies: History - Our Timeline
Social Studies: History - Quakers
Social Studies: History - The Gettysburg Address
Social Studies: History - General McClellan
Social Studies: Career Path - Photographer*
Language Arts: John Greenleaf Whittier
Language Arts: *Uncle Tom's Cabin*
Language Arts: Writing and Discussion Question
Language Arts: Vocabulary
Fine Arts: Daguerreotype

Social Studies: History - Our Timeline

Remember that our book takes place over the course of 100 years. In chapter 1 we looked at ways to deduce the time frame of a story—technology, fashion, historic notes, etc.

In these chapters, we find ourselves reading about the Civil War. We read about Ruth's gentleman friend, John Norton, fighting with General McClellan. What does this say about the current time frame of our story? Can you figure out what year it is now? You can certainly narrow it down to just a few years. Hitty's memoirs have now brought us to somewhere between 1861-1865. How do we know this? If you study General McClellan, you will discover that McClellan served as a general during those years. (Note: An introduction to this general is included in this chapter's lessons.)

If our story began around the turn of the 19th century, then we are now over halfway through Hitty's first hundred years!

If you enjoy art projects, making a timeline (either notebook or wall hanging) of our story would be an excellent project. What things have you learned that could be included on your timeline? (Ideas: poke bonnets, fountain pens, whaling, try-pots, ships, trains, Carib Indians, John Greenleaf Whittier, Charles Dickens, etc.)

Social Studies: History - Quakers

Clarissa and her family are Quakers. If you studied *Betsy Ross* in FIAR Vol. 5, you may remember learning about the Quaker faith. Here is a brief review:

A man named George Fox founded the Religious Society of Friends, or the Quakers, in England in the late 1600s. The term "Quaker" was originally a derogatory term coined by Fox's opponents and was derived from Fox's belief that people should "tremble at the Word of the Lord."

The most significant defining features of the Quaker faith are 1) a simple lifestyle, 2) pacifism, 3) an emphasis on education and learning, and 4) equality for all people.

Social Studies: History - The Gettysburg Address

In chapters 10 and 11 we see the Civil War discussed in relation to the Pryce family and their involvement in war relief and anti-war campaigns. (An excellent book to explore as you review the Civil War is *If You Lived at the Time of the Civil War* by Kay Moore.)

In this lesson, however, we will look at the Civil War from a different perspective. We will study the words of the most significant figure in the Civil War, Abraham Lincoln.

Many consider Abraham Lincoln to be our country's greatest leader. He served as president of the United States from 1860-1865.

Lincoln was chiefly self-taught and homeschooled. His formal education did not last even one year. He believed in education and worked very hard to become not only literate, but also well read. He succeeded in becoming well educated, and Lincoln's writings and speeches are still considered some of the most eloquent and moving texts ever written.

If you have never studied the Gettysburg Address, now would be an excellent time. The writing is stunning. The Gettysburg Address is also a wonderful choice for memorization and oral readings!

As you look over the Gettysburg Address, consider when and where it was given. It is famous and also very short. President Lincoln delivered the speech during the Civil War on November 19, 1863 at the site of the Battle of Gettysburg in Pennsylvania. Lincoln wrote the speech to help rally the North and remind people of the purposes for fighting the war. The Gettysburg Address is carved in stone inside the Lincoln Memorial in Washington D.C.

Here is the complete text of the Gettysburg Address:

Four score and seven years ago our fathers brought forth upon this continent, a new nation, conceived in liberty, and dedicated to the proposition that all men are created equal.

Now we are engaged in a great civil war, testing whether that nation, or any nation so conceived and so dedicated, can long endure. We are met on a great battlefield of that war. We have come to dedicate a portion of that field, as a final resting place for those who here gave their lives that this nation might live. It is altogether fitting and proper that we should do this.

But, in a larger sense, we cannot dedicate—we cannot consecrate—we cannot hallow—this ground. The brave men, living and dead, who struggled here, have consecrated it, far above our poor power to add or detract. The world will little note, nor long remember what we say here, but it can never forget what they did here. It is for us, the living, rather, to be dedicated here to the unfinished work which they who fought here have thus far so nobly advanced. It is rather for us to be here dedicated to the great task remaining before us—that from these honored dead we take increased devotion to that cause for which they gave the last full measure of devotion—that we here highly resolve that these dead shall not have died in vain—that this nation, under God, shall have a new birth of freedom—and that this government of the people, by the people, and for the people, shall not perish from the earth.

Read through the speech again. Do you know how many years "four score and seven" is? (A score is 20 years. Four score and seven equals 87 years.) What does it mean when we say our nation was "conceived in Liberty"? What did Lincoln mean when he says we cannot dedicate, consecrate or hallow the ground? Why does he say the "brave men" have consecrated it? What does it mean that "these dead shall not have died in vain"? You will gain a far greater appreciation for this speech if you understand these ideas and words.

The Gettysburg Address is an excellent passage to memorize and recite. Perhaps you can put together a small (or long) report on Lincoln or the Battle of Gettysburg and present it to your family or friends.

Social Studies: History - General McClellan

Ruth Pryce's heart belongs to a young man named John Norton. She has promised to marry John when he returns from the war and his position under General McClellan.

George Brinton McClellan (1826-1885) was a general in the Union army during the Civil War (1861-1865). He quickly became known as a popular and strong leader—excellent at organizing and training troops. He was even known as the "Young Napoleon," after the French military general Napoleon I. McClellan became so respected, he even ran as the Democratic candidate in 1864 against Abraham Lincoln. He lost, but remained very popular. McClellan did serve in public office as the governor of New Jersey from 1878-1881.

Social Studies: Career Path - Photographer*

Clarissa enjoys getting her daguerreotype taken by the photographer. Although daguerreotypes are very rare these days, you may have experience with a professional photographer.

Do you enjoy photography? Playing with light and shadow, posing people, or catching interesting scenes are just a few of the things good photographers do each day.

There are many different areas in which you can work as a professional photographer. Which do you think sounds the most interesting?

Commercial photographers take pictures for websites, magazines, books and other publications. The pictures can be used for advertisements or just as illustrations. Look at a local grocery store advertisement that you receive in the mail or view online. Do you see the pictures of lettuce or ground beef? A commercial photographer took those pictures. Fashion photography is also considered commercial photography. Commercial photographers must be highly skilled and able to work in a variety of situations.

Portraitures are made by the kind of photographer who takes "family photos." Portrait photographers work in small or large studios, in the outdoors at parks and other locations, or at people's houses. taking pictures of people—individuals, families, weddings, baby pictures, etc. A portrait photographer must like people and be creative in arranging people in a variety of poses.

There are other photography career options, including aerial photography, real estate photography, news and military photography, nature photography, research, film processing, layout and art direction, and scientific photography. This last type of photography is highly specialized and includes medical photography—microscopes, x-ray machines and cameras are used to help doctors diagnose illnesses.

If you like to take pictures and enjoy photography as an art form, looking at photography as a career path is an excellent option to explore. You can learn more about photography by researching online, getting books on the subject, looking into local photography classes or even visiting a local portrait studio or commercial photography site.

Language Arts: John Greenleaf Whittier

This chapter introduces you to the American poet John Greenleaf Whittier.

John Greenleaf Whittier was born in 1807 in Haverhill, Massachusetts and is often known as "the Quaker Poet." His parents were Quaker farmers and his poetry reflects his Quaker heritage. Much of Whittier's work centers on life in New England during the 1800s. He also worked for peace and an end to slavery.

Whittier died in 1892, but his poetry is still read and loved by adults and children alike.

The poem Clarissa learns for Mr. Whittier is his poem entitled "Telling the Bees." Here are the first four stanzas of that poem:

Here is the place; right over the hill
Runs the path I took;
You can see the gap in the old wall still,
And the stepping-stones in the shallow brook.

There is the house, with the gate red-barred,
And the poplars tall;
And the barn's brown length, and the cattle-yard,
And the white horns tossing above the wall.

There are the beehives ranged in the sun;
And down by the brink
Of the brook are her poor flowers, weed-o'er-run,
Pansy and daffodil, rose and pink.

A year has gone, as the tortoise goes
Heavy and slow;
And the same rose blows, and the same sun glows,
And the same brook sings of a year ago.

You may enjoy learning these first few stanzas or some stanzas from another of Whittier's poems. One of Whittier's most famous poems is the long "Snow-Bound," which tells the story of a Quaker family homebound during a blizzard.

Language Arts: *Uncle Tom's Cabin*

The Pryce family, like almost all Quaker families, does not believe in violence or war. In this chapter, we see the family reading aloud the book *Uncle Tom's Cabin*.

228

Published in 1852, this book was written by Harriet Beecher Stowe. Stowe believed slavery was a national sin and wrote the book in order to criticize the pro-slavery movement. The book has become a classic and deals with slavery and southern life in pre-Civil War America.

If you have a deep interest in the Civil War, reading *Uncle Tom's Cabin* may be appropriate. The book features excellent writing, but also includes intense images and strong themes.

Language Arts: Writing and Discussion Question

Hitty writes, "...and though I lived in a Quaker household, which was not sending men away to fight, still we all felt it, too." What do you think Hitty means? Have you ever witnessed a sad or tragic event? Even though you weren't directly involved, how did it make you feel? Write or discuss your answer.

Language Arts: Vocabulary

brow   The part of the face above the eyes; the forehead.

fichu   A three-cornered lace cape for women, worn with the ends fastened or crossed in front.

furbelow   A flounce or ruffle, a showy ornamentation.

leghorn   A straw hat, typically broad-brimmed.

whatnot   A stand with several shelves for books and curios.

Fine Arts: Daguerreotype

Hitty is thrilled to have the Artist take her picture! Have you ever heard of a daguerreotype? Daguerreotype portraits were popular during the middle of the 19th century (1840s and 1850s). A French theatre designer, Louis J. M. Daguerre, created and perfected the photographic process in 1837. Daguerreotypes were the first practical method of photography.

The process of daguerreotypes used a very thin piece of copper that had been plated in silver. The silver, which had been treated with iodine, became sensitive to light. The copper sheet was placed in the camera and then exposed to light (and the subject being photographed). Later, the sheet was removed from the camera and treated with mercury. The image was then "fixed" (or made permanent) on the copper plate. This process was much faster than any previous method of photography, but it still took an exposure time of nearly one hour.

Just four short years after Daguerre announced his new process, the photographic world had already invented a new process which cut the exposure time down to less than a minute. This process was invented by a British inventor, William H. Fox Talbot, and involved light-sensitive paper, not copper plates. Talbot's friend, fellow inventor Sir John Herschel, coined a new phrase and named the patented process "photography."

Daguerreotypes are still collected by people all over the world. Daguerreotypes can be quite beautiful and they hearken back to a simpler time.

Chapters Twelve and Thirteen

"In Which I Go Into Camphor, Reach New York, and Become a Doll of Fashion"

"In Which I Spend a Disastrous New Year's and Return to New England"

Teacher Summary

When Clarissa Pryce is sent away to boarding school, Hitty is put into mothballs, packed away in a box, and sent to the Pryces' cousins, the Van Rensselaers, in New York City. The Van Rensselaers' seamstress, Miss Milly Pinch, discovers Hitty a couple of years later. She is delighted with the small doll and dresses Hitty in the finest fashions.

The Van Rensselaer's young daughter, Isabella, discovers Hitty and wants her. Mr. Van Rensselaer pays Miss Pinch for Hitty and the small doll takes up residence in Isabella's nursery.

It is with Mr. Van Rensselaer and Isabella that Hitty meets Charles Dickens on the street one day. Isabella is so shocked by seeing her favorite author in person that she drops Hitty nearly on his feet. Mr. Dickens kindly picks Hitty up and hands her back to Isabella. Both the child and the doll are thrilled to have met the famous writer.

New Year's Eve arrives and Isabella is told she is too young to take part in the festivities. She disobeys her parents and decides to go out anyway. Just a short while after she and Hitty have been walking, Isabella is attacked by a group of street urchins. They taunt and tease her and steal Hitty. One of the boys, Tim Dooley, decides to give Hitty to his little cousin, Katie. It is with Katie and her mother that Hitty travels to Rhode Island. There, she and Katie play a great deal and Hitty enjoys herself.

Unfortunately, the fun ends soon enough. One day Katie and her friends take a hayride and Hitty is lost on the wagon. The next day the hay, along with Hitty, is thrown into the hayloft, and it is in the hayloft that Hitty spends the next several years.

What we will cover in these chapters:

Social Studies: History - The Industrial Revolution*
Language Arts: Charles Dickens
Language Arts: Writing and Discussion Question
Language Arts: Vocabulary
Research Project: Revising Your Work

Social Studies: History - The Industrial Revolution*

Katie and her mother take a train back to Rhode Island. Hitty is fascinated by this new mode of transportation. She remembers horse-drawn stagecoaches. We see Katie's mother and another woman discussing the advantages of traveling by steam.

Steam engines, like those used in the train Katie is traveling in, revolutionized the lives and jobs of people around the world. Steam engines were first introduced in the late 17th century, but weren't perfected until nearly 100 years later. James Watt, of Scotland, perfected and patented the first steam engine in 1785. The steam engine was just one of the important advancements and inventions that all comprised a vital time in America and around the world. This time is known as the **Industrial Revolution**.

Before the Industrial Revolution in the 18th century, most manufacturing of any kind was done by hand. Wagon wheels, tools, tables, shoes, jewelry, fabrics and textiles were all made by craftsmen in smaller shops and were made one piece at a time. Generally, one craftsman made each item from beginning to end. For example, a woodcarver would begin with a solid trunk of oak and continue the project until he had a finished bed that he would then sell. This way of making and producing goods took time and made things very expensive. After all, if you spent several weeks building a bench wouldn't you want to charge top dollar for it? But what if, instead, you were able to build a machine that did much of the labor and was able to assemble 20 benches a day? Suddenly, the cost drops and productivity increases. This is what happened during the Industrial Revolution. The Industrial Revolution saw many power-driven pieces of machinery introduced into the marketplace and suddenly the production of goods increased dramatically and the price for each item became far more reasonable.

There are so many interesting and important aspects and effects of the Industrial Revolution here in America and globally. Here are some more examples of things you may wish to research further for a writing or speech project:

- the concept of division of labor
- the textile industry
- coal and iron and their part in the Industrial Revolution
- the role of capital
- how the Industrial Revolution affected the working and upper classes
- the railroad and how it played a part in the Industrial Revolution

Language Arts: Charles Dickens

Isabella and her father enjoy spending time together and reading great books, such as Charles Dickens' book *Nicholas Nickleby*. Isabella is thrilled when she accidentally runs into and meets Charles Dickens.

Charles Dickens was an English novelist and is still one of the most popular authors of all time. His books delight both adults and children. A few of his most famous works are *David Copperfield*,

Great Expectations, Oliver Twist, A Tale of Two Cities, and *A Christmas Carol*. Dickens' books are filled with detail, warmth and clever humor.

Charles Dickens (Charles John Huffam Dickens) was born in Portsmouth, England on February 7, 1812. The Dickens family moved to London when Charles was only two years old.

The Dickens family was very poor and Charles had to quit school on several occasions to work and help his family. When he was only 12 years old, Charles worked in a factory pasting labels on bottles of shoe polish. The work was hard and the factory was not a pleasant place to be. Although he only held that job for a few months, the terrible experience stuck with Charles for his entire life.

Charles Dickens quit school entirely at age 15 and went to work as a newspaper reporter soon after. He had a natural and expert ability at writing, and he quickly gained experience working at the newspaper and magazines. When he was only 24 years old, he published his first success entitled *The Posthumous Papers of the Pickwick Club*. It was a series of stories published monthly and was later combined into a book entitled *The Pickwick Papers*. Immediately, Charles Dickens was famous and remained so for his entire life.

Charles Dickens married Catherine Hogarth in 1836. The couple had 10 children, but their marriage was weak. They divorced in 1858.

Besides being a great writer, Charles Dickens loved giving dramatic readings. He often read at charity benefits, enjoying both the performance and helping others.

Charles Dickens died of a stroke at the age of 58 on June 9, 1870.

If you are unfamiliar with Charles Dickens' work, a wonderful place to begin is with *A Christmas Carol*. It is a fabulous story any time of the year! Written with compassion, wit and humor, the story has become a classic.

Like Charles Dickens, you may enjoy giving your own reading performance or dramatic reading. Perhaps you can set up a "literary night" with your family, with each member reading a favorite passage, poem or story. Unlike oral reports, a dramatic reading does not require memorization. Instead, the performer reads directly from the book. There are, however, some tips to remember as you give a dramatic reading.

Charles Dickens

- Select a story you truly love.
- Know the story well.
- Use a pleasant, strong voice when speaking.
- Try to incorporate "character" voices to distinguish between the characters. Make eye contact with your audience. Speak clearly and with energy.

If you want to learn more about Charles Dickens, here are some books to look for:

Who Was Charles Dickens? by Pam Pollack
Charles Dickens and Friends: Five Lively Retellings by Marcia Williams (an illustrated introduction to Dickens' works)

Language Arts: Writing and Discussion Question

Miss Pinch doesn't seem to like working for the Van Rensselaer family very much, does she? Where do you think she would rather work? What would she rather be doing? Write or discuss your answer.

Language Arts: Vocabulary

aggrieved   Being or feeling injured or wronged.

barouche   A four-wheeled carriage with a driver's seat, two passenger seats facing one another, and a folding top.

basque   A woman's close-fitting bodice that extends below the waist.

camphor   A white substance with a strong odor; used to protect clothing from moths and for medicinal purposes.

effigy   An image or statue, usually of a person.

ether   A colorless, sweet-smelling liquid that evaporates quickly; its fumes cause unconsciousness when deeply inhaled.

modiste   A person who makes or sells fashionable women's hats and dresses.

pelisse   A long coat or cloak lined with fur.

portiere   A curtain hung across a doorway.

Research Project: Revising Your Work

You've worked hard on your research paper and now you're in the home stretch! You still have a bit of work left to do, however, and the next section is revising your work. Revising your work involves two things.

First, it involves **proofreading**. Proofreading means to very carefully read through your paper and change any misspellings, grammar errors, or mistakes in spacing or indenting, etc.. It helps to proofread several times yourself, and then have a friend or family member proofread it for you, too. You will be amazed at how many errors your eyes fail to pick up after looking at it several times.

The second phase of revising involves **documenting your sources**. Now that you know what pieces of research and quotes you've included in your paper, you can go back and add in documentation using the Modern Language Association, or MLA, format. Write each quote, statistic, or piece of information accurately and then give full and accurate attribution. If you haven't already gotten a book or website to help you with the MLA format, now is the time to do that. In short, the MLA form cites references within the body of the text, instead of in footnotes. A simple "Works Cited" page with each author or work title listed alphabetically will also be used.

Chapters Fourteen and Fifteen

"In Which I End My Hay-Days and Begin a New Profession"

"In Which I Learn Much of Plantations, Post Offices, and Pin Cushions"

Teacher Summary

It is not Amos who discovers and saves Hitty from the hay, but a young boy. He takes Hitty into the house. The farm family doesn't think much of Hitty, but one of their boarders does. He is a young artist named Mr. Farley and he adopts Hitty. He asks one of his models to make a new outfit for Hitty. In this way, Hitty becomes an artist's model herself. Mr. Farley often uses Hitty while doing his still life work. And anytime he works on a painting of a family or of children he has them hold Hitty.

Eventually, Hitty and Mr. Farley go to New Orleans during Mardi Gras. Mr. Farley enjoys the festivities and then must be off for a month or two to paint portraits for several plantations in the area. Instead of dragging Hitty along, he asks a sweet pair of old ladies, Miss Hortense and Miss Annette, if they would keep Hitty. They are delighted and even work on a new outfit for her. They take their family heirloom, a lacy wedding handkerchief, and fashion Hitty an amazing wedding gown. Their city is hosting a large cotton Exposition and they loan Hitty, in her new cotton finery, as an example of the best woven cotton cloth in the world. Hitty is placed in a glass case of honor and everyone at the Exposition loves her. Unfortunately, so does a particularly sly little girl named Sally Loomis. Her father is a steamboat captain and they are in New Orleans to visit the Exposition. While the specially appointed guard for Hitty's case isn't looking, Sally takes the doll and leaves the Exposition. Hitty finds herself that evening hidden in the young girl's cabin aboard the *Morning Glory*.

One day as she and Sally are visiting a plantation church, they hear a sermon on sinning. Sally is filled with remorse for stealing Hitty and decides to return the doll to God as penance. She flings Hitty, along with the little basket in which the doll is resting, into the river. Hitty floats along for some time and is discovered by a young slave boy as he is fishing. He takes Hitty back to his house and she becomes the boy's little sister's doll. The little girl is named Car'line. Car'line is very enchanted with Hitty and is devastated when her owner discovers the doll. The plantation owner's wife recognizes Hitty from a picture that was in the paper a few months before. The Exposition had placed a "missing" ad and had offered a ransom for the return of Hitty. She tells Car'line the doll must be returned—that Hitty's real owners are missing her. Indeed, she returns Hitty to the Exposition organizers, but, unfortunately, they don't know where to send Hitty. Miss Hortense and Miss Annette are unable to locate Mr. Farley. After all, Hitty truly belongs to him. Finally, Hitty is sent to an old address for Mr. Farley in New York. It is no use. He has moved and Hitty remains in her wooden box in the dead-letter office at the post office for some time.

Eventually, the postal employees hold a raffle of sorts with the left parcels. Someone gets Hitty but he is disappointed. With many twists and turns, Hitty ends up with a new couple. The wife decides to use Hitty to make a doll pincushion. She makes Hitty into an emerald green silk pincushion from the waist down and loves the effect. She decides to enter Hitty as an item at the annual church fair sale.

What we will cover in these chapters:

Social Studies: Geography - New Orleans*
Social Studies: Geography - Vicksburg
Language Arts: Writing and Discussion Question
Language Arts: Vocabulary
Fine Arts: Playing the Guitar

Social Studies: Geography - New Orleans*

Mr. Farley and Hitty wind up in an interesting and busy city known as New Orleans. Look on a map of Louisiana and locate New Orleans. Do you see how it hugs the Mississippi River? New Orleans is often called the "Crescent City" because its original section lays along a giant curve along the Mississippi. Sieur de Bienville founded the city of New Orleans in 1718.

New Orleans' French Quarter is the most famous section of New Orleans. French colonists originally settled the area, also known as *Vieux Carre* (vee yoo cair RAY), meaning "Old Square." It is interesting to note that in the late 1700s horrendous fires destroyed much of the French Quarter. At that same time, Spain ruled Louisiana. When the French Quarter was rebuilt it was under Spanish rule. Therefore, it was redone following a Spanish style of architecture. Today, the French Quarter still resembles a Spanish area with patios and wrought-iron balconies and not a Parisian street.

It is virtually impossible to talk about New Orleans and not discuss Creole cooking and jazz music. New Orleans is known throughout the world as the home of Creole cooking. Creole cooking is a spicy and delicious blend of French and Spanish cuisine. Creole cooking often features seafood (chiefly shrimp and crayfish), as well as delicious sausages. Ingredients include bell pepper, onions, celery and a fascinating spice known as *filé* (fee LAY) powder. File powder is made from ground sassafras leaves. It lends a deep, smoky flavor to many dishes. It also operates as a thickening agent.

If you are interested in the foods of New Orleans, you might want to look up Creole vs. Cajun cooking and read about these two important influences in the foods of southern Louisiana.

New Orleans is also known as the birthplace of jazz music. In the early 1900s, both black and white musicians would get together in the French Quarter and play. From this wonderful blending of styles, jazz was born. Today, many of the most famous jazz clubs are still located along the streets of the French Quarter. If you would like to have a taste and sense of New Orleans without having to travel, listen to some old New Orleans style jazz music and make one of the quintessential New Orleans dishes—dirty rice. Who knows? Perhaps Miss Hortense and Miss Annette dined on just such a dish.

Dirty Rice

(This recipe calls for ground chicken livers and chicken gizzards. Any butcher at a supermarket meat counter can do this for you easily and for free. You may also use a combination of ground beef or sausage as a substitute for the liver and gizzards, if you'd like.)

Seasoning Mix:

2 tsp. ground red pepper (cayenne)
1 tsp. salt
1 1/2 tsp. black pepper
1 tsp. paprika
1 tsp. dry mustard
1 tsp. ground cumin
1/2 tsp. dried thyme

Other ingredients:

2 Tbs. vegetable oil
1/2 lb. chicken gizzards, ground
1/4 lb. ground pork
1/2 tsp. dried oregano
2 bay leaves
3/4 cup finely chopped onions
1/2 cup finely chopped celery

236

1/2 cup finely chopped green bell peppers
2 tsp. minced garlic
2 Tbs. unsalted butter
2 cups chicken stock
1/2 lb. chicken livers, ground
3/4 cup uncooked converted rice

Combine the seasoning mix ingredients in a small bowl; set aside. In a large skillet, cook the gizzards, pork, oregano and bay leaves in the oil over high heat until meat is thoroughly browned. Stir in seasoning mix. Cook the seasoning with the meats for at least 1 minute to allow the spices to fully release their flavors. Add onions, celery, bell peppers and garlic. Stir thoroughly. Add butter and stir until melted. Reduce heat to medium and cook about 8 minutes.

Add the stock and deglaze*. Cook 8 minutes over high heat, stirring once. Stir in chicken livers and cook about 2 minutes. Add rice and stir thoroughly. Cover pan and turn heat to very low; cook 5 minutes. Remove from heat and leave covered until rice is tender, about 10 minutes. Remove bay leaves. Serves 6.

*Deglazing is a chef's term for adding a liquid to a hot pan in which meats or vegetables have been cooked and scraping the bottom to stir up more flavor for sauces, gravies, etc.

Social Studies: Geography - Vicksburg

Miss Hortense might have been married, but sadly, her true love died in the Battle of Vicksburg. Throughout Five in a Row, we have looked at the Civil War from many angles. Here is yet another opportunity to review and learn about one of the most important Civil War battles.

Often referred to as the Siege of Vicksburg, the battle took place in the spring of 1863. General Grant knew he wanted to capture the city of Vicksburg. Vicksburg was (and is) a major Mississippi River port. It was the major port between Memphis and New Orleans. First, Grant launched his capture from the north. He did this several times, but the marshy and muddy areas north of New Orleans bogged down his men. In April, 1863, Grant decided upon a new course of action. During the dark of night, Union artillery sea vessels and supply ships floated past the Confederate artillery along the river and established a base on the south side of New Orleans. With this new area in his grasp, Grant's troops then marched down the west side of the river and crossed over by ship to dry ground on the east side south of the city. After many attacks and battles, Vicksburg finally surrendered on July 4, the day after the Southern defeat at Gettysburg. Grant's plan worked. The North now controlled the Mississippi River. Why would this be an important strategy in the course of the Civil War?

Look at a map of the United States. The Mississippi River divides the southern (or at the time, the Confederate) states in half. If the Union army could gain control of the Mississippi River in this area, they could, in essence, cut the Confederate power in half, as well. Think about it for a moment. How would the Confederate states get tax dollars and funds back and forth to one another? They certainly couldn't go north. How would the Confederate states get supplies, guns and food between themselves? Grant's strategy in Vicksburg was brilliant and helped him toward the end goal—winning the Civil War.

Language Arts: Writing and Discussion Question

Sally Loomis feels ashamed of herself for stealing Hitty after she hears the sermon on stealing. She throws Hitty into the river and runs home. Do you think she told her father what she did? Why or why not? Support your answer with facts found in the text relating to Sally's character.

Language Arts: Vocabulary

detected   Found out; discovered.

formidable   Hard to overcome, hard to deal with; to be dreaded.

mar   To spoil the beauty of; to damage.

Mardi Gras   The last day before Lent; Shrove Tuesday. It is celebrated in New Orleans and other cities with parades and celebrations.

plied   Past tense of ply—to go back and forth again and again.

roused   Awakened; stirred up.

tapering   Becoming gradually smaller at one end.

Fine Arts: Playing the Guitar

One of Hitty's favorite things about her life on the plantation with Car'line is listening to the men playing their guitars and banjos and singing. Do you play an instrument? Even if you are already taking lessons for some other istrument, learning to play the guitar can be a lot of fun.

With a book from your local library or a few videos online, you can learn to play a few simple chords and be playing a song in no time. Learning to play complex and beautiful songs on a guitar takes years of practice and dedication, but any beginner can learn a few basics and enjoy the experience.

Hitty: Her First Hundred Years

Chapters Sixteen and Seventeen

"In Which I Return to Familiar Scenes"

"In Which I Am Sold at Auction"

"And Last Remarks"

Teacher Summary

Hitty is bought by a young woman at a church fair and given to the young woman's Great-Aunt Louella as a birthday gift. Great-Aunt Louella lives in Boston and Hitty can't help but feel good about returning to the New England area—so near her birthplace of Maine. Unfortunately, Great-Aunt Louella doesn't take a shine to Hitty as pincushion. A guest of the old lady's does, however, and undresses Hitty to uncover her beautiful wooden legs and feet. The guest, Miss Pamela, falls in love with Hitty. She dresses her in a new gown and takes her wherever she goes.

One day Miss Pamela goes for a drive and Hitty is sadly thrown from the car by mistake. Although they look and look for the small doll, the knot of an old tree hides her and they must leave her behind. A few years go by. One day some young people are having a picnic near the tree. They spy Hitty and think she is quite the funny old doll. They take her with them, but soon forget her and she is left behind in the rented stage. The carriage owner finds Hitty and allows his daughter, Carrie, to have the small doll. Carrie, much to Hitty's excitement, takes the small doll with her to her hometown of Portland, Maine. Hitty is thrilled! Portland is so very near to her birthplace. Portland was the town and harbor that Captain Preble so often visited and from where he set sail on his voyages.

Carrie soon decides to hold a sale of her things and an older woman at the sale takes a liking to Hitty.

She likes Hitty's expression and takes her home. Much to Hitty's amazement the old woman's home used to belong to the Prebles. Just as she has always hoped, Hitty has returned to her roots. The Prebles are long gone, but the ancestral pine still blows in the wind and the "P" is still roughly cut over the fireplace.

Hitty stays in the home for several years, but in the end is auctioned off after the old woman's death. A man purchases Hitty for over $50 and takes her back to a shop owned by Miss Hunter. Miss Hunter had sent him to buy some new things for her shop and is delighted with Hitty. Of course, Miss Hunter's shop on Eighth Street in New York is where our story began. In this way, we find out how Hitty came to be in Miss Hunter's shop and we can only speculate as to her next set of adventures.

What we will cover in these chapters:

Social Studies: History - The Horseless Carriage
Social Studies: History - The Time Frame at the End of Our Story
Language Arts: Writing a Complete Story
Language Arts: Personification
Language Arts: Writing and Discussion Question
Language Arts: Vocabulary
Research Project: Preparing the Final Draft
Service Project: Reviewing Your Efforts*

Social Studies: History - The Horseless Carriage

In this chapter, Hitty sees a car for the very first time. When automobiles first came out, they were called "horseless carriages." Automobiles were exciting! In brief, Gottlieb Daimler and Karl Benz developed the first of the gasoline engines in 1885. Benz and Gottlieb later formed an alliance and began producing cars under the Mercedes-Benz name. Perhaps one of the most famous names in automobile history, Henry Ford, built his first successful gasoline powered car in 1886. Then, in 1904 he founded the Ford Motor Company. It was this company that produced the Model T Ford (in 1908). This was the first car that was mass-produced using a moving assembly line. With this technology, Ford was able to offer a quality car at a reasonable price, right around $300. The Model T was the top selling car in America for over 20 years and people affectionately called it the "Tin Lizzie."

At first, only the wealthy owned cars. In the early 1900s, farmers became the first mass group of car buyers. Cars allowed them to sell their products much faster and to a larger region. If their farms were several miles from two different towns, cars allowed the farmers to travel to both—even in one day! This was something unimaginable in the days of horse-drawn wagons.

Take some time to investigate a new subject regarding cars. You can write a paper or develop a speech on a related subject. Here are few ideas that can get you started:

Car Safety (i.e., highway speed limits, drinking and driving, seatbelts and air bags, safety technology, driver instruction classes, etc.)

Environmental Impact of Cars (i.e., fuel emissions, gasoline and oil spills)

Foreign Imports and How They Compare to Domestic Cars (what makes and models of cars are produced in Great Britain, Sweden, Germany, France, Japan, and South Korea?)

Cars of the Future (i.e., hybrids, electric, driverless, concept cars, etc.)

Social Studies: History - The Time Frame at the End of Our Story

In our lessons in chapter 1, we discussed how to deduce the time frame of a story when no specific date is given. Technology, fashion and foods were all cited as items to look for in a story to help figure out what the time period is.

In chapter 1, we decided that Hitty's memoirs begin sometime during the first several years of the 19th century. Now that we are at the end of the book, we know that airplanes have been invented. This "clue" leads us to know that Hitty is now living in the early years of the 20th century. Her first hundred years have passed and she is now in another century. It is now yet another century for us—the 21st century. Do you think if Hitty were a real doll she might still be around? What do you think her adventures have been during her second hundred years? Do you think she has traveled by airplane?

Take some time to think about what Hitty may have experienced since the book ended. Write a short summary or begin a short story depicting these events. You could write a simple paragraph, but you might enjoy your writing and begin a "sequel" to Rachel Field's book.

Language Arts: Writing a Complete Story

Our author, Rachel Field, writes a wonderful story, doesn't she? She weaves so many adventures into the life of one small doll. Field introduces us to a colorful and memorable cast of secondary characters, as well. Remember Captain Preble? The Old Peddler? Bill Buckle? Miss Pinch? Field also knows how to write a complete story—a story that leads the reader through a tale with a beginning, middle and an ending.

Hitty: Her First Hundred Years is a complete story. The beginning of our story is truly when Hitty begins her memoirs about the Old Peddler and Maine. The middle of the story is when Hitty is lost in India. And finally, the end of the story begins in chapter 13 as Hitty is returned to New England. As you read other books, see if you can identify the beginning of the story, the middle of the story and where the ending begins.

Not all stories end with the character returning to where he began (like Hitty returning to Maine and the old Preble house), but all excellent stories end with a character learning something about himself. Hitty returns to her roots in Maine before she ends up in a new locale at the Eighth Street Antique Shop. Before she arrives there, however, she learns all about the world, other people and, most of all, about herself and what she can handle. Hitty is a brave doll. She is a doll of character and a doll that has a purpose—to write her memoirs.

As always, you can improve your writing skills by reading other authors' works and learning from their styles. In this book, you can learn from Field's skill in writing a complete tale. She doesn't leave any loose ends, but, instead, weaves a wonderful ending.

Language Arts: Personification

If you have used previous volumes of Five in a Row, you've seen examples of personification many times. Certainly, *Hitty: Her First Hundred Years* is a dramatic example of personification. After all, the main character is a doll! Personification is just that—giving a nonliving thing human characteristics and feelings.

Think back to Hitty. What can Hitty do that is like a person? She can think. She can write (using her brain and hand). She can see, but she apparently does not blink because no one notices this. She can't move her head, but she can move her leg a bit. Remember when she's lost in the Preble family church and she uses her leg to make a sound? Can Hitty speak? Well, she certainly doesn't talk in the book, so we can assume she cannot. Hitty can most definitely feel, however. Her feelings are hurt when people refer to her as ugly and worn, and they are built up when people think she is attractive or when she is called a doll with "character."

If you want to try your own hand at personification, you can choose any inanimate object and give it human characteristics. Here are some questions you can answer about your object that might help you brainstorm ideas for your story. Some of these questions may apply to your character, and some may not.

What is your object's name?
What gender is your object?
Who are his/her parents?
Where is he/she from?
What does he/she love to eat? Hate to eat?
What does he/she do for fun?
What is his/her favorite sport?
What is his/her favorite type of music?
Where does he/she love to go on vacation?
What was his/her hometown like?
What is his/her greatest accomplishment?
What is his/her greatest fear?
What is his/her favorite time of day?
What is his/her best childhood memory?
What would he/she like to be when he/she grows up?
Where does he/she want to be in 10 years?

As you can see, by simply answering a list of questions you begin thinking about your new character. As you look over your answers a story may begin forming in your mind, and as you write you can refer back to your list for specifics or for new ideas.

Language Arts: Writing and Discussion Question

In the lessons for chapter 1, you were asked to think about how Hitty might have come to be in Miss Hunter's antique shop. Now that the story has ended, you know what truly happened. How did your deduction and the end of our story match or disagree? Do you like the way Rachel Field, our author, wrote the ending?

Language Arts: Vocabulary

bric-a-brac   Interesting or curious trinkets used for decoration.

burnished   Made shiny; polished.

junketing   Going on a pleasure trip; traveling by means of someone else's expense.

Research Project: Preparing the Final Draft

Your research paper is nearly finished! Aren't you proud of your work? It will be exciting to present this major writing assignment to your parent/teacher. You still have just a few details to finish up.

First, you need to make sure you are completely satisfied with the paper. Have you checked it for any last-minute revisions you wish to make? Next, you need to prepare a final copy for presentation. This includes double-spacing all the pages, numbering your pages, and creating your "Works Cited" page. You also need to create a title page, which will include your name and the date. Finally, you might want to add a dust jacket or folder for a more professional look.

You've done it! You've completed your research paper. Well done!

Service Project: Reviewing Your Efforts*

Your service project should be well underway now. You may decide to stop or continue if you are enjoying your new-found service. How has the project gone? Do you feel good about what you've done and who you have helped? Perhaps to finish the project you can write a poem, story, or paper about your experience with your service project and the people you've met.

Use this page to jot down relevant info you've found for this
Five in a Row chapter book, including favorite lessons, go-along
resources, field trips, and family memories.

HITTY: HER FIRST HUNDRED YEARS

Dates studied: _____

Student: _____

Favorite Lesson Topics:

Social Studies:
_____
_____
_____

Science:
_____
_____
_____

Language Arts:
_____
_____

Fine Arts:
_____
_____
_____

Life Skills:
_____
_____
_____

**Relevant Library Resources:
Books, DVDs, Audio Books**

_____
_____
_____
_____
_____
_____
_____

Websites or Video Links:

_____
_____
_____
_____
_____
_____

Related Field Trip Opportunities: _____
_____
_____

Favorite Quote or Memory During Study: _____
_____
_____

244

Research Paper Information

The Research Paper lesson introduced you to the opportunity to write a research paper and some research paper topics that you might choose from. Using the outline below, you can begin your research paper process and prewriting background work.

Teacher's Note: This page is meant to merely be a basic outline for your student. There are many writing resources available to your student for more in-depth instruction. You are strongly encouraged to obtain one of these resources for your student to use in conjuction with this unit. One which is highly recommeneded is *Writers Inc.: A Student Handbook for Writing and Learning* (by Senbranek, Meyer and Kemper). In this book, the Modern Language Association (MLA) form for citing sources is explained. You can also find other research paper writing resources at your local library.

1. Gathering Information and Prewriting

Choose your subject.
Gather information.
Create a thesis statement.
Make notes.
Create a bibliography.

2. Creating a Writing Plan

Prepare an outline.
Develop your writing plan.
Revise your work.

3. Writing a First Draft

Write the introduction.
Write the body of the paper.
Write the conclusion.

4. Revising Your Paper

Revise your paper at least three times. (Proofread each time!)
Create documentation for all your sources (using MLA form).

5. Preparing the Final Paper

Proofread.
Arrange and number the pages.
Add a title page, including name and date.
Prepare final copy of the paper.
Add a folder or dust jacket , if you'd like. Make it look as good as it can!

Language Arts: **Vocabulary Words**

Throughout Five in a Row volumes 5-8, vocabulary review has been done with crossword puzzles and the vocabulary sorting activity (as used in the *Neil Armstrong* unit). In the *Hitty: Her First Hundred Years* unit we want to introduce a different type of vocabulary review. You may choose to use this review format or continue with the sorting activity review if you would rather.

Below you'll find a diagram with blank sections. Draw a picture that represents the meaning of each vocabulary word in a chapter into each blank section. Some words will be easier to draw than others; just do your best to come up with something that represents each word visually for yourself. Make one or more copies of the page below for each chapter's vocabulary words. You can enlarge the image if desired.

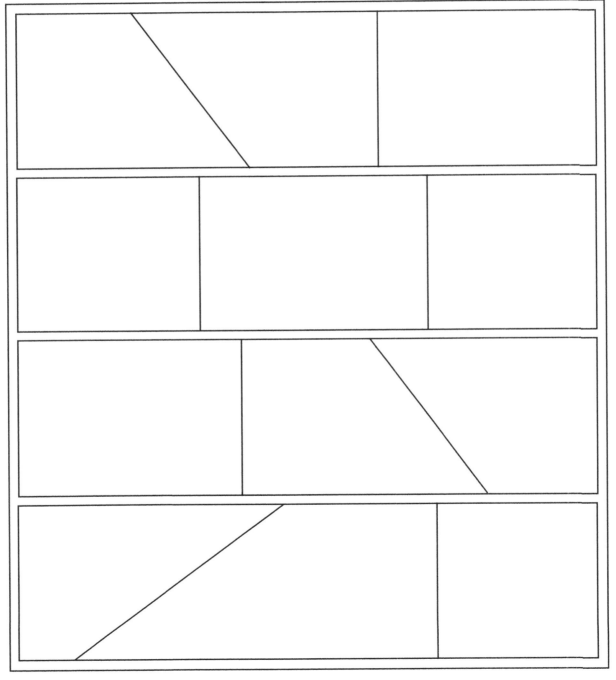

246

Hitty: Her First Hundred Years - Chapter 3

Name:

Date:

Science: **Vestibular Input**

In the lesson **Science: Motion Sickness**, you learned that the vestibular system (located in the inner ear) is partially responsible for reporting to our brain what is happening around our body. Our balance can be affected when there is too much motion and our vestibular system is overwhelmed.

Our vestibular system is receiving input constantly as we move our heads—the greater the movement, the higher the vestibular input that we receive.

Some people prefer lots of vestibular input (they love swinging, jumping on a trampoline, etc.) while others do not enjoy activities that produce high vestibular input. There are many vestibular activities that you can try that can help to build your balance, could feel calming to you, or could be energizing to you.

- Swinging
- Jump rope
- Somersaults
- Rocking chair
- Jumping on a trampoline
- Riding a roller coaster
- Standing on a balance board
- Hanging upside down

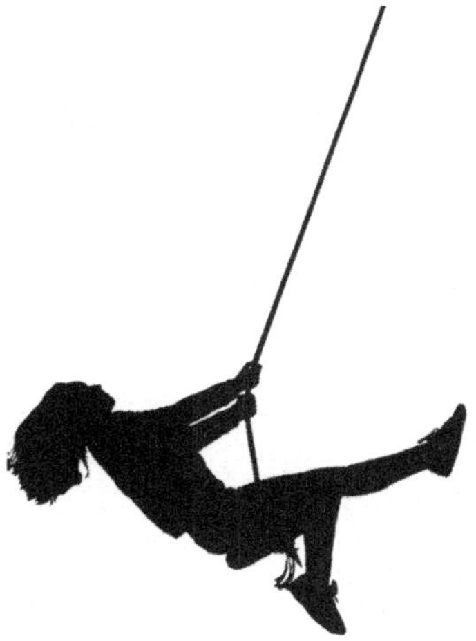

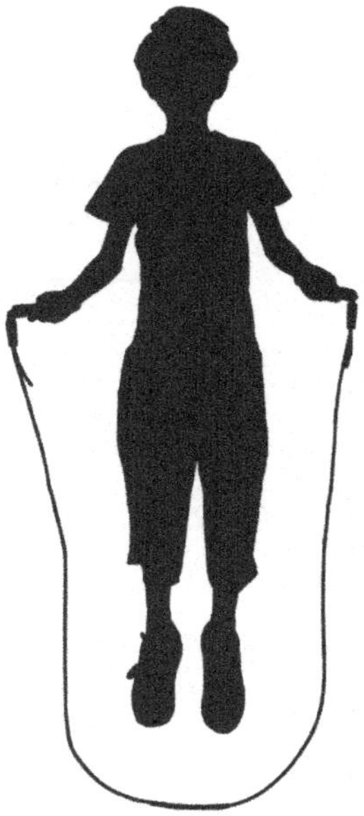

Research online, "vestibular activities for kids."
Record more ideas that you find through your research below:

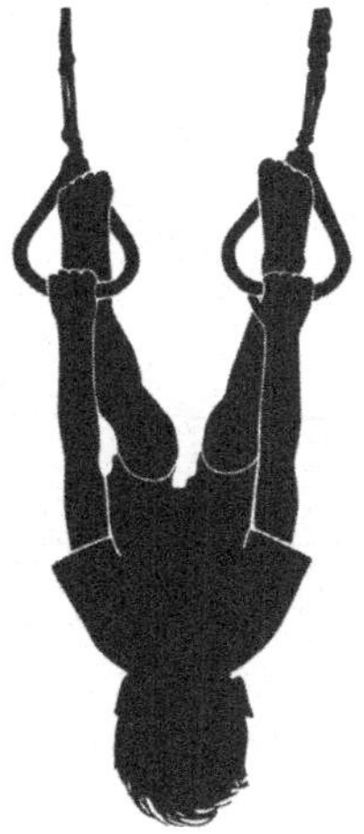

Name:

Date:

Language Arts: **Dynamic, Static and Stereotypical Characters**

In the lesson **Language Arts: Characters - Dynamic, Static and Stereotypical**, you were introduced to three types of characters found in many fictional stories. Use a fictional story that you are familiar with (it could be *The Boxcar Children* or *The Saturdays* from FIAR Volumes 5 and 6, or a different story that you've read) to fill in blanks below.

Book Title:

_____

Dynamic Character(s):

_____

_____

_____

248

Static Character(s):

_____

_____

_____

Stereotypical Character(s):

_____

_____

_____

Hitty: Her First Hundred Years - Chapter 4
Research Project Outline

Topic _____

Introduction _____

_____

_____

Thesis Statement _____

_____

_____

1st Major Point _____

   1. _____

   2. _____

   3. _____

2nd Major Point _____

   1. _____

   2. _____

   3. _____

_____

3rd Major Point _____

   1. _____

   2. _____

   3. _____

Conclusion _____

_____

_____

Name:

Date:

Science: **Biography - Who Am I?**

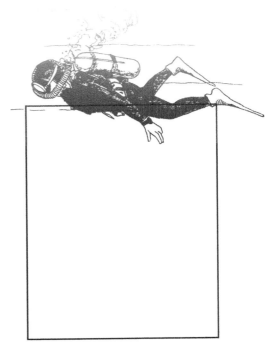

Marine biologists choose a speciality within their field. These specialties include: phycology, ichthyology, invertebrate zoology, marine mammalogy, fishery biology, marine biotechnology, marine microbiology or marine ecology. To dig deeper, after completing the lesson **Career Path: Marine Biologist,** you can learn about Eugenie Clark, a woman who dove into the field and specialized in ichthyology (the study of fish).

Two go-along books that you could use for research are:

Shark Lady: The True Story of How Eugenie Clark Became the Ocean's Most Fearless Scientist
    by Jess Keating (picture book)
Shark Lady: True Adventures of Eugenie Clark
    by Ann McGovern (chapter book)

Print and paste an image of Eugenie Clark into the frame. Write information gathered through your research into the spaces below.

250

Name: _____

Lived: _____

Known for: _____

_____

_____

_____

Connections to story: _____

_____

_____

_____

_____

Name:

Date:

Science: **Coral Reefs**

Virtual 🖥 FIELD TRIP

In the lesson, **Science: Coral Reefs**, many interesting facts about coral reefs are provided for you to learn more about these colorful habitats. Take a virtual tour to introduce yourself to the visual beauty and wonder within the coral reefs. Search online for, "coral reef virtual tour." Take notes below, and include any information that you find particularly interesting. Take a screenshot during the virtual tour and paste an image into the frame above (or search online for an image of something you learn about in the virtual tour to print and paste).

_____

_____

_____

_____

_____

Name:

Date:

Science: **Bioluminescent Animals—Photo Scavenger Hunt**

After completing the **Science: Bioluminescence** lesson, you can use this page to go on a photographic scavenger hunt of six different sea or land animals that utilize bioluminescence.

Search online for the following: "bioluminescent animals." Print and paste images of each animal you choose into the spaces below and label each photograph.

252

Hitty: Her First Hundred Years - Chapter 8

Name:

Date:

Language Arts: **Sensory Descriptions**

The **Language Arts: Sensory Descriptions** lesson discusses ways to incorporate the five senses into your writing to make it come alive for the reader. Write one or two paragraphs based on the prompts below, and circle which senses you were able to fit into your paragraph after writing it.

Writing Prompt: You arrive on a desert island and find yourself sourounded by new plants, animals, and foods. Write about your imaginary experience.

Circle which senses you used in the paragraph: sight   hearing   touch   smell   taste

_____

_____

_____

_____

_____

_____

_____

Writing Prompt: You're traveling through a busy city on your way to visit friends. You notice lots of traffic, food stands, people walking their pets, etc. Write about your imaginary experience.

Circle which senses you used in the paragraph: sight   hearing   touch   smell   taste

_____

_____

_____

_____

_____

_____

_____

Name:

Date:

Social Studies: **Biography - Who Am I?**

To dig deeper, after completing the lesson **Social Studies: Missionaries**, research a missionary and learn more about them. Use the go-along books listed below or search online.

A good go-along book:
Great for God: Missionaries Who Changed the World by David Shibley

A good missionary series to choose a book from:
Christian Heroes Then and Now
   by Janet and Geoff Benge

254

Print and paste an image of the missionary you chose into the frame.
Write information gathered through your research into the spaces below.

Name: _____

Lived: _____

Known for: _____

_____

_____

_____

Connections to story: _____

_____

_____

_____

_____

Name:

Date:

Fine Arts: **Photography**

In the lesson **Career Path: Photographer**, many types of professional photography were mentioned. Photography is an fulfilling hobby even if it isn't a probable career path. Learning what makes a photograph look good can be helpful to everyone. Search, "basic photography skills for kids," online or use the resource book below to learn more about photography. If you have access to a digital camera or phone camera, you can practice what you learn! Print and paste a photograph that you take in the frame below and note any particular tips or lessons that you learned about photography through your research.

A good go-along book:
National Geographic Kids Guide to Photography by Nancy Honovich and Annie Griffiths

What lessons, tips or tricks did you learn about photograhpy in your research?

_____

_____

_____

_____

_____

Name:

Date:

Social Studies: **Industrial Revolution**

In the **Social Studies: Industrial Revolution** lesson, you learned that from about 1760 through the early 1800s, the United States and western Europe transitioned to new manufacturing processes that changed people's lives dramatically. Below is a list of five inventions that resulted from the Industrial Revolution. Choose one of these and research who invented it and when; how, where, and by whom it was used; how it transformed daily life, etc. Print and paste a picture by your summary.

Choose from:

• assembly line
• telegraph
• steam engine
• sewing machine
• internal combustion engine

256

Industrial Revolution Invention: _____

_____

_____

_____

_____

_____

_____

_____

_____

_____

_____

Hitty: Her First Hundred Years - Chapters 14 & 15

Name:

Date:

Social Studies: **Foods & Finds - New Orleans: Photo Scavenger Hunt**

In the **Social Studies: New Orleans** lesson, you learned some basic facts about New Orleans. Now you can embark on a photographic scavenger hunt of this famous city and see for yourself some of the sights.

Search online for the following: "photograph of _____" (fill in the blank with the items listed next)—Cafe du Monde beignet, Jackson Square New Orleans, St. Louis Cathedral New Orleans. Print and paste images into the spaces below and label each photograph.

Service Project: **Documentation and Memories**

It's time to document what you've done with your **Service Project** and the memories that you've made. Print a few photographs of yourself doing your service project, or, you could print and paste images or information from the website of the organization you served into the frames below.

List memories you made or facts about your service in the blanks provided.

258

Chapter Book

Sample **Lesson Planning Sheet**

Neil Armstrong: Young Flyer and *Marie Curie and the Discovery of Radium* have more suggested lessons per chapter than you will probably want to (or be able to) cover. The sample planning sheets below and on the following pages show ideas that *could* be chosen for the first two weeks of the **Neil Armstrong** study. You are free to choose any of the lesson ideas and keep track of your choices by noting them on the reproducible, blank Lesson Planning Sheet (following these pages). For more ideas on making the best use of your Five in a Row curriculum, be sure to read the *Tips and Advice for Five in a Row Chapter Book Studies* section as well as *How to Use Five in a Row Volume 8* earlier in this volume.

Week __1__	Monday	Tuesday
Title: *Neil Armstrong: Young Flyer* **Author:** Montrew Dunham	Read Chapter 1 together, then: **Language Arts** Review quotation marks in book and also using example from manual **Social Studies** Discuss time frame of story Do activity sheet	**Language Arts** Discuss numerical prefixes and come up with some examples (orally) **Social Studies** Tri-motor airplanes: Read lesson, look at some onlines Tie in to Science lesson on aluminum and alloys

Wednesday	Thursday	Friday
Read Chapter 2 together, then: **Social Studies** Wright brothers – look up Kill Devil Hills and Kitty Hawk online Read go-along book from library on Wright brothers Talk about discussion question: invention vs. discovery	**Science** How airplanes fly Do activity sheet	**Language Arts** Sort vocabulary words on sheets **Social Studies** Review England and discuss King Edward VIII Listen to his abdication speech online Tie in to Life Skills lesson on a sense of duty – give an example from my life

Chapter Book

Sample **Lesson Planning Sheet: Week 2**

Week **2**	Monday	Tuesday
Title: *Neil Armstrong: Young Flyer* **Author:** Montrew Dunham	**Read Chapter 3 together, then:** ### Language Arts Sort vocabulary words on sheets Review synonyms, antonyms, and homonyms Do activity sheet	**Life Skills** Discuss being content from lesson (ask: what do you need to be content with in your life right now?) Tie it in to "difficult decisions" from last chapter's Life Skills lesson

Wednesday	Thursday	Friday
Read Chapter 4 together, then:	**Social Studies**	**Fine Arts**
Social Studies		OR
	Castle Garden and Ellis Island	**Creative Writing**
Prussia – look up a historical map online	Do activity sheet	(give a choice)
Language Arts		Drawing from memory vs. drawing from life (firefly)
		OR
Sort vocabulary words on sheets		Creative writing: Beginning with one item

Chapter Book Lesson Planning Sheet:

Week ___	Monday	Tuesday

Title:

Author:

Wednesday	Thursday	Friday

Index

Social Studies

Science

Language Arts

Research Project

Title index

Author index

Fine Arts

Life Skills

Supplemental Book List

Neil Armstrong: Young Flyer

The Wright Brothers: How They Invented the Airplane by Russell Freedman
If Your Name Was Changed at Ellis Island by Ellen Levine
Find The Constellations by H. A. Rey
The Ashley Book of Knots by Clifford Ashley
Starry Messenger by Peter Sis
Carrying the Fire: An Astronaut's Journeys by Michael Collins
Liftoff! by Michael Collins
The Far Side of the Moon by Alex Iruine
Flying to the Moon and other Strange Places by Michael Collins
Disney Maps: A Magical Atlas of the Movies We Know and Love by Disney
Constellations by F. S. Kim
Constellations, The Story of Space Told Through the 88 Known Star Patterns in the Night Sky
   by Govert Schilling
The Digestive System by Jennifer Prior
The Digestive System by Christine Taylor-Butler
How Food Travels in the Body: Digestive System by Biology Books for Kids
Harry S. Truman (Childhood of Famous Americans Series) by George E. Stanley
Hidden Figures: Young Readers' Edition by Margot Lee Shetterly
Chasing Space: Young Readers' Edition by Leeland Melvin

Marie Curie and the Discovery of Radium

The Iridescence of Birds: A Book About Henri Matisse by Patricia MacLachlan
Henri Matisse: Drawing with Scissors by Jane O'Connor
Henri's Scissors by Jeanette Winter
Colorful Dreamer by Majorie Blain Paker
Elements: A Visual Exploration of Every Known Atom in the Universe by Theodore Gray
The Periodic Table: Elements with Style! by Simon Basher and Adrian Dingle
Alfred Nobel: The Man Behind the Peace Prize by Kathy-Jo Wargin
The Nobel Prize: The Story of Alfred Nobel and the Most Famous Prize in the World by Michael Worek
Alfred Nobel: Inventive Thinker by Tristan Boyer Binns

Hitty: Her First Hundred Years

Stellaluna by Janell Cannon

The Advetures of Tom Sawyer by Mark Twain

Moby-Dick by Herman Melville

D'Aulaires' Book of Greek Myths by Ingri and Edgar d'Aulaire

Draw 50 Sharks, Whales, and Other Sea Creatures by Lee J. Ames and Warren Budd

The Swiss Family Robinson by Johann David Wyss

Rikki-Tikki-Tavi by Rudyard Kipling

Christian Heroes: Then & Now by Janet and Geoff Benge

Hero Tales: A Family Treasury of True Stories from the Lives of Christian Heros
   by Dave and Neta Jackson

If You Lived at the Time of the Civil War by Kay Moore

Uncle Tom's Cabin by Harriet Beecher Stowe

A Christmas Carol by Charles Dickens

Who Was Charles Dickens? by Pam Pollack

Charles Dickens and Friends: Five Lively Retellings by Marcia Williams

Writers Inc.: A Student Handbook for Writing and Learning by Senbranek, Meyer and Kemper

Shark Lady: The True Story of How Eugenie Clark Became the Ocean's Most Fearless Scientist
   by Jess Keating

Shark Lady: True Adventures of Eugenie Clark by Ann McGovern

Great for God: Missionaries Who Changed the World by David Shibley

National Geographic Kids Guide to Photography by Nancy Honovich and Annie Griffiths

Scope of Topics

Neil Armstrong: Young Flyer

History
Tri-motor airplane
1930s
Kittyhawk, North Carolina
Wright Brothers
King Edward VIII
England
Prussia
Germany
Castle Garden
Ellis Island
Pearl Harbor
Steam engine
President Harry S. Truman
Atom bomb
Truman Doctrine
Fair Deal
Korean War
NASA
Sir Isaac Newton
Michael Collins
Edwin "Buzz" Aldrin

Geography
Kittyhawk, North Carolina
England
Prussia
Germany
Castle Garden
Ellis Island
Pearl Harbor
Pacific Islands
Korean War
Capes

Career Path
Chef
Baker
Pilot
Astronaut

Science
Aluminum
Alloys
Eardrum
Flight
Rubber
Research
Constellations
Campfires
Stars
Digestion
Science fair projects
Conduction
Convection
Radiation
Galaxies
Solar system
Air travel
Sound travel
Gravity experiment
Moon
Rockets

Language Arts
Dialogue (punctuation)
Numerical prefixes
Synonyms
Antonyms
Homonyms
Metaphors
Similes
Personification
Summarizing
Interviewing

Vocabulary Words

mono, uni

bi

tri

quad

quint, pent

sex, hex

sept

octa

deca

cent

abdicate

duty

synonyms

antonyms

homonyms

metaphors

similes

contentment

kaiser

masticator

vulcanization

latex

scale

symbol

Melanesia

Micronesia

Polynesia

Pearl Harbor

cartography

digestion

saliva

esophagus

acid

personification

conduction

convection

radiation

air

outer space

galaxy

solar system

NASA

orbit

thrusters

roll

re-entry

splashdown

docking

lunar

calculus

maria

crater

waxing

waning

perigee

apogee

tide

cape

rocket

solid fuel

liquid fuel

propellant

Fine Arts

Model airplane

Designing a book cover

Cooking Yorkshire pudding

Drawing

Map making

Knot making

Cooking outside

Making musical instruments

Life Skills

Difficult decisions

Contentment

Helping others

Creativity

Compromise

Determination

Dealing with death

Bravery

Teamwork

Goals

Marie Curie and the Discovery of Radium

History
Late 1800s
Russian rulers
Polish culture
Henri Becquerel
Spanish-American War
Irene Joliot
Albert Einstein
Treaty of Versailles

Geography
Poland
French Riviera
Polish culture
Alps
Carpathian Mountains
Baltic Sea
Spanish-American War

Science
Tuberculosis
Geology
Malachite
Barometer
Physics
Louis Pasteur
Chemistry
Nutrition
Magnets
Crystals
Uranium
Questioning
Radioactive materials
Kidneys

Language Arts
Research
Foreign languages
Thesis writing
Transitional words and phrases

Vocabulary Words
malachite
physics
physics apparatus
aneroid
lake
kulig
zloty
sugar beet
gaiety
crystal
magnet
radiation poisoning
treaty
kidney
nephron
ureter

Fine Arts
Storytelling
Kulig streamers and sleigh bells
Line drawing
The Thinker

Life Skills
Concentrating
Self-sacrifice
Education
Persistence
Cooperation
Generosity

Hitty: Her First Hundred Years

History
1800s
Antiques
Native Americans
Whaling
Ships
Horsehair
Carib Indians
Hinduism
Missionaries
Tailor-made clothing
Quakers
Gettysburg Address
General McClellan
Industrial Revolution
Horseless carriage

Geography
Ireland
Northeast United States
Cape Hatteras
Carribean Islands
India
Philadelphia
New Orleans
Vicksburg

Career Path
Marine biologist
Photographer

Science
Bats
Conch shells
Prairie flowers
Motion sickness
Ocean waves
Sailing
Whales
Coral reefs
Distillation
Bioluminescence
Cobras

Language Arts
Point of view
Onomatopoeia
Understanding verse
Foreshadowing
Greek mythology
Sea jargon
Characters
Ship jargon
Sensory descriptions
John Greenleaf Whittier
Uncle Tom's Cabin
Charles Dickens
Writing a complete story
Personification

Vocabulary Words
confidante
infirmity
memoir
muff
prowlishly
reprove
tippet
wadgetty
bereft
cove
disconsolately
dory
foraging
ignominiously
gig
gullet
tantilizing
turnpike

cabin
cabin boy
cargo
crew
"fitting out"
hull
mast
masthead lantern
stern
"weigh anchor"
chart
gale
harbor
port
wharves
doleful
aftercabin
amidships
berth
bowsprit
crow's nest
figurehead
foc's'le
ratlines
rigging
topsail
try-works
try-pots
yardarm
"batten down the hatches"
"heave to"
mate
combers
enlivening
scud
"in fast"
harpoon
gamming
concocted
wallowing
buffetings
gesticulating

gimcracks
marlinspike
providence
cutting
phosphorescent
porringer
skirmish
stealth
talisman
bazaar
bullock
fakir
flageolet
foreboding
gaped
precarious
voluminous
balustrade
calomel
catechism
devious
dimity
fan rope
merino
brow
fichu
ferbelow
lakehorn
whatnot
aggrieved
barouche
basque
camphor
effigy
ether
modiste
pelisse
portiere
detected
formidable
mar
Mardi Gras

plied
roused
tapering
bric-a-brac
burnished
junketing

Fine Arts
Quill pens
Drawing animals
Cooking raspberries
Cooking gingerbread
Illustrating text
Watercolor
Daguerreotype
Playing guitar

Life Skills
Conscience
Courage
Loyalty

Research Project
Beginning the process
Creating your writing plan
Writing a first draft
Revising your work
Preparing the final draft

Service Project
Choosing your project
Beginning your project
How is it going?
Reviewing your efforts

Inspired learning through great books.

Five in a Row is a complete,* well-rounded, literature-based curriculum that takes your child from pre-K through middle school.

Before *five in a Row*

For ages 2-4

Before Five in a Row is a rich treasury of creative ideas that help you gently, consistently prepare your children for the lifelong adventure of learning. Now in a revised second edition, this bestselling volume is the foundation for inspired learning through great books and future studies with the entire Five in a Row curriculum.

More Before *five in a Row*

For ages 3-5

More Before Five in a Row inspires your child's learning through extraordinary children's picture books while nurturing your relationship with them and making memories to last a lifetime! Designed for ages 3 through 5, this preschool and kindergarten curriculum is filled with lessons for you and your child to enjoy together and prepare your child for the lifelong adventure of learning.

Five *in a Row*

For ages 5-12

Five in a Row is an easy-to-follow, highly effective instructional guide for teaching Social Studies, Language Arts, Art, Applied Math and Science using outstanding children's literature as the basis for each unit study. Lessons are designed for children ages 5 through 12, and include discussion guide and questions, teacher answers, hands-on activities and suggestions for further study. Visit www.fiveinarow.com to view suggested age ranges for each volume.

Five in a Row Bible Supplement (for Vols. 1-4)

The *Five in a Row Bible Supplement, 2nd Edition* provides hundreds of lessons in character development with accompanying Bible references. Each story has numerous lessons to choose from, all in an easy-to-use format.

Five in a Row Bible Supplement for Vols. 5-8 coming soon!

Full-Color, Laminated Story Disks

Available for *Before FIAR*, *More Before FIAR*, and *FIAR Volumes 1-5*.
Storybook Maps are also available for *Before FIAR* and *More Before FIAR*.

Digital Resources

Available from fiveinarow.com

FIAR Mini Units

Five in a Row Mini Units are digital unit studies based on children's picture books that include lessons for ages 2-12, designed to be used for one week.

FIAR Planner

The *Five in a Row Combined Family and Academic Planner* was created to give you access to school planning pages specific to the Five in a Row curriculum.

Notebook Builder

More than 120 pages of notebooking templates for all ages, appropriate for any topic or unit of study.

FIAR Nature Studies
(Spring, Summer, Fall, Winter)

FIAR Nature Studies encourage your entire family to enjoy and explore the outdoors in all four seasons. It is a true unit study approach to nature studies; suggestions introduce you and your child to poetry, music, and art that tie in to the season.

You will need to add math and phonics/reading instruction to **Five in a Row.*

www.fiveinarow.com

Made in the USA
Columbia, SC
24 January 2023